Dongsan Library Old Books Translation Series No. 5
English Translation Series No. 1

RECORD OF THE WORDS AND DEEDS OF YUHANDANG SA-SSI

(*Yuhandang Sa-ssi ŏnhaengnok*)

An annotated translation

RECORD OF THE WORDS AND DEEDS OF YUHANDANG SA-SSI
(*Yuhandang Sa-ssi ŏnhaengnok*)
An annotated translation

Printed 2022. 6. 20
Published 2022. 6. 30

Translator Michael C. E. Finch
Editor Lee Jonghan
Publisher Synn Ilhi
Published by Keimyung University Press
Room 105 Bosangwan, Keimyung University
1095 Dalgubeoldaero, Dalseo Gu, Daegu 42601
TEL. +82-53-580-6233 FAX. +82-53-580-6235
Homepage. www.kmupress.com
Registration 1970. 9. 1 (#347-1998-1)
ISBN 979-11-6516-145-3 93810 Price ₩20,000

This book has been published with the support of the University Innovation Support Project for the 2022 academic year administered by the Ministry of Education of the Republic of Korea and the National Research Foundation of Korea.

Dongsan Library Old Books Translation Series No. 5
English Translation Series No. 1

RECORD OF THE WORDS AND DEEDS OF YUHANDANG SA-SSI
(*Yuhandang Sa-ssi ŏnhaengnok*)
An annotated translation

Translated by Michael C. E. Finch
Edited by Lee Jonghan

KEIMYUNG UNIVERSITY PRESS

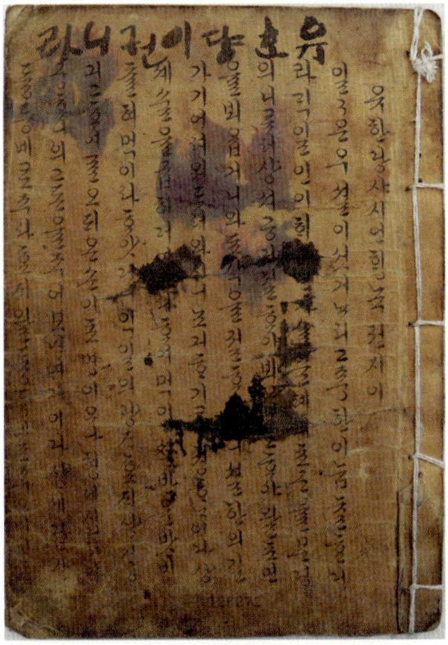

Yuhandang Sa-ssi ŏnhaengnok (*Record of the Words and Deeds of Yuhandang Sa-ssi*)
Keimyung University Dongsan Library

Translator's Preface

Record of the Words and Deeds of Yuhandang Sa-ssi (*Yuhandang Sa-ssi ŏnhaengnok*) is the first English translation of a series of translations of old books in the possession of Keimyung University Dongsan Library. This book contains anecdotes of the childhood, youth, middle age, and old age of the fictional female character Yuhandang Sa-*ssi*. The setting of the work is Ming dynasty China during the reign of the Wanli Emperor (萬曆, 1573–1620). The setting of novels in China was customary among Chosŏn dynasty novels.

Yuhandang is a fictional female character, who would have been considered an ideal woman by the noble families of the Chosŏn dynasty. Yuhandang is born into a family that had revered Confucian learning from generation to generation and had an outstanding family tradition. Not only is she intelligent from an early age, but she also loves learning. After greeting her parents early every morning, she immerses herself in learning all day long. From the age of seven or eight, her academic level surpasses that of grown men, and by the time she is nine years old, when the anecdote of *'wangyŏŏ'* (C.

wangyuyu 王餘魚: 'king's remaining fish') appears, she has reached the point of being able to surpass any other scholar.

After her marriage, she and her husband honor her parents-in-law with filial piety, perform ancestral rites with sincerity, and treat the servants with kindness and in this way garner praise from their relatives. She suggests to her husband that they should save money through frugality and in this way increase the family's wealth and then use the increased wealth to establish a 'righteous storehouse', so that her parents-in-law could do charitable deeds. Through Yuhandang's conversations with the people around her, the knowledge and methods that would have been necessary for the running of a *yangban* family, such as prenatal education and childcare, childbirth and hospitality, health care and disease prevention, as well as admonishments in words and deeds, are all explained in detail.

Yuhandang directly teaches various Confucian texts and classics to her seven sons, grandsons and granddaughters, great-grandsons and great-granddaughters. Through anecdotes involving questions asked by her offspring and other relatives that are answered by Yuhandang, her erudite knowledge is clearly revealed. Nevertheless, Yuhandang repeatedly emphasizes that the purpose of study is to put into practice what has been studied, rather than just to learn for the sake of learning.

In her old age, Yuhandang leads her granddaughters, grandsons' wives and other members of her extended family on a tour of the family's private estate, including Wanshu Garden (萬樹園) and Shuiyue Pavilion (水月亭), and on one occasion composes poetry at a family gathering. At the end of the work, Yuhandang's eldest son Ilbong celebrates his sixtieth birthday. As both his grandfather Minister Tu and his father Tu Ch'ŏnbok are still alive, this is a rare occasion for the members of three generations to celebrate a sixtieth birthday together. The feast is attended by thousands of relatives, including over a thousand descendants of Minister Tu. The work concludes with Wi Ch'ŏn'gyŏng, the son-in-law of Minister Tu, writing 'Preface to a Sixtieth

Birthday Banquet' (*Su yŏn sŏ* 壽宴序) to commemorate the blessings enjoyed by Minister Tu's family.

The author of *Record of the Words and Deeds of Yuhandang Sa-ssi,* which depicts the nobility's view of an ideal woman Yuhandang in the Chosŏn dynasty, is still unknown. Regarding the genre to which this book belongs, scholarly opinions are divided among the genres of 'ethics', 'question-and-answer encyclopedia' and 'women's didactic novel' (*kyuhun sosŏl* 閨訓小說). Further in-depth research on this point needs to be conducted in the future.

Translating Professor Kim Dongwook's modern Korean translation of *Yuhandang Sa-ssi ŏnhaengnok* and its abundant annotations into English, the translator could not help but be impressed not only by the erudite knowledge of the author of the original work, but also by that of Professor Kim in his elegant translation and meticulous tracking down of the countless references to classical Chinese texts that appear in this work. I have also greatly benefited from the careful reading of the manuscript by Professor Lee Jonghan, whose many corrections and suggestions for improvements have greatly increased the scholarly value of the translation. It is my sincere hope that, despite any remaining shortcomings due to my own limitations, readers of this translation will experience the same pleasure in exploring the Confucian intellectual, ethical and aesthetic worldview of Yuhandang and her many family members that I experienced as I translated it.

April 2022

Michael C. E. Finch

Explanatory Notes

1 This book is an annotated translation of *Yuhandang Sa-ssi ŏnhaengnok* in the possession of the Byeogoh Old Books Repository (碧梧古文獻室) of Keimyung University Dongsan Library (童山圖書館). *Yuhandang Sa-ssi ŏnhaengnok* (*Record of the Words and Deeds of Yuhandang Sa-ssi*) is set in China during the reign of the Wanli Emperor (1573–1620) of the Ming dynasty and portrays the ideal female figure of the Chosŏn dynasty through the fictional female character Yuhandang Sa-*ssi* as its main protagonist.

2 Annotations are numbered sequentially from beginning to end as footnotes. These mainly contain names of people, the names of books, the sources of key terms and phrases, and related background knowledge. However, romanized terms and Chinese characters have also been placed in parentheses in the main text.

4 The dates in this book are all according to the lunar calendar.

5 In the main text, Chinese characters have been included in parentheses whenever deemed necessary to increase the clarity of meaning of proper nouns or key terms.

6 The typographic conventions of this translation follow the recommendations of the 17th edition of the *Chicago Manual of Style*.

7 McCune-Reischauer romanization has been used for Korean words and Pinyin for Chinese words. As the novel is set in Ming China and contains the names of many Chinese historical personages as well as many Chinese geographical and other terms, the translator decided to romanize the names of the key fictional characters such as Yuhandang and her family members using McCune-Reischauer romanization to reflect the fact that this work is a vernacular Korean work by an anonymous Korean author written in Han'gŭl, while rendering all other non-fictional Chinese names that appear in the text using Pinyin romanization.

8 In the footnotes, the translations of the Chinese Classics, namely, *Book of Odes* (*Shijing*), *Book of History* (*Shujing*), *Book of Rites* (*Liji*), *Book of Changes* (*Yijing*), *Analects* (*Lunyu*), *Mencius* (*Mengzi*), *Great Learning* (*Daxue*), and *Records of the Grand Historian* (*Shiji*) have been based on the translations of James Legge that have been made available on-line at China Text Project (https://ctext.org/). Translations of other Chinese works in the footnotes have been largely based on the Korean translations by Professor Kim Dongwook.

Table of Contents

Fascicle 1

Fascicle 2

Fascicle 3

Fascicle 1

Yuhandang's Birth

Yuhandang (幽閒堂) of the Sa descent group (Sa-*ssi* 謝氏) was the daughter of Scholar (Ch'ŏsa 處士)[01] Sa Kwanghan (謝光翰), while her mother was from the No descent group (No-*ssi* 盧氏)[02] and was the daughter of the Hanlin Academy scholar No Wŏn'gyŏng (盧元景). The Sa family generally excelled in scholarship and was looked up to by people in the world, and the No family members were also outstanding in their conduct and words, and from generation to generation, it was a family that occupied high rank and was exceptional in its moral behavior.

---

01 Ch'ŏsa (處士) is a term for a scholar without an official government position. In the original text Sa Kwanghan is referred to simply as 'Ch'ŏsa' and occasionally 'Chŏsa kong'. The former appellation is translated throughout as 'Scholar Sa' and the latter as 'Lord Scholar Sa'.

02 In Chosŏn times it was usual for women from the gentry (*yangban* 兩班) class to be referred to by their family name followed by the term '*ssi*' (氏), meaning 'descent group'.

Lady No gave birth to Yuhandang on the 19th day of the fourth lunar month of the Chŏngch'uk Year (C. Dingchou nian 丁丑年, 1577) in the fifth year of the reign of the Wanli Emperor (萬曆), Shenzong (神宗) of the Ming dynasty. The family was upright and prominent (*ch'ŏnghyŏn* 清顯)[03] and strict in its morals. Yuhandang was intelligent and concentrated on studying from a young age, so all her relatives said, "The intelligence and ability of personages in this world is born from their seeds."

Yuhandang's eldest brother Sa Manch'un (謝萬春) was a vice director (K. *wŏnoerang*; C. *yuanwailang* 員外郎).[04] Because he loved his younger sister's innate qualities, outstanding character and splendid talent, he taught her the *Elementary Learning* (*Xiaoxue* 小學) and all the Confucian classics. When Sa-*ssi* became six or seven years old, her studies progressed every day and every month (*ilch'wi wŏlchang* 日就月將), and there were few fully grown men who could compare with her ability.

As Sa-*ssi* got up early every day, washed and greeted her parents and immersed herself in her studies without a break from start to finish.

---

03 *Ch'ŏnghyŏn* (清顯) is a term used to refer to an official position (*ch'ŏnghwan* 清宦) in which integrity is emphasized and which is a prominent post (*hyŏnjik* 顯職).

04 *Wŏnoerang* (C. *yuanwailang* 員外郎) was the title of a vice director and was a junior 5 rank post in the Ming dynasty. In the original text Sa Manch'un is referred to simply by his title '*Wŏnoerang*,' which is translated throughout as Vice Director Sa.

Vice Director Sa marveled at this and gave her the studio name (*tangho* 堂號) 'Yuhandang'.[05] But she declined saying, "Even a man only gets a studio name after 'accomplishing the Way and establishing virtue' (*tosŏng tŏngnip* 道成德立), so how can a woman have a studio name at the age of seven or eight?"

Nevertheless, from that time forward the members of the household and her relatives always called her Yuhandang, and in this way Yuhandang became her brush name (*pyŏlho* 別號).

Prognostication of the Japanese Invasion of 1592

Scholar Sa had been good at astronomy from his childhood. Every night he would take Vice Director Sa to look at the stars, and the father and son would discuss them together. In the spring of the Kyemi Year (癸未年, 1583) Scholar Sa looked at the stars and said, "The star in the east with a deep red aura has moved, so if we discuss the star's 'degree number' (K. *tosu*; C. *dushu* 度數),[06]

---

05 *Tangho* (堂號) is a place name that is used to refer to a person.

06 'Degree number' (K. *tosu*; C. *dushu* 度數) is the position occupied by a star measured in 'degrees' (K. *to*; C. *du* 度).

it looks as though something will happen ten or eleven years from now. You look carefully."

After ascending the raised pavilion (K. *nudae*; C. *loutai* 樓臺) and looking carefully, Vice Director Sa said, "The red star's aura is directed towards China, but its position is very far away, so a war (*pyŏngnan* 兵亂) could arise in a foreign country, but China does not need to be anxious about it."

Yuhandang, who was at their side accompanying them, added, "If a war occurs, it looks as though the country of the inferior people (*soin* 小人) will invade the country of the superior people (*kunja* 君子)."

Vice Director Sa said, "How can a seven-year-old child, who has not even seen an astronomy book, know about inferior and superior people?"

"In an old text it states, 'In the Years of the Dragon and Snake (*sejae yongsa* 歲在龍蛇), the superior man sighs and laments' (*kunja ch'at'an* 君子嗟歎).[07] Ten and eleven years from now will be the Imjin Year and the Kyesa Year,

---

07 'Biography of Zheng Xuan' (Zheng Xuan zhuan 鄭玄傳), *History of the Later Han* (*Hou Hanshu* 後漢書): "In the spring of the fifth year of Jian'an (建安) Confucius appeared in Zheng Xuan's dream and said, 'Get up! Get up! This is the Year of the Dragon and next year is the Year of the Snake.' Awakening from his dream, Zheng Xuan corroborated the prophecy, realized that his life was coming to an end and soon afterwards fell ill." (五年春, 夢孔子告之曰, '起, 起! 今年歲在辰, 來年歲在巳.' 既寤以讖合之, 知命當終, 有頃寢疾.) Concerning this, Li Xuan in his commentary quoted *Gaocai buyu zhuan* (高才不遇傳) by Liu Zhou (劉晝) of Qi of the Northern Dynasties (Beiqi 北齊) saying, "Chen (辰) is a dragon and Si (巳) is a snake. When the Year of the Snake and the Year of the Dragon arrive, the wise lament, so Zheng Xuan's interpretation of the prophecy is more or less saying the same thing." (辰爲龍, 巳爲蛇. 歲至龍蛇賢人嗟, 玄以讖合之, 蓋謂此也.)

and are they not the Years of the Dragon and the Snake?[08] If the superior people are made to lament, the side that mobilizes its army will be the inferior people."

Scholar Sa laughed out loud and said, "This seven-year-old child's reading of characters and interpretation of their meaning is extremely subtle."

Ten years afterwards in the Imjin Year, Japan invaded Chosŏn (朝鮮), so Chosŏn's envoys came requesting reinforcements. The emperor granted a special favor and dispatched a general, so Lord Scholar Sa hearing this praised her.

"At that time I listened carefully to what my daughter said. As now is the time of the Years of the Dragon and Snake, and from long ago Chosŏn has been called a nation of superior people and Japan a land of raiders from beyond the sea, what she said was truly correct."

---

08 The Imjin Year (壬辰年, 1592) in which the Japanese invasion of Chosŏn occurred was the Year of the Dragon and the following Kyesa Year (癸巳年, 1593) was the Year of the Snake.

Questions and Answers on the *Elementary Learning* I

After Yuhandang read the *Elementary Learning* (K. *Sohak*; C. *Xiaoxue* 小學), she asked, "It is right that the words of Wang Zhu (王蠋), 'A loyal minister cannot serve two sovereigns' (*ch'ungsin pulsa igun* 忠臣不事二君) come under the heading 'Righteousness between a Ruler and His Ministers' (*kunsin chi ŭi* 君臣之義) and that the words, 'A faithful wife cannot have two husbands' (*yŏllyŏ pulgyŏng ibu* 烈女不更二夫) come under the heading 'The Relationship Between a Husband and Wife' (*pubu chi ryun* 夫婦之倫). But would it be wrong for them both to be placed under the heading 'A Loyal Minister Cannot Serve Two Sovereigns'?"[09]

Vice Director Sa said, "Indeed that is true. It is arranged that way because these words are spoken by the same person, and also, even though the book is divided into Fascicle 1 and Fascicle 2, which are both different, the end of Fascicle 1 is connected to the meaning of Fascicle 2, so the meaning of the words is connected and unbroken. As a woman, your reading of books is extraordinary and praiseworthy."

---

09 'Illustrating the Cardinal Principles' (Minglun 明倫), *Elementary Learning* (*Xiaoxue* 小學). When the Yan (燕) general Yue Yi (樂毅) invaded Qi, he heard of the virtue of Wang Zhu (王蠋), a minister of Qi, and advised him to surrender. But Wang Zhu refused to surrender saying, "A loyal minister cannot serve two sovereigns, and a faithful wife cannot have two husbands." (忠臣不事二君, 烈女不更二夫.)

Questions and Answers on the *Elementary Learning* II

When Yuhandang read the 'Subject Matter of the *Elementary Learning*' (*Xiaoxue* tici 小學題辭),[10] Vice Director Sa asked Yuhandang, "'The great and originating' (*wŏn* 元), 'the penetrating' (*hyŏng* 亨), 'the advantageous' (*li* 利), and 'the correct and firm' (*chŏng* 貞) follow the order of spring (*ch'un* 春), summer (*ha* 夏), autumn (*ch'u* 秋) and winter (*tong* 冬), but the order of benevolence (*in* 仁), righteousness (*ŭi* 義), courtesy (*ye* 禮) and wisdom (*chi* 智) is different. Benevolence belongs to spring, righteousness belongs to autumn, courtesy belongs to summer, and wisdom belongs to winter, so even though the order ought to be "benevolence, courtesy, righteousness and wisdom," it is "benevolence, righteousness, courtesy and wisdom." Do you know why this is so and what it signifies?"

Yuhandang replied, "There is no particularly deep significance. 'The great and originating', 'the penetrating', 'the advantageous', and 'the correct and firm' are mentioned in accordance with the order of the four seasons,

---

10 '*Xiaoxue* tici' (小學題辭) forms part of the introduction of the *Elementary Learning* and was written by Zhu Xi (朱熹). The first sentence of 'Subject Matter of the *Elementary Learning*' (*Xiaoxue* tici 小學題辭) is as follows: "'The great and originating', 'the penetrating', 'the advantageous', and 'the correct and firm' are the unchanging principles of Heaven's law. Benevolence, righteousness, courtesy and wisdom are the guiding principles of human nature." (元亨利貞, 天道之常, 仁義禮智, 人性之綱.)

while benevolence, righteousness, courtesy and wisdom are mentioned in accordance with the order of east, west, south and north because benevolence is associated with the east (*tong* 東), righteousness is associated with the west (*sŏ* 西), courtesy is associated with the south (*nam* 南) and wisdom is associated with the north (*puk* 北)."

Vice Director Sa then asked with deliberation, "Wouldn't it be possible to say 'east, south, west and north' as well as 'east, west, south and north'?"

"As 'the great and originating', 'the penetrating', 'the advantageous', and 'the correct and firm' are listed in heaven's natural order, we say them in that order, and because east, west, south and north are geographical terms, they are referred to in that way based on the directions that are facing each other. How is it that you do not know 'the principle of the orderly passage of time and the pairing of opposites' (*yuhaeng taedae chi li* 流行待對之理)?"[11]

Vice Director Sa struck his knee in admiration and praised her, saying, "Even among men who read books, there are only a few who know about 'the principle of the orderly passage of time and the pairing of opposites'. Even though you are just a young girl, you already know such things. How extraordinary you are!"

---

11 In the phrase *yuhaeng taedae chi li* (流行待對之理), *yuhaeng* (流行) refers to the orderly passage of time, and *taedae* (待對) refers to the pairing of opposites.

Questions and Answers on *Elementary Learning* III

One day after reading the first part of the *Elementary Learning*, Yuhandang asked Vice Director Sa, "'When sleeping do not lie down on your side; when sitting do not lean to one side; do not look at immoral things with your eyes; do not listen to lewd things with your ears.'[12] As men's academic scholarship is also like this, how can it only refer to women? And as it also pertains to women's daily life, how can it only be applicable when they are pregnant?"

"Your question is truly precise and deep. Whether a man or a woman and at whatever time, if they are people who study, shouldn't they all behave in this way? It is just that when women in *Biographies of Women* (*Lienü zhuan* 列女傳) were pregnant, they did this for the reason of prenatal education of the fetus in the womb."

---

12 'Entry into Learning' (Lijiao 立敎), *Elementary Learning*: "When sleeping do not lie on one side; when you sit down do not lean to one side; when you stand do not stand on one foot; do not eat food with an impure taste; do not eat meat if it has not been cut properly; if the seat is not upright, do not sit there; do not look at immoral things with your eyes; do not listen to lewd sounds with your ears." (寢不側, 坐不邊, 立不蹕. 不食邪味, 割不正, 不食, 席不正, 不坐, 目不視邪色, 耳不聽淫聲.) The original source is 'Three women of the Zhou family' (Zhoushi sanmu 周室三母), *Biographies of Women*.

Writing about Doors

Yuhandang was standing to one side of the doorway of the wooden-floored living area (*maru*), when Vice Director Sa came in from the outside and asked, "Why are you standing to one side of the door?"

"Elder brother all your life you have avoided walking in the middle of a pathway. You always walk to one side, and you have always put into practice the teaching, 'While parents are still living, never walk in the middle of a pathway.'[13] How could I not follow the teaching about not standing in the middle of a doorway? Since the age of nine, I have never stood in the middle of a doorway."

"As you have already begun by talking about 'doors' (*mun* 門), can you tell me what was said about 'doors' in the teachings of people in the past?"

"There are the words, "do not step on the threshold" (*haeng puli yŏk* 行不履閾)[14] and 'when going through a doorway (*ch'urip munho* 出入門戶), always allow an

---

13 'Illustrating the Cardinal Principles', *Elementary Learning*: "When your parents are still living never occupy the place where they usually sit; when you sit down do not sit in the middle of a room; when you are walking do not walk in the middle of the pathway; when you are standing do not stand in the middle of the doorway." (爲人子者, 居不主奧, 坐不中席, 行不中道, 立不中門.) The original source is 'Summary of the Rules of Propriety' (Quli 曲禮), *Book of Rites* (*Liji* 禮記).

14 'In His Native Place' (Xiangdang 鄉黨), *Analects* (*Lunyu* 論語): "Confucius never stood in the

elder person to go through first' (*p'il hu changja* 必後長者),[15] but the words 'if the door is open, also leave it open' (*hogae yŏkkae* 戶開亦開) and 'if the door is closed, then also close it (after you)' (*hohap yŏkhap* 戶闔亦闔) are truly good teachings."[16]

Vice Director Sa also asked, "Can you tell me about any writings concerning doors in the *Records of the Grand Historian* (*Shiji* 史記)?"

"There are so many writings in the *Records of the Grand Historian*, so how could I refer to them all? There are the elderly mother of Wangsun Jia (王孫賈) leaning against the doorway[17] and the child of Tao Yuanming (陶淵明) coming out of the doorway.[18] One became a mother and attained benevolence, and one became a child and attained filial piety.[19] Those

---

middle of a doorway and never trod on a threshold." (立不中門, 行不履閾.)

15 'Entry into Learning' (Lijiao 立敎), *Elementary Learning*: "From the age of eight children must be taught modesty without fail from the outset by always ensuring their elders go in and out of doorways first and begin eating first." (八年, 出入門戶, 及卽席飮食, 必後長者, 始敎之讓.)

16 'Respecting the Body' (Jingshen 敬身), *Elementary Learning*: "When you are about to go through a doorway lower your gaze without fail, take hold of the door handle with both hands, and do not look behind you. If the door is already open then leave it open; if the door was closed then close it (after you); if there is someone entering after you, you must not close it completely." (將入戶, 視必下, 入戶奉扃, 視瞻毋回, 戶開亦開, 戶闔亦闔, 有後入者, 闔而勿遂.)

17 'Studying the Classics' (Jigu 稽古), *Elementary Learning*. Wangsun Jia served King Min of Qi (齊閔王), but when the king was defeated and fled, Wangsun Jia returned home. At that time Wangsun Jia's mother said as follows: "When you went out in the morning and returned home late, I leaned on the doorway waiting for you; when you went out in the evening and did not return, I leaned on the village entrance gate and waited for you. How could you return home when the king you now serve has fled and you do not know where he is?" (女朝出而晩來, 則吾倚門而望, 女暮出而不還, 則吾倚閭而望. 女今事王, 王出走, 女不知其處, 女尚何歸?) The original source is 'Strategy of Qi' (Qi ce 齊策), *Strategies of the Warring States* (*Zhanguo ce* 戰國策).

18 In Tao Yuanming's 'Ode on Returning Home after Resigning' (Guiqulai ci 歸去來辭), there is the phrase "a young child waiting in the doorway." (稚子候門.)

19 *Great Learning*: In the *Great Learning* there is a passage praising the virtue of King Wen of Zhou (周文王) as follows, "Becoming a child, he attained filial piety; becoming a father, he

two doorways were private doorways that were hardly worth looking at, but is it not good that their names have been passed down to succeeding generations because of a mother's love and a son's filial piety?"

Vice Director Sa was overjoyed, and filled with admiration said, "As you have referred to human conduct even in ordinary words, I can indeed see how you behave yourself in daily life."

The Origin of the Phrase 'Born in the Year of the Pig' (*Sokchŏ*)

When Vice Director Sa's third youngest brother was ten years old, he read a passage, and when his elder brother Vice Director Sa asked him the meaning of the characters '*sokchŏ*' (屬猪), the third youngest brother was unable to answer. Vice Director Sa suddenly lost his temper and rebuked him excessively.

Yuhandang, who was sitting next to him, said, "When an elder brother intends to teach a younger brother with all his heart, friendship is

---

attained benevolence." (爲人子止於孝, 爲人父止於慈.)

most important, so suddenly changing one's words and facial expression demonstrates that something is lacking in a scholar's studies. Furthermore, if you wish to teach children to read and write, showing impatience through words and facial expressions is not the right way to teach them."

Vice Director Sa apologized, saying, "Even though the characters '*sokchŏ*' are not difficult, my younger brother forgot them, so I was naturally unable to prevent myself from scolding him with angry words and an angry facial expression. My younger sister's words are, of course, correct, and I feel ashamed of myself."

Yuhandang asked, "What does the word '*sokchŏ*' mean?"

"They say *sokchŏ* refers to the Song (宋) dynasty."

"What is its origin?"

"I don't know its origin."

Yuhandang laughed and said to Vice Director Sa, "If you want to know the origin of the word *sokchŏ*, I will tell you. Song Taizu (太祖) Zhao Kuangyin (趙匡胤) was born in the Chŏnghae Year (丁亥生, 927), and because *hae* (亥) means 'pig', he was referred to as '*sokchŏ*' (Born in the Year of the Pig).'[20]

---

20 Emperor Taizu (太祖) of Song (Zhao Kuangyin 趙匡胤, 927–976), the founder of the Song dynasty, and also Emperor Taizong (太宗) of Song (Zhao Jiong 趙炅, 939–997), the second emperor of the Song dynasty, were both born in the Year of the Pig (K. Kihae nyŏn; C. Jihai nian 己亥年), so the characters '*sokchŏ*' (C. *shuzhu* 屬猪: 'born in the Year of the Pig') came to

Vice Director Sa was overjoyed. "Because my younger brother forgot the meaning of *sokchŏ*, he was rebuked by me, and because I did not know the origin of the word *sokchŏ*, how could I avoid being rebuked by my younger sister?"

16th Day of the Tenth Lunar Month

On the 16th day of the tenth lunar month, the moon was shining on the pine tree branches between the eaves of the houses, and the chrysanthemum wine was well fermented. Lord Scholar Sa took Vice Director Sa and his brothers to drink wine together, and after the father and sons had discussed their essays, Vice Director Sa asked Yuhandang, "Did you know that today is the same day of the year that Su Dongpo (蘇東坡) enjoyed and then wrote about in 'Second (Ode on the) Red Cliff' (Hou Chibi 後赤壁)?"

"Because my elder brother venerates literary composition, he thinks of the scenery in the poetic essay 'Second Ode on the Red Cliff' (Hou Chibi fu 後

be used as another name for the Song dynasty.

赤壁賦),[21] but I am thinking of something else."

"What is that?"

"Wasn't it on a moonlit night on the 16th day of the tenth lunar month that Master Zhu Huian (朱晦庵)[22] went with Xu Jinzhi (許進之) to the banks of a stream and, while listening to the *kŏmun'go*, composed 'Beckoning a recluse to play' (Zhaoyin cao 招隱操)?[23] I think of the work of Huian, but elder brother's thoughts do not go beyond the composing of beautiful sentences. As elder brother already thought of enjoying himself at the Red Cliff, I will wash the cup and pour some more wine for you."

Wiping the cup clean, she filled it to the brim and brought it to him. Vice Director Sa received and drank it and in good humor leaned against the balustrade and said, "I have just thought of someone else who enjoyed himself on the 16th day of the tenth lunar month. Was it not on this day

---

21 Su Shi (蘇軾, 1037–1101) was a Northern Song literatus whose brush name was Dongpo (東坡). On the 16th day of the seventh lunar month, 1082, while living in exile, Su Dongpo wrote 'First Ode on the Red Cliff' (Qian Chibi fu 前赤壁賦) about an enjoyable time he spent at Red Cliff (Chibi) on the upper reaches of the Yangtze River, and in the tenth lunar month of the same year he wrote, 'Second Ode on the Red Cliff' (Hou Chibi fu 後赤壁賦).

22 Huian (晦庵) was the brush name of the Southern Song Confucian scholar Zhu Xi (朱熹, 1130–1200). He is also respectfully referred to as Zhuzi (朱子: Master Zhu).

23 'Beckoning a recluse to play' (Zhaoyin cao 招隱操), *Collected works of Huian* (Huian ji 晦庵集). On the 16th day of the tenth lunar month Xu Jinzhi visited Zhu Xi with his *kŏmun'go* (C. *guqin* 古琴) and played it for him, inspiring Zhu Xi to compose the work 'Beckoning a recluse to play' (Zhaoyin cao).

that Wu Longhan (吳龍翰) enjoyed himself at Mt. Huang (黃山)?"[24]

Yuhandang laughed and replied, "Once again elder brother is thinking about the composition of beautiful sentences. I also have something else in mind."

"What is that?"

"Was it not on the 16th day of the tenth lunar month that Yan Ruoyu (顔若愚) published the *Classic of Mind-and-Heart* (*Xinjing* 心經) and gave a sermon on it to scholars at a county (*kun* 郡) Confucian school?"[25]

Vice Director Sa laughed out loud and praised her, saying, "It is indeed wonderful how you only think of the deeds of wise and superior men. As Su Dongpo (蘇東坡) wrote the 'First Ode on the Red Cliff' (Qian Chibi fu 前赤壁賦) on the 16th day of the seventh lunar month, can you tell me any other scholar of the past who wrote something on the 16th day of the seventh lunar month?"

---

24 Wu Longhan (吳龍翰, 1233–1293) was a Song dynasty literatus. According to 'Record of a Journey to Mt. Huang' (Huangshan jiyou 黃山紀遊) in his anthology *Posthumously Collected Works of Gumei* (*Gumei yigao* 古梅遺稿), Wu Longhan toured around Mt. Huang together with Bao Yunlong (鮑雲龍) and Song Fuyi (宋復一) on the 16th day of the tenth lunar month, 1268.

25 On the 16th day of the tenth lunar month, 1234, Yan Ruoyu (顔若愚) completed a new set of printing woodblocks for the *Classic of Mind-and-Heart* and wrote the essay, 'In Praise of the *Classic of Mind-and-Heart*' (*Xinjing zan* 心經贊).

"There is someone. Elder brother said that the first and second odes on the Red Cliff were written on the 16th day of the seventh and tenth lunar months, and just now I mentioned the *Classic of Mind-and-Heart*, so I reply by saying the *Classic of Mind-and-Heart*. Cheng Minzheng (程敏政) wrote the preface to the *Classic of Mind-and-Heart* on the 15th day (*porŭm*) of the seventh lunar month."[26]

Vice Director Sa burst out laughing and said, "Your intelligence is truly exceptional, so even if we stayed up all night, it would be difficult for me to outdo you."

Studying How to Stop Drinking Alcohol

Vice Director Sa enjoyed drinking alcohol both when he went touring around beautiful landscapes and when he met friends on a flowery morning or a moonlit evening. As he often drank too much and became drunk, every

---

26 Cheng Minzheng (程敏政, 1446–1499) was a Ming dynasty literatus. He wrote the preface to the *Annotated Classic of Mind-and-Heart* (*Xinjing fuzhu* 心經附註) on the 15th day of the seventh lunar month.

time he did so, his father Lord Scholar Sa admonished him and forbade him to drink alcohol.

Yuhandang remonstrated with him and said, "Elder brother you have always liked the *Book of Changes* (*Yijing* 易經), so how is it that you cannot put into practice the three words '*chŏl ŭmsik*' (節飲食: 'moderation in drinking and eating')?"[27] According to the words of Confucius (Kongzi 孔子) 'Parents only concern is that their children might become ill',[28] so if you cannot control your drinking and sometimes become ill, think of how much anxiety you will cause our father."

As she remonstrated with him sincerely, Vice Director Sa replied, "As my younger sister's words are truly correct, how can I not follow them?"

From that moment he stopped drinking alcohol, wrote 'Admonition to Give up Alcohol', pasted it to the wall and said to Yuhandang, "If I ever drink alcohol again from now on, please remonstrate with me."

So Yuhandang praised him over and over again, and then a long time later Yuhandang asked him, "Elder brother, don't you sometimes think about alcohol?"

---

27 'Lower Jaw Hexagram' (Yigua 頤卦), *Book of Changes*: "Thunder below the mountain; the superior man observes this and is careful in his words and moderate in his drinking and eating." (象曰. 山下有雷, 君子以愼言語, 節飲食.)

28 'On governing' (Weizheng 爲政), *Analects*: "When Meng Wubai (孟武伯) asked about filial piety, Confucius said, 'Parents only concern is that their children might become ill.'" (孟武伯問孝, 子曰, '父母唯其疾之憂.')

"I gave my word to my younger sister, so how could I think about alcohol again?"

"After you made up your mind, you had no intention of drinking again, but a long time later, it would be easy to think about it."

Then ten years after he had stopped drinking, Vice Director Sa went to a place where some of his friends had gathered, and on his return he said, "At today's party the cups were filled to the brim with good wine, and its fragrant aroma pervaded the raised pavilion, so I really wanted to drink today."

Laughing Yuhandang said, "That easily happens. In the past when Master Cheng Mingdao (程明道), who had always enjoyed hunting, suddenly stopped at the age of sixteen and said 'I will never think about it again', Master Zhou Lianxi (周濂溪)[29] said, 'How can you easily say that? After lying dormant and never arising, such thoughts can suddenly start again one day, and you will be back where you first started.' And then twelve years later Master Cheng Mingdao was passing a field at dusk where he saw some people hunting, and without realizing it, he experienced a feeling of joy in

---

29 Lianxi (濂溪) was the brush name of the Northern Song dynasty Confucian scholar Zhou Dunyi (周敦頤, 1017–1073), who wrote *Explanation of the Diagram of the Supreme Ultimate* (Taiji tushuo 太極圖說).

his mind and said to himself, 'Now I know that I am incapable.'[30]

Elder brother when you said before that you had no intention of drinking alcohol, it was an easy thing to say. Now the disturbance that you felt in your mind when you saw the alcohol was like the joy that arose in Master Cheng Mingdao's mind when he saw the hunting scene. Master Cheng Mingdao firmly took control of his mind so that thoughts of his enjoyment of hunting would no longer arise. Likewise, if elder brother maintains his determination to stop drinking alcohol for a long time, so that even if you encounter good wine, you have no desire to drink it, then you will be able to see that even trivial things like food are relevant to a scholar's studies."

Vice Director Sa marveled and expressed his gratitude, "As the example you cited is truly to the point, how could I not take your words to heart?"

---

30 'Promoting Goodness and Correction' (Qianshan gaiguo 遷善改過), *Annotated Classic of Mind-and-Heart*: When Cheng Mingdao was sixteen or seventeen years old, he stopped hunting, which he had enjoyed, and thought that he had lost all interest in it, so Zhou Lianxi told him that his desire was just hidden. These are the words Cheng Mingdao spoke when twelve years later he saw people hunting in a field and feelings of joy once again arose in his mind.

How to Write Well

When Scholar Sa was studying, he collected all the instances of when wise men of old referred to the character for benevolence (*in* 仁), compiled a book in two fascicles that he named *Record of Writings on Benevolence* (K. *Ku'il lok;* C. *Juren lu* 具仁錄) and called all his sons together and had them write the foreword (*sŏmun* 序文). After Scholar Sa had once looked over what they had written, he showed it to Yuhandang, asking for her critical opinion on the level of the composition. So Yuhandang said, "They have written so well that even the masters of the Six Dynasties (Liuchao 六朝)[31] could not have excelled them. Nevertheless, even though the writing is good, it is lacking not only because the sentences in the lower section (of the text) are not as good as those in the upper section, but it is also flawed insofar as the lower section does not connect properly with the meaning of the upper section."

Scholar Sa laughed out loud and said, "I showed it to you just to test you, and I see your opinion is exactly the same as mine. As you are only a

---

31 The 'Six Dynasties' (Liuchao 六朝) was the name given to the six dynasties south of the Yangtze River in the era of the Wei, Jin and North-South Dynasties (Wei Jin Nan Bei chao 魏晉南北朝, 221–589), namely, Wu (吳), Eastern Jin (東晋), Song (宋), Qi (齊), Liang (梁) and Chen (陳). They all had Jiankang (建康: present-day Nanjing [南京]) as their capital.

woman, how do you know about the rule of 'interlocking the beginning and end' (*sangha kwanswae* 上下關鎖) when composing a piece of writing?"

"I learned this from looking at some literary works previously."

"In which literary works did you notice this?"

"There are no literary works that do not employ the art of 'interlocking the beginning and end'. First of all, if we just look at Zhu Xi's 'Introduction to the Subject Matter of the *Elementary Learning*', in the upper section we have the words "In all of these from the very beginning" (C. *fan ci jue chu* 凡此厥初), "there is nothing which is not good" (C. *wu you bu shan* 無有不善),[32] and in the lower portion we have the words "one would finally recover the beginning (i.e. the original perfection of human nature)" (C. *nai fu qi chu* 乃復其初),[33] so we can see that the single character *chu* (K. *ch'o* 初) connects the upper and lower (portions of the text). Also, in the upper portion there are the words "... is called holding to one's inborn nature" (C. *shi yue bing yi* 是曰秉彝)[34] and below are the

---

32 'Introduction to the Subject Matter of the *Elementary Learning*' (*Xiaoxue* tici 小學題辭), *Elementary Learning*: "In all of these, from the very beginning, there is nothing that is not good. Therefore, like a verdant growth the Four Beginnings are stirred, move in response and appear." (凡此厥初, 無有不善, 藹然四端, 隨感而見.)

33 'Introduction to the Subject Matter of the *Elementary Learning*', *Elementary Learning*: "The bright Mandate would shine forth; there would come to be no distinction between one's interior dispositions and external conduct; virtue would become lofty and one's accomplishments broaden, and one would finally recover the beginning (i.e. the original perfection of human nature)." (明命赫然, 罔有內外, 德崇業廣, 乃復其初.)

34 'Introduction to the Subject Matter of the *Elementary Learning*', *Elementary Learning*: "Loving one's parents, reverencing one's older brother, being loyal to one's ruler, and showing respect to

words “Fortunately, the inborn nature of man” (C. *xing zi bing yi* 幸玆秉彝).[35] As both phrases include the characters *bing yi* (K. *pyŏng yi* 秉彝) by looking at this one piece of writing alone, we can understand the overall system of how to write.”

Scholar Sa called Vice Director Sa and said, “Your younger sister looked at this piece of writing and said, ‘The lower section is not as good as the upper section, and the meanings of the upper section and lower section are not connected’, so her opinion of your writing is apposite.”

“My younger sister’s words are correct. When I was writing it, after writing half of it, my younger brother looked it over and said he would write the lower half. But after it was written, it was clumsy, because this was the first time he had ever written a foreword, and so it ended up like this. I will rewrite the lower section correctly.”

---

elders is called ‘holding to one’s inborn nature’ (*bing yi* 秉彝).” (愛親敬兄, 忠君弟長, 是曰秉彝.)

35 ‘Introduction to the Subject Matter of the *Elementary Learning*’, *Elementary Learning*: “Fortunately, the inborn good nature of man will not perish as long as Heaven lasts.” (幸玆秉彝, 極天罔墜.)

Wangyŏŏ

One day Vice Director Sa and his brothers had gathered together to engage in writing and viewing the scenery of flowers and willow trees, so Yuhandang acquired some fish and served sliced raw fish.

"Elder brother, do you know the name of this fish?"

Vice Director Sa said, "It is called *panmyŏnŏ* (C. *banmianyu* 半面魚) and also *pimogŏ* (C. *bimuyu* 比目魚)."[36]

"Does it have another name?"

"I have never heard of one, but if you know, tell me."

"Another name is *wangyŏŏ* (C. *wangyuyu* 王餘魚).[37] Long ago the king of Yue caught fish at Qiantang Lake (錢塘湖),[38] prepared sliced raw fish and ate it and then threw away half into the water where the fish came back to life, so they

---

36 *Panmyŏnŏ* and *pimogŏ* refer to flatfish with eyes on one side of their body, such as flounder and halibut.

37 'Sliced fish' (Kuaican 膾殘), *Record of the Origins of Matters and Things* (Shiwu jiyuan 事物紀原) compiled by the Song dynasty scholar Gao Cheng (高承): "When King Goujian of Yue was defending Kuaiji (會稽), he had just prepared sliced raw fish when he heard that the Wu army had arrived, so he threw the remaining fish into the river, where they changed back into live fish. But because they had the appearance of sliced fish, 'they were called '*kuaican*' (sliced fish). They were also called the 'king's remaining fish' (*wangyuyu* 王餘魚)." (越王句踐之保會稽也, 方斫魚爲膾, 聞有吳兵, 棄其餘於江, 化而爲魚. 猶作膾形, 故名膾殘. 亦曰王餘魚.)

38 Qiantang Lake (錢塘湖): West Lake (Xihu 西湖) to the west of Hangzhou (杭州) in Zhejiang Province, China.

called them 'half-sided fish' (*panmyŏnŏ*), and because they were what remained after the king had eaten them, they were also called the 'king's remaining fish' (*wangyŏŏ*)."

The brothers all laughed out loud and said, "People of the world say that we brothers have read a lot of books, but today there is no way we can match up to you, our younger sister, so whenever we see your intellectual ability, we feel it is such a pity that you were born as a woman."

"Even a man has to pay attention to his conduct; if someone is famous just because he has read a lot of books, how valuable is he? As a woman refrains from learning, how strange it would be to pretend that this is fair. I have read a few books, but how can I match the ability of my elder brothers? In the end, I was just preparing sliced raw fish when the thought came to me, and as we are gathered together as brothers and sisters with no one else from outside the family, I accidentally spoke out. Listening to your praise, I feel embarrassed."

A few months later the emperor was viewing blossoms and fishing at Taiye Pond (太液池)[39] while also gathering the scholars and holding the civil examination. Yuhandang's third eldest brother was in the palace courtyard

---

39 Taiye Pond (C. Taiyechi; K. T'ae'aekchi 太液池): The name of a lotus pond in the imperial palace.

(taking the examination); the theme for the civil examination essay was the three characters '*wang*' (王) '*yŏ*' (餘) and '*ŏ*' (魚). Because none of the scholars who packed the courtyard knew the origin of the word '*wangyŏŏ*', they were unable to write an appropriate essay. But because the third eldest brother had heard about it from his younger sister, he wrote it down and submitted it.

When the emperor went up to the viewing platform to personally evaluate the essays, he saw this essay and, greatly praising it, awarded him the highest mark in the examination. Then he called him, and bestowing wine upon him, gave him a generous reward and asked, "In which book did you see the explanation about '*wangyŏŏ*'?"

Because the highest ranking candidate (*changwŏn*) had not heard the name of the book, he just replied that his sister had told him, so the emperor said, "You and your brothers have all made names for yourselves as scholars, as your younger sister is like that, she is indeed worthy of being the younger sister of her elder brothers!"

When Yuhandang's third eldest brother returned home and related these words, there was no one in the household who did not congratulate him and celebrate the honor, but Yuhandang alone spoke in the following way, "In the *Book of Rites* (*Liji* 禮記) it states, 'In the place where public affairs are attended to, do not speak about matters relating to women',[40] so how could you speak about your younger sister in the court. In ordinary times I avoid any praise of myself being heard outside the home, so how could I welcome being praised at the court? Furthermore, it is a pity that my elder brother's first words upon advancing in the world should be counter to the *Book of Rites*."

Her third eldest brother apologized for his mistake.

Regretting Being Born as a Woman

One day when Vice Director Sa and his brothers visited to pay their respects to their parents and then looked for their younger sister, his wife said, "She visited to pay her respects and then went."

When the brothers found Yuhandang, she was sitting quietly at a desk without reading and with a sad expression, so the brothers asked, "Younger sister what kind of day is it today that you are sitting alone, and what is it

40 'Summary of Ceremonies II' (Quli xia 曲禮下), *Book of Rites*: "In the place where public affairs are attended to, do not speak about matters relating to women." (公庭, 不言婦女.)

that you are worrying about?"

Yuhandang sighed and answered, "When I think about my life, I can never become a man but will always be a woman. All the natural world is good, and viewing many famous mountains and streams is the pleasurable occupation of men, but I cannot do that. Widely reading the works of history of past generations and thoroughly examining the historical records about the political upheavals of all the ages increases the wisdom of men, but I cannot do that. Collecting many extraordinary writings and books (*kimun pyŏksŏ* 奇文僻書), stacking them up in a raised pavilion, planting unusual flowers and all kinds of grasses in a garden and sitting in their midst composing sentences is the wonderful occupation of men, but I cannot do that.

Passing the civil examination in one's youth, offering a lifetime of experience and helping the nation from above to achieve peace and an era of sagely rule, while from below preserving the family name and glorifying oneself as a man of letters are the occupations of men, but I cannot do such things. I am afraid to walk down the hallway. I worry that my words might spread abroad. All I can do is embroidery and sewing, which is no more significant than just preparing food. I know things in my mind, but I cannot write down a single one of them. As this is the case, how can I not feel deep resentment about my lot if I compare it to the diverse occupations of men?"

Vice Director Sa replied, "After heaven and earth separated, the masculine heavenly way (Qiandao 乾道)[41] revered movement, and this principle is clearly stated by the masculine creative hexagram (Qiangua 乾卦) and the feminine receptive hexagram (Kungua 坤卦). From ancient times learned women have never accomplished anything by insisting on engaging in the affairs of the world, so are you lamenting now that you are the only one? Even among men in the world, not every man achieves distinction and accomplishments. Even among men, there are countless ones who live as though they were in a dream or inebriated and then die.

Concerning such people, it would be better to be a woman, pay attention to oneself, perfect one's nature and eradicating faults all one's life, obtain a name for oneself as a wise wife in this world—so how can you envy foolish men. Apart from the literary composition and occupations that you mentioned, the foremost is scholarship. How is academic study any different for a man or a woman? Younger sister you have an outstanding character, and also you are skilled in writing and worldly affairs, but nevertheless you were born a woman. When our parents and we saw your

---

41 Qiandao (乾道): 'Creative hexagram' (Qiangua 乾卦), *Book of Changes* (*Yijing*), "Heaven, in its motion, (gives the idea of) strength. The superior man, in accordance with this, nerves himself to ceaseless activity." (天行健, 君子以自彊不息.)

exceptional wisdom and your intelligent writing, we always felt heartrending pity, and now upon hearing your words, my heart is even more sorrowful. Your character is already close to the Way, and the teachings of our family are all based on scholarship, so exert yourself in the pursuit of scholarship, and if you become a 'superior person among women' (*yŏ jung kunja* 女中君子), how could your parents and brothers not admire you?"

The Reason for Standing in Front of the Ancestral Shrine Doorway

When Yuhandang was nine years old, a fire broke out on one side of Scholar Sa's house. All the people in the household were shocked, and after the fire was put out, they found that Yuhandang was not in her room. The people searched for her high and low, and then they found that Yuhandang had opened the central door of the ancestral shrine and was standing inside the central doorway with the key in her hand. When the people asked her the reason, Yuhandang replied, "Everyone in the whole family was at their wits end and preoccupied with trying to put out the fire, but as I am a child, I am not able to put out a fire. But if the fire came close to the ancestral shrine,

I was worried that in the rush the adults would be falling over themselves trying to open the door, so I opened the central door of the ancestral shrine, and as I could not leave it unattended after already having opened it, I remained to guard it."

Everyone considered this to be admirable, and also Lord Scholar Sa upon hearing this said, "As your thoughts are always outstanding in this way, it is regrettable that you were not born a man."

Yuhandang's Marriage

Once Yuhandang had come of age there were many people among the wealthy and noble families in the district that sought her hand in marriage. Scholar Sa declined them all and said to Vice Director Sa, "The filially pious and fraternal conduct of Tu Wŏnyong (C. Du Yuanyong 杜元庸) who is now a minister (K. *sangsŏ*; C. *shangshu* 尙書), is clear from a distance. His family and character also are in accord with my will. They say his eldest son Ch'ŏnbok (C. Tianfu 天復) has received his parents' teaching and is outstanding, so what do you think about contracting a marriage between him and Yuhandang?"

"Indeed he is worthy. When my younger sister was born there were unusual omens in the form of dreams (*mongjo*). While she was growing up, her thoughts were deep and calm, and she never transgressed the Way. Her demeanor is mild and composed, so her descendants will flourish greatly. As Minister Tu's family tradition is extremely benevolent and it is a family that will have many descendants, it is right that we seek each other out."

Finally, when the marriage was contracted with Minister Tu's family, Minister Tu was overjoyed and said, "Concerning the duty of intermarriage between scholars and superior persons, discussing wealth is the custom of barbarians, and coveting power is something scholars have guarded against. Not only have I always had a deep friendship with Scholar Sa, but I consider his character and conduct to be extremely beautiful, so how could this marriage contract between our two families be a chance happening?"

Having agreed upon the marriage, Scholar Sa's family intended to select an auspicious day (*t'aegil*). At that time in the home of Imperial Censor (K. *siŏsa*; C. *shiyushi* 侍御史) Liu Huang who was a descendant of Chengyibai (誠意伯) Liu Ji (劉基),[42] a book on the art of choosing auspicious days had been

---

42 Chengyibai (誠意伯) Liu Ji (劉基): The courtesy name of Liu Ji (1311–1375) was Bowen (伯溫). As a scholar who lived around the end of the Yuan dynasty and the beginning of the Ming dynasty, he made meritorious contributions to the foundation of the Ming dynasty and was invested with the title 'Chengyibai'. He was also well versed in the art of divination (*myŏngnihak*

handed down from generation to generation, and its methodology was extremely precise.

As fortune would have it, Censor Liu and Scholar Sa had a relationship that was as 'strong as steel and as fragrant as orchids' (K. *kŭmnan chi kyo*; C. *jinlan zhi jiao* 金蘭之交),[43] so when he visited Scholar Sa, and while they were enjoying themselves by sharing a cup of wine together, Scholar Sa said, "How would it be if you selected an auspicious day for the marriage of my young daughter?"

Censor Liu agreed to this saying, "There are three levels in the method of selecting an auspicious day, namely, upper, middle and lower, so upper-level people cannot use middle- and lower-level dates, and middle- and lower-level people cannot use upper-level dates. The people of the world do not know about this law and just want to choose an auspicious day because they do not know about this principle of harmonization. With which family will the marriage be contracted?"

命理學).

43 *Kŭmnan chi kyo* (金蘭之交): 'A relationship as strong as steel and as fragrant as orchids.' 'Treatise on the Appended Remarks I' (Xici zhuan shang 繫辭傳上), *Book of Changes* (*Yijing*). "The comradeship of two people is sharp enough to cut through metal; the words of comradeship have a fragrance like orchids." (二人同心, 其利斷金, 同心之言, 其臭如蘭.)

"With the family of the eldest son of Minister Tu Wŏnyong."

Censor Liu was overjoyed and said, "Minister Tu is my lifelong friend. Not only is our friendship deep, but his family tradition is most benevolent, and his descendants will surely prosper. Indeed, we will be able to use an upper-level auspicious day. How could I refuse to select the date for the marriage ceremony on behalf of my two friends?"

Finally, he selected the date and said, "I have selected the 24th day of the second lunar month of next year, the Sinmyo Year. That day is the so-called 'case of two butterflies pairing up and flying together' (*ssangbi hojŏp kyŏk* 雙飛胡蝶格),[44] so not only will the couple's descendants be wealthy and noble, but among their offspring they will give birth to many intelligent and wise men and wives."

With gratitude Scholar Sa said, "The marriage has been contracted with the family of a friend, and a close friend has selected the date. This is truly an extraordinary thing."

---

44 *Ssangbi hojŏp kyŏk* (C. Shuangfei hudie ge 雙飛胡蝶格): This is a special term in divination for weighing up and evaluating the Five Elements (K. *Ohaeng*; C. *Wuxing* 五行) of the Four Pillars (K. *Saju*; C. *Sizhu* 四柱), and literally means the 'case of two butterflies pairing up and flying together'.

A Frugal Marriage Ceremony

As Scholar Sa's wife wanted to have an elaborate marriage ceremony, Scholar Sa said, "Having raised a child and arranged her marriage, how could parents not want to hold an extravagant marriage ceremony? But excessively splendid things provoke jealousy in the Creator (Chomulchu 造物主) and easily cause disasters, whereas it is said that frugality brings blessings. This is not just an ancient saying. I myself have observed its veracity over many years in this world in the families of relatives and friends (*chig'u* 直友).[45] Among the families that venerated luxury by competing amongst each other, there are few families that have always favored splendor and never met disaster, so I cannot help but be wary of this. Also, Minister Tu's household is renowned throughout the world for being honest and frugal. Because they have held high positions from generation to generation, it is a house that the people of the world admire. Our family is also a family that has been said to be pure and virtuous from generation to generation. Now that our two families have

---

45 *Chig'u* (直友): A friend with whom one can talk in a straightforward way. 'Jishi' (季氏), *Analects*. "There are three types of beneficial relationships. It is beneficial to associate with an honest person, with a sincere person, and with someone with much learning." (益者三友, 友直, 友諒, 友多聞, 益矣.)

our children married, people will open their eyes and watch us, so how can we now forsake our family traditions for the sake of our young daughter's marriage? Absolutely do not buy any silk or jade, as it would be best to follow the example embodied in the phrase 'a thorn tree hairpin and burlap skirt' (*hyŏngch'ae p'ogun* 荊釵布裙).'[46]

Vice Director Sa said, "As it has become customary for the world to be extravagant in these times, there are many superior men who read books who deplore this. Also, because Minister Tu's family and our family are both renowned in the world, it is right to try to be frugal so that the world can follow our example."

Lady No said to Vice Director Sa, "It is right for the children to be frugal and preserve their blessings. Might it not be that by making the marriage ceremony of our two families a frugal one, the trend towards luxury in the world will be changed?"

"We are not discussing whether the world will imitate us or not; it is just right for our family at least to preserve our family tradition. In ancient times Guo Linzong (郭林宗)[47] was a renowned scholar, and because he wore

---

46 *Hyŏngch'ae p'ogun* (荊釵布裙): A thorn tree hairpin and burlap skirt. This expression refers to dressing in a frugal manner.

47 Guo Linzong (郭林宗): Guo Tai (郭泰, 128–169). Guo was a well-known personage in the Later Han era whose courtesy name was Linzong (林宗). One day he was walking along a

a hat that was broken on one side, the people of the world imitated him by wearing hats that were broken on one side, and this hat was called a 'dog-eared turban' (K. *chŏlgak kŏn*; C. *zhejiao jin* 折角巾). Even though Guo Linzong was such a simple and modest (*ch'ŏngdam* 淸淡) scholar, people admired him and so this happened. If, in the house of a gentleman who reads, manners are taught and frugality is revered, how can there be no benefit to the way the world is governed? In addition, it is said that the eldest son of Minister Tu, Ch'ŏnbok, excelled in filial piety before he was ten years old, and he is said to be a filial son (*hyoja*) by all from far and near. As a sixteen-year-old boy, he was not only famous for his literary composition and learning, but also for his knowledge of etiquette, gentle behavior and obedience to his father's teachings, so people have called him 'a son who takes after his father'. It will not please his heart if the marriage ceremony is carried out in an extravagant way."

"Even knowledgeable young people like splendid things."

---

road when it started to rain, and one edge of his headwear became bent, so other people imitated this.

"Young persons may like luxury, but it is right for adults to forbid it. Since Tu Ch'ŏnbok[48] is well-educated, how could we be extravagant and lead him into the wrong way?"

"This is what your father said, and as this is what you say, too, how can I not do it? My heart rejoices at this, too."

Returning the Silk

A long time ago, Scholar Sa's friend Drafting Adviser (*Sain* 舍人) Chin had had to have a funeral for his parent, and being in poverty, he was unable to hold the funeral. Hearing about this, Scholar Sa sent 200 pieces of silver so that he could hold the funeral ceremony, and afterwards Drafting Adviser Chin became Governor of Shujun (Shujun taishou 蜀郡太守).[49] So when he heard that

48 From this point in the original text Tu Ch'ŏnbok is referred to as Tu *hyoja* (filial son Tu) or simply *hyoja*. Rather than referring to him with the rather cumbersome appellation in English as Filial Son Tu (Tu *hyoja*) and the vague appellation Filial Son (*hyoja*), the translator has opted to refer to him by his family name and given name Tu Ch'ŏnbok when he is referred to as Tu *hyoja* and as Ch'ŏnbok when he is referred to just as *hyoja*.

49 Shujun taishou (蜀郡太守): Shujun is a region in present-day Sichuan Province (四川省) and has been famous for its silk since ancient times.

Scholar Sa's daughter was getting married, he sent fifty bolts of silk from the Shu region. Scholar Sa refused to receive them, and after sending them back, he went into the inner quarters and said to his wife, "Governor Chin said he was sending the silk to support the marriage of our daughter. Such silk is difficult to find in this world, so it could be well used for the marriage."

"We decided not to use silk for this marriage, so how could we use it just because it was sent by someone else? Even though we have already decided not to use it, it could not be clearer when a superior person has to decline or accept something. It seems it would be better to send it back."

Laughing, Scholar Sa said, "I already sent it back before hearing your words. As you responded in this way, it seems that we are both of the same mind."

When Governor Chin saw Scholar Sa's letter in reply and that the silk he had sent had been returned, overwhelmed with embarrassment, he praised Scholar Sa's humble heart saying, "I know this person's integrity in his daily life, but to have this much integrity is an illness."

A Mother's Entreaty

After several months had passed the auspicious day arrived, and when they returned from greeting Yuhandang's parents-in-law (*ch'inyŏng* 親迎), her mother No-*ssi* admonished Yuhandang, "When you enter the home of your in-laws, even after you have done everything with respectful and careful (*tongdong ch'okch'ok* 洞洞屬屬) sincerity, do not be at ease. As there are many women in this world who are unable to attend their parents-in-law as if they were their own parents, this is extremely lamentable. When parents are raising a daughter, they always know that they will send her to another person's home, so they do not think of entrusting her to their own family. Parents-in-law first welcome their new daughter-in-law, and as the descendants of the family are completely entrusted to the daughter-in-law, the parents-in-law both love the daughter-in-law, and their expectations of her are weighty. If you become a daughter-in-law, how can you be careless regarding such expectations? As one should have nothing but devotion and respect when attending one's parents-in-law, after going to the home of your parents-in-law, you should get up early and go to bed late (*sukhŭng yamae* 夙興夜寐), be careful and respectful, and concerning every word and deed, you must first report to your elders before carrying them out. Only trust your mother-in-law's love and do not be careless in your mind in the slightest, and if you serve with sincerity, you will come to be called a virtuous daughter-in-law. You will also come to be called a virtuous wife of a superior man; and giving birth to sons and daughters, if you teach them and guide them in the way of righteousness, you will be called a virtuous mother. So these three things are your duty. The enjoyment of prosperity, honor and blessings of your descendants all depends upon your mind. If you strive to be benevolent and pursue righteousness in your conduct, Heaven will bless you, so all the fortune and misfortune of people arises from their own body. Who does not know to serve one's parents-in-law with all one's sincerity? But there are only a few women in this world who study the classics, so they are ignorant of the study of righteousness. But what you have seen and heard at home is different from what other ignorant people have seen and heard in their homes, and as your benevolent and filially pious character and intellectual talent is far beyond that of others, we not only love you with all our heart but also completely trust you. Think of your parents-in-law as your own parents, your husband's brothers as your own brothers and relatives. If there is no good deed left undone, we will see the efficacy of our parental teaching."

Yuhandang listened to these words with her head bowed, and when she arrived at her parents-in-law's home, she offered the formal greeting to her parents-in-law (*hyŏn kugo rye* 見舅姑禮).[50] Minister Tu was extremely delighted and said to his wife, "I heard the rumor that the bride had an extremely benevolent and filially pious character; her eyebrows and eyes are very distinct, and her behavior is very calm, so she is truly a vessel that will receive many blessings. This will add to our family's honor?"

"Her parents' teaching was very devoted. A young woman enters her new home for the first time, and her behavior is this beautiful, so how could that be if her innate personality was not outstanding. This is truly fortunate."

Yuhandang's Physiognomy

Minister Tu's elder female maternal cousin Chu-*ssi* (C. Zhu-*shi* 朱氏) was the wife of Vice Director of the Ministry of Personnel (K. Ibu sirang; C. Libu shilang 吏部侍郎) Ha Munjung (C. He Wenzhong 賀文中). From her childhood she had been gifted at physiognomy, but thinking this was inappropriate for

---

50 *Hyŏn kugo rye* (見舅姑禮): A ceremony in which the daughter-in-law greets her parents-in-law for the first time after the marriage ceremony.

women, she had never spoken out about it throughout her life. Minister Tu also considered it to be akin to sorcery and had never engaged in discussion about it, but on this day he was so delighted upon seeing the bride that he said to Lady Chu, "Our brothers and sisters have gathered at the feast today, and even in the eyes of an ordinary person, our new daughter-in-law's appearance and presence is out of the ordinary. What if my elder sister breaks her vow and engages in a discussion about the bride's physiognomy?"

Laughing Chu-*ssi* said, "All my life my lord has admonished me never to speak about physiognomy, but as you are ordering me to speak about it for the first time today, is this because you are overjoyed at seeing your daughter-in-law for the first time? As my lord's daughter-in-law is no different from my own daughter-in-law, how could I refuse? But as the bride is a person from a family learned in scholarship and virtuous conduct, if we speak about this kind of sorcery, she will be laughing at us inside."

"In ancient times Confucius' maternal grandfather observed the physiognomy of Shuliang He (叔梁紇)[51] and considered him worthy to be his

---

51 Shuliang He (叔梁紇): 'The Family of Confucius' (Kongzi shijia 孔子世家), *Records of the Grand Historian*. "Shuliang He had an illicit relationship with the daughter of Yan-*shi* (顏氏), who gave birth to Confucius." (紇與顏氏女, 野合而生孔子.)

son-in-law; Lord Lü (呂公)[52] saw the physiognomy of Han Gaozu (漢高祖) and Fan Kuai (樊噲) and chose them as his sons-in-law, so since ancient times has there not been discussion of physiognomy?"

Chu-*ssi* propounded, "The art of physiognomy does not depend upon examining the face alone; observation of the whole body, the way of walking and moving is paramount. This bride's overall appearance is like that of a turtle; her way of walking and moving her hands and feet is extremely serious and calm, and as there is not the slightest sense of frivolity about her, this is indeed extremely valuable. Her lifespan is infinite and the prosperity of her descendants unfathomable. In ancient times Hua Fengren (華封人) blessed Emperor Yao (堯) with 'long life (*su* 壽), wealth (*pu* 富) and many sons (*ta namja* 多男子)'.[53] Is there more anyone could wish for than these three? Speaking about the face, the Five Peaks (K. *Oak;* C. *Wuyue* 五嶽)[54] are well rounded and have an auspicious aura; although the two eyes are mild,

---

52 According to the 'Biography of Gaozu' (Gaozu benji 高祖本紀) in the *Records of the Grand Historian*, Lord Lü was adept at assessing people's physiognomy and is said to have chosen Han Gaozu as his son-in-law. Fan Kuai (樊噲), who was Han Gaozu's general, was married to Lord Lü's younger daughter.

53 According to 'Heaven and Earth' (Tiandi 天地), *Zhuangzi* (莊子), Hua Fengren was a person who guarded the Hua (華) region, from whom Emperor Yao received three kinds of blessings, namely, 'long life (C. *shou*; K. *su* 壽), wealth (C. *fu*; K. *pu* 富) and many sons (C. *duo nanzi*; K. *ta namja* 多男子)'.

54 *Oak* (C. *Wuyue* 五嶽) refers to the 'Five Sacred Mountains' in Daoism: In physiognomy this term signifies the forehead, nose, chin, and the left and right cheekbones.

they have a brilliance, so her character is kind, and she is also outstandingly talented. Her nose indicates wealth, and it also reveals the character of her mind. Her nose is extremely well-proportioned and substantial, so her mind will be benevolent and compassionate, and she will also have sufficient wealth. Her mouth is an even rarer type. In the art of physiognomy, it is a goblet of the type that can consume all kinds of difficulties. As the ears cannot be seen by a person sitting next to them, they are not only a precious type, but as they are also whiter than her face, her name will be known all over the world. I have seen a succession of physiognomies of many maternal and paternal women relatives, but this is the first time I have seen a person with such a combination of precious physiognomic features as this bride has. Congratulations, as the descendants of the house of my lord will be even more prosperous."

Minister Tu was extremely delighted and said, "My thoughts are the same. My elder sister's words are indeed clear. It is a great blessing for our family. I never usually drink alcohol, but today I will drink."

He then ordered the bride to present the wine cup, and he drank three cups.

Taking Care of Her Sick Mother-in-law

Yuhandang had already spent a long time at the home of her parents-in-law. She attended her parents-in-law with filial piety and was obedient towards her husband. She was extremely friendly towards her brothers-in-law and sisters-in-law, and she treated her relatives and servants with benevolence, so people in her neighborhood all sang her praises. Minister Tu and his wife considered the sagacity of their eldest daughter-in-law to be quite out of the ordinary. One day Minister Tu's wife became slightly ill, so for over a day she was unable to get up from her bed. Yuhandang exerted all her sincerity day and night, personally tasted her medicine and never left her side. The outstanding virtue of the filially pious daughter-in-law was such that people who witnessed it were all deeply impressed.

Minister Tu also considered this to be extraordinary and said to his wife, "As the conduct of the bride is not such that can be attained by a young woman, if she had not been born as a noble lady how could this be possible?"

"As I experienced this illness, the way she boiled tea and porridge with her own hands in a way suitable for my sick body as well as the way she sat me up and laid me down were well beyond the strength of a child. In spite of my daughter-in-law's weak body, she was able to ease my difficulties, and I was able to recover from this illness easily. How could this not be considered to be extraordinary?"

Making Her Father-in-law's Court Attire

One day Minister Tu's wife had to cut out the minister's court attire (*chobok* 朝服)[55] and was going to have it sewn it together.

"As an official robe is different from other garments, please sew it in front of me."

On receiving this order, Yuhandang picked up a ruler and scissors and after cutting out the cloth, she discussed the measurements with her husband's younger sister, and as her hands moved so quickly as they sewed, the task was completed before the sun set. Minister Tu's wife considered this to be astounding. The following morning Minister Tu attended the

55 *Chobok* (C. *chaofu* 朝服) was the attire worn by officials when attending to government affairs in the court.

morning audience at the court (*choboe* 朝會)[56] wearing it, and it fitted him very well. From that time forward Yuhandang was put in charge of making Minister Tu's clothes, and nothing ever lacked as all the clothing for the four seasons was made in advance.

Questions and Answers on the *Book of Odes*

One day Yuhandang arose and read a piece of writing and as Tu Ch'ŏnbok had also awoken and arisen, sitting down he asked, "What text are you reading?"

"It is the *Book of Odes* (*Shijing* 詩經)."

Then after reading one or two phrases, the cock crowed. Yuhandang asked, "In 'Zhengfeng' (鄭風) in the *Book of Odes*, the lady who wrote the passage 'The woman says the cock is crowing and the man says the dawn has brightened faintly'[57] was extremely wise, but the woman who wrote

56 *Choboe* (C. *chaobui* 朝會) was a morning meeting in the court at which the officials greeted the king/emperor.

57 'The Woman Says the Cock is Crowing' (*Nü yue jiming* 女曰鷄鳴), 'Odes of Zheng', *Book of Odes*. "The woman says the cock is crowing and the man says the dawn has brightened faintly.

the passage, 'The wind and rain rage and the cock crows' was extremely immoral. Both are writings by people from the country of Zheng, and the sound of cocks crowing in Zheng would not be different. It is strange that people's nature in terms of good and evil should differ so greatly."

"That is correct. Therefore, Mencius (Mengzi 孟子) said, 'the people who get up when they hear the cock crow and diligently carry out good deeds belong to the followers of Emperor Shun (舜),[58] but the people who get up when they hear the cock crow and diligently pursue profit belong to the followers of Brigand Zhi (盜蹠).'[59] Also, he admonished that 'if one gets up when the cock crows, thoughts gradually arise.'"[60]

Arise, Sir, and look at the night sky, if the morning star be not shining. Bestir yourself, and move about, to shoot the wild ducks and geese." (女曰鷄鳴, 士曰昧旦. 子興視夜, 明星有爛, 將翶將翔, 弋鳧與雁.)

58 'Wind and Rain' (Fengyu 風雨), 'Odes of Zheng', *Book of Odes*. "The wind and rain rage and the cock crows. But now that I have seen you, how could my illness not be cured?" (風雨瀟瀟, 鷄鳴膠膠. 旣見君子, 云胡不瘳.)

59 'Wholeheartedness I'(Jinxin shang 盡心上), *Mencius* (*Mengzi* 孟子). "Mencius said, people who get up when they hear the cock crow and diligently carry out good deeds belong to the people of Emperor Shun (舜); people who get up when they hear the cock crow and diligently pursue profit belong to the people of Brigand Zhi (盜蹠)." (孟子曰, 鷄鳴而起, 孳孳爲善者, 舜之徒也, 鷄鳴而起, 孳孳爲利者, 蹠之徒也.)

60 'Admonition on rising early and going to bed late' (Suxing yemei zhen 夙興夜寐箴) by the Song-dynasty Confucian scholar Chen Bai (陳栢). "If the cock crows and you awaken, thoughts gradually arise." (鷄鳴而寤, 思慮漸馳.)

Giving Birth to Seven Sons

One day Daoist Master Chang, who had previously been acquainted with Minister Tu, visited Minister Tu and said, "In the past when my lord held your grandfather's funeral, I selected the mountain (for the gravesite). As it was unusually auspicious in all the world not only will your descendants prosper, but you will have countless descendants who will be sages and superior persons. Furthermore, the *ansan* (案山)[61] is a seven-peaked mountain (*ch'ilbongsan* 七峰山), and as the first peak is even more magnificent, seven male descendants will be born in the future; these seven male descendants will all be noble and outstanding at literary composition; and due to the influence of the seven peaks,[62] it has been said that the eldest male descendant would be born as a superior person. This year is the thirtieth year, so it would not be inappropriate to discuss the destiny of the mountains. Has a grandson been born to my lord this year?"

---

61 As a geomantic term, *ansan* refers to a small and low mountain in front of a grave (*hyŏl* 穴) that is like a low table placed in front of someone who is sitting down.

62 The content from 'seven peaks……' in this section to '……After Yuhandang became pregnant Lady Won admonished her to avoid certain foods' at the beginning of the following section is missing in the Keimyung University version of the text, so it was supplemented here with content from the edition prepared by Nason (羅孫) Kim Tonguk (金東旭, 1922–1990), a pioneering scholar of premodern Korean literature.

"This year spring has gone and summer has arrived, but no child has been born in our household."

"That mountain is a renowned mountain under heaven, and I put my whole heart into selecting it, so within this year a precious male descendant will be born."

Minister Tu was overjoyed and went into the inner quarters and asked, "Are any of our daughters-in-law pregnant?"

"Our eldest daughter-in-law Sa-*ssi* has been pregnant for five months."

Minister Tu was greatly pleased and came out and told Daoist Master Chang, who said, "That is right. In the past the *ansan* of the tomb of the great-great grandfather of Cai Jiufeng (蔡九峰)[63] had nine peaks, and the middle peak was particularly high and well proportioned. So Cai Jiufeng had nine sons, and as Cai Jiufeng's scholarship was renowned, people said this was the "energy of the high middle peak," and so Cai's brush name came to be Jiufeng (Nine Peaks). Also, among the seven peaks of my lord's household's mountain, the first peak is the highest and most graceful, and as all the remaining peaks are also graceful and extraordinary, all seven brothers will in turn be born and be virtuous people, famous for their

---

63 Cai Jiufeng (蔡九峰): The Song-dynasty scholar Cai Chen (蔡沈, 1167–1230), whose brush name was Jiufeng (九峰). He was said to be well-versed in the *Book of History* and numerology.

literary skill. This year the eldest son will be born, next year the second son will be born, and every year afterwards the remaining seven sons will be born."

After that indeed seven sons were born in the same number of years. Minister Tu named them after the mountain peaks, Ilbong (First Peak), Ibong (Second Peak), Sambong (Third Peak), Sabong (Fourth Peak), Obong (Fifth Peak), Yukpong (Sixth Peak) and Ch'ilbong (Seventh Peak).

A Mother-in-law's Requests Concerning Prenatal Education

After Yuhandang became pregnant Lady Wŏn admonished her to avoid certain foods saying, "When you became pregnant, you had already read in *Biographies of Women* such admonitions as 'When standing do not stand on one leg; when sitting do not lean to one side; do not look at anything immoral with your eyes; and do not listen to lewd sounds with your ears.'[64] Also, in the medical books (*ŭisŏ* 醫書), there are many foods mentioned that are

64 "When standing …": See footnote 12.

forbidden. All kinds of foods such as dog meat, pork, fish without scales,[65] crabs, Job's tears, barley malt, buckwheat, purslane greens, mushrooms in general, ginger, mustard and garlic are all forbidden.[66] Also, she must dress neither too warmly nor too coolly; she must not eat too much; she must not drink too much; she must not go up to a high place; she must not lift heavy things; she must not work too hard; and in the final month of pregnancy, she must not wash her hair, and she must not raise her voice.'[67] All these words are from famous physicians from ancient times who clearly understood the energy of the harmony of heaven and earth and the principles of conceiving

---

65 "Fish without scales" refers to eels, loaches, squid, and so on.

66 'Miscellaneous diseases' (Chappyŏng 雜病), *Exemplar of Korean Medicine* (*Tongŭi pogam* 東醫寶鑑). "If a pregnant woman eats dog meat, her child will not be able to make a sound; if she eats rabbit meat, the child will have a hare lip; if she eats fish without scales, the delivery will be difficult; and if she eats crabs, she will deliver prematurely. …… If she eats ginger sprouts, the baby will have too many fingers; if she eats Job's tears, she will miscarry; if she eats barley malt, the energy required for the growth of the fetus will be diminished; if she eats purslane greens, she will miscarry; and if she eats garlic, the energy required for the growth of the fetus will be diminished. …… if she eats various kinds of mushrooms, the child will die prematurely from convulsions." (食犬肉, 令子無聲, 食兎肉, 令子缺脣. 食無鱗魚, 難産, 食螃蟹, 令子橫生. … 食薑芽, 令子多指. 食薏苡, 墮胎. 食麥芽, 消胎氣. 食莧菜, 墮胎. 食蒜, 消胎氣. … 食諸般菌蕈, 令子驚風而夭.) The original source is *Introduction to Medicine* (*Yixue rumen* 醫學入門) by the Ming dynasty physician Li Chan (李梴).

67 *Book of Obstetrics in Korean Translation* (*Ŏnhae t'aesan chibyo* 諺解胎産集要). "In the *Married Woman's Comprehensive Collection* (C. *Furen daquan*; K. *Puin tajŏn* 婦人大全) it states, a pregnant woman should not dress too warmly, should not eat to the point of satiety, should not drink too much, should not take medicine recklessly, should not receive acupuncture or moxibustion treatment recklessly. She should not lift heavy things or go up to high or rocky places, and she should not sleep or lie down too long. She should walk around occasionally without fail, and in the final month of pregnancy, she should not wash her hair." (婦人大全曰, 衣毋太溫, 食毋太飽, 飮毋大醉, 勿妄服湯藥, 勿妄用鍼灸, 勿擧重登高涉險, 勿多睡臥. 須時時行步, 臨月不可洗頭.)

a child. How could you violate them in the slightest? If you break these taboos through carelessness, and a child is conceived in that year, even if that child is still a fetus in the womb, it is your own child, and as a mother how could you violate in the slightest these words that protect your child. It is more difficult to heal the illness of the young than it is to heal them once they have grown up, and as it is more difficult to heal the illness of a fetus in the womb than it is to heal a young child, it is right to thoroughly comply (with these taboos). Even if children hurt or injure themselves while playing together, parents feel distress, so how could you harm your own child because you ate a forbidden food or did a forbidden action. It is extremely displeasing that after many women in this world give birth to a child, they are so overflowing with love for them that they carry, hug and bother them in unreasonable and excessive ways, but because they are unaware of the child in their womb right before birth, they are careless in their eating and behavior."

Yuhandang replied, "Listening to the words with which you are now warning and admonishing me, I am reminded of the words from *Biographies of Women* and the *Elementary Learning*. 'When standing do not stand on one leg; and when sitting do not lean to one side.' Such words are not only for pregnant women but are also for men who engage in scholarship. The phrase 'Do not look at immoral things, and do not listen to lewd sounds' is not mentioned in *Biographies of Women* alone. The saying, 'The superior person does not stay his ears and eyes on deceitful sounds and dazzling colors',[68] is widely found in the classics. The words 'do not go up to a high place' and 'do not go near a precipitous place' were the teachings of ancient sages who said, 'While your parents are alive do not go up to a high place, and do not go near a precipitous place.'[69] As the words 'do not eat too much' are in the *Analects*, 'When you eat, do not eat to the point of satiety.'[70] I wonder if I will be able to take all the teachings of the sages and admonitions of the medical texts to heart and personally put them into practice. The reason it is difficult to cure a child if it becomes ill when it is a fetus in the womb (*t'aejung* 胎中) can be found in the words of Master Zhu (Zhuzi 朱子) in which he made a comparison with a child becoming ill while a fetus in the womb.[71] All the words you have spoken are very appropriate, so

---

68 'Respecting the body (General Decorum)', *Elementary Learning*. "The superior person does not permit his mind to be attracted to deceitful sounds and seductive colors." (君子, 姦聲亂色, 不留聰明.) The original source is 'Record on the Subject of Music' (Yueji 樂記), *Book of Rites*.

69 'Illustrating the Cardinal Principles', *Elementary Learning*. "(When parents are still living) do not go up to a high place, do not go near to a precipitous place, do not scold in a loud voice and do not laugh loudly." (不登高, 不臨深, 不苟訾, 不苟笑.) The original source is 'Summary of the Rules of Propriety I' (Quli shang), *Book of Rites*.

70 'To Learn' (Xue'er 學而), *Analects*. "Confucius said, he who aims to be a man of complete virtue, in his food does not seek to gratify his appetite, nor in his dwelling-place does he seek the appliances of ease; he is earnest in what he is doing, and careful in his speech; he frequents the company of men of principle that he may be rectified—such a person may be said indeed to love to learn." (子曰, 君子, 食無求飽, 居無求安, 敏於事而愼於言, 就有道而正焉, 可謂好學也已.)

71 'Disciples of Master Cheng' (Chengzi menren 程子門人), *Collection of Conversations of Master*

how could I not take them to heart? However, because I have not spent my whole life engaging in scholarship, I fear that I might betray the teachings of the sages and misinterpret their admonitions."

Way of Managing Household Affairs and Establishing a 'Righteous Storehouse'

In the way they treated one another, Tu Ch'ŏnbok and Yuhandang were extremely respectful as though they were each other's guests. Even when they were enjoying a harmonious and loving relationship in the inner quarters, there was no careless teasing or laughter. Also, whenever the couple engaged in a discussion, it was always about how they could make sure that Yuhandang's parents-in-law's food and clothing was neither too cold nor too warm. One day Yuhandang said to Tu Ch'ŏnbok, "The reason for

---

Zhu (*Zhuzi yulei* 朱子語類). "Scholars believe that ailments of the temperament are the most difficult to cure. … Long ago, I saw one doctor who was good at acupuncture who said, 'This illness can be treated by acupuncture, but illnesses contracted by the fetus in the womb are difficult to treat.'" (學者氣質上病最難救. … 向見無爲一醫者, 善用鍼, 嘗云, '是病可以鍼而愈, 惟胎病爲難治.')

being filially pious towards one's parents and serving them, which includes providing them with food and clothing, has not departed from the four characters Confucius spoke to Zengzi (曾子), namely, 'cultivate character, moderate consumption' (C. *xiushen jieyong*; K. *susin chŏlyong* 修身節用). Now in our house we practice the principles of filial piety and serving elders, so we also have to think deeply about the teaching concerning moderating consumption. My parents-in-law's innate character is benevolent. If they see anyone among their relatives or friends in need, they strive to generously provide for them. As there is never enough to share with others, is it not now time to be concerned about how to provide for the wealth of the household? We have to regulate the family fortune separately, and as we will be giving to others, we have to prepare for that. Is this not the 'way of nourishing the will' (K. *yang chi chi to*; C. *yangzhi zhi dao* 養志之道)?'"[72]

---

72 'Li Lou I' (Lilou shang 離婁上), *Mencius*. "Zengzi, in nourishing his father Zeng Xi (曾皙) was always sure to have wine and meat provided. And when they were being cleared away, he would ask respectfully to whom he should give what was left. If his father asked if there was anything left, he was sure to say, 'There is.' After the death of Zeng Xi, when Zeng Yuan (曾元) came to nourish Zengzi, he was always sure to have wine and meat provided. But when the things were being cleared away, he did not ask to whom he should give what was left, and if his father asked if anything was left, he would answer 'No.' As he intended to serve them again. This is what is called 'nourishing the mouth and body.' We may call Zengzi's practice 'nourishing the will'." (曾子養曾皙, 必有酒肉, 將徹, 必請所與, 問有餘, 必曰有. 曾皙死, 曾元養曾子, 必有酒肉, 將徹, 不請所與, 問有餘, 曰亡矣, 將以復進也. 此所謂養口體者也, 若曾子, 則可謂養志也.)

"As I have also thought of this principle in my heart, my wife's words are indeed appropriate. Please think carefully about how we should go about managing these things."

"Hwangunp'yŏng (黃雲坪) estate in Namgwak (南郭) exchanged one year's harvest for 3,000 gold pieces; from what was gained from another estate enough to eat for one year was harvested, and the income from Hwangunp'yŏng was used up every day and ran out. From now on I think it would be good if the young people in our home and even the servants economize on clothing and food. The income from Hwangunp'yŏng will then be more than enough, so if we save for three years, we will have 10,000 pieces of gold. If we combine the income from both places, it will amount to 6,000 pieces of gold every year. Let's not use all of this on food and clothing but save the Hwangunp'yŏng produce separately, build a 'righteous storehouse' (*ŭigo* 義庫) and entrust it to a diligent person so that it can be used when my parents-in-law take care of others."

Tu Ch'ŏnbok praised her, "My wife's insight is indeed discerning. As the building of a righteous storehouse is set forth in the rules and regulations for righteous storehouses (*ŭich'ang* 義倉) by Confucian scholars in the past, let us do the same."

"Now even though we have an income of 6,000 pieces of gold, it will not suffice for what is disbursed, so we have to think of a plan to increase it gradually. In general, the principle for using wealth can only be established if regulations are decided upon from the beginning, so we have to decide upon those regulations precisely."

"I have decided upon this plan from long ago, but as it is happening through my wife's strength today, my wife should also decide upon the regulations."

"We do not have to make many regulations. The disbursement of wealth from the righteous storehouse should be organized into five levels. To anyone among our relatives who is extremely destitute and experiencing ill fortune, we will disburse wealth according to the first level; next we will give according to the second level; then the third level, the fourth level, and the fifth level, step by step reducing the amount given, so that in a year we will be able to cope with just 6,000 pieces of gold. In the future, if we add more and prepare, and it becomes 10,000 pieces of gold, then after that would we not be able to manage to afford almost everything? As there are several brothers in the household, the income from their official positions inside and outside the court can also be accumulated and become wealth handed down from generation to generation. What remains of the salary from their official positions inside and outside the court should not be used to gather more wealth but be put it into the righteous storehouse, and if this is gradually collected, in the future the wealth in the righteous storehouse will increase from 30,000 to 70 or 80,000 pieces of gold. Afterwards, we can gradually plan to increase the amount we can disburse, and if we give an appropriate amount not just to relatives but also to people passing along the road, we will not just be serving the heart of my parents-in-law who want to give now, but will it not also become a means for our children and grandchildren to do righteous deeds in the future?"

Tu Ch'ŏnbok was overjoyed and said, "Ordinary women in this world truly cannot match my wife's management. As I previously heard my father always say that the righteous granary system was good, my wife's opinion today is the same as what I have heard my father say in the past."

So after three years the Hongunp'yŏng (紅雲坪) estate was newly purchased. The income from the two separate estates was 7,000 pieces of gold per year, and as Hongunp'yŏng had been purchased, the income that came into the righteous storehouse in one year was now more than 10,000 pieces of gold. If the parents-in-law met and wanted to support the destitute, Tu Ch'ŏnbok gave instructions for disbursements to be graciously given out according to the first level or the second level. From this time forward relatives and friends came to look upon the wealth in the righteous storehouse just as if it was their own wealth.

Tu Ch'ŏnbok's Dream

One day the Jade Emperor (Okhwang sangje 玉皇上帝) sent a pair of boys wearing crimson clothes to meet Tu Ch'ŏnbok in a dream, so perplexed, Ch'ŏnbok followed the boys. The clouds of five colors were verdant and lush (*ch'ongnong* 葱蘢), abounding in all directions with exotic flowers and plants, and the gates were made of jade. Standing next to the gates were Daoist immortal officials (*sŏn'gwan* 仙官) wearing crimson robes who said, "The Jade Emperor has been waiting a long time, so how could you be so slow!"

And when he was rebuked, Ch'ŏnbok became even more perplexed and followed the boy through the gate.

The stairs were made of blue jade. A raised pavilion was made of crimson jade, and in a lofty place surrounded by a jade balustrade sat the Jade Emperor. Daoist immortal officials were lined up on the left and right, and twelve pairs of boys wearing blue clothes stood on the left and right sides bearing brightly colored phoenix fans (*ch'aebongsŏn* 彩鳳扇). The courtyard was paved with jade of five colors, and its splendor was dazzling. As Ch'ŏnbok was even more awe-stricken and was barely able to look up, the emperor ordered the boys to instruct him to raise his face. Ch'ŏnbok lifted his face for a moment, and the emperor laughed and said, "You, Ch'ŏnbok, when you were down on earth (*hat'o* 下土), were easily able to understand the principle of loving your parents and were no different from the Daoist immortals (*sinsŏn* 神仙) who have heavenly knowledge, and your virtuous wife's insight in establishing a 'righteous storehouse' is indeed in accordance with my desire to aid living beings. For this reason, I have called you here to offer you wine."

Thereupon, he ordered the Daoist immortal boys to give him wine to drink. One Daoist immortal boy went to the jade wine jar and poured some osmanthus wine (*kyehwaju* 桂花酒) into a lotus-shaped wine cup; another boy filled a plate shaped like a lotus leaf with jujubes and gave it to Ch'ŏnbok. Overawed Ch'ŏnbok received the wine and drank it all, and after eating some of the jujubes, he left many of them on the plate. Ch'ŏnbok arose, bowed four times and said, "As these jujubes are truly extraordinary, I would like to take them home to give to my parents to eat."

"How could I not listen to Ch'ŏnbok's words that proceed from his utmost sincerity of heart?"

The emperor ordered the boy to give them to him. The boy wrapped them in a blue silk wrapping cloth (*pojagi*) and placed them inside his sleeve, weighing it down.

The emperor spoke again, "As your seven sons correspond to the seven stars of the Big Dipper (Puktu Ch'ilsŏng; C. Beidou Qixing 北斗七星), your grandsons will correspond to the Twenty-eight Constellations (Isipp'alsu 二十八宿)."

And he ordered a Daoist immortal boy to pick crimson flowers from a cinnamon tree (*kyesu namu*), and he gave four or five bunches to him.

"Share them out among your offspring."

As Ch'ŏnbok was about to depart, the emperor said, "Although I gave you many cinnamon tree blossoms, it is still not enough. I will give you some cinnamon tree blossom seeds, so you can plant them by your house, and they will grow from generation to generation so that your father and your offspring can share them."

One of the boys received the cinnamon tree seeds wrapped in a five-colored flower-patterned wrapping cloth, brought them down from the tower and gave them to him. Tu Ch'ŏnbok arose, knelt down to receive them respectfully and then arose again holding them in his arms. As the emperor ordered the boy to lead the way, the boy went out of the gate. The Daoist immortal officials who had been standing guard at the gate when they had entered said to the boy, "Who is this person that he not only received so many of his majesty's *tongmyŏng hwajo* (洞冥火棗) jujubes, but also how could he have received so many cinnamon tree blossom seeds when even one seed is rarely bestowed upon an ordinary person?"

"This person's conduct is extraordinary and accords with the will of his majesty, so that is why he gave him so much. Even though we have attended his majesty for thousands of years, today is also the first time that we have seen him reward anyone so generously."

Tu Ch'ŏnbok followed the boy back to his home, and after gathering his parents and brothers, and all his male and female paternal and maternal relatives in the wooden-floored living area and embracing them and telling them how proud he was, he awoke and realized it had all been a dream. After Tu Ch'ŏnbok awakened from the dream, the aroma of jujubes came from his mouth; his left and right sleeves appeared weighed down, and he felt as though he was holding cinnamon tree blossom seeds to his chest. Sitting up he fell into deep thought and then the cock crowed.

Tu Ch'ŏnbok Gives up the Civil Examination

Tu Ch'ŏnbok's two younger brothers passed the civil examination. One of them placed first in the exam, and his glory was immeasurable. Yuhandang said to Tu Ch'ŏnbok, "Father achieved the official position of Minister in the Board of Rites (K. Yebu sangsŏ; C. Libu shangshu 禮部尙書), and two members of our household have passed the civil examination. As one is a drafting adviser (K. *sain*; C. *sheren* 舍人)[73] in the Baihuguan (K. Paekhogwan 白虎觀),[74] and one is a compiler (K. *p'yŏnsugwan*; C. *bianxiuguan* 編修官) in the Hanlin Academy (C. Hanlinyuan; K. Hallimwŏn 翰林院), they are devoted to making names for themselves as men of letters. There are only a few people who covet wealth and social rank in this world and are not wary of being excessive who do not later suffer failure. Our house has long been called a house of learning, so how can we not be vigilant not to exceed our bounds today? What greater joy could there be in this world than quitting preparing for the civil examination, adopting the study of the Classics as your task, and steadily teaching writing and virtuous conduct to all your sons and nephews to make them famous Confucian scholars?"

---

73 A drafting adviser (K. *sain*; C. *sheren* 舍人) was a senior 4th rank official.
74 Baihuguan (白虎觀) was the place where Emperor Zhangdi (章帝) of Han (漢) gathered scholars to lecture on the Five Classics (K. Ogyŏng; C. Wujing 五經).

"To stop preparing for the civil examination is a way of guarding against being excessive. As my two younger brothers have risen in the world and gained official positions, there is only one person remaining to attend to all the needs of our parents. How can I leave my parents for the sake of a temporary official position? People of old said, 'How could I exchange the task of caring for my parents for a single day with the official position of one of the three advisers to the king (*samgong* 三公)?' So how could I exchange caring for my parents every day for the position of one of the three advisers to the king? From this day forward, I will stop worrying about getting an official post, and I have made up my mind to stay by my parents' side from morning until evening and to take care that they are neither too hot nor too cold in their daily life. My wife's words now are in accord with righteousness. As someone who has studied the *Book of Changes* all her life, you are well-versed in the hexagram 'Modesty' (Qiangua 謙卦)."[75]

"As a woman I just happened to read the *Book of Changes*, but how can you call that studying? Shouldn't even people who have never studied it at least know this much?"

---

75 'Modesty hexagram' (C. Qiangua 謙卦), *Book of Changes*. "Having already possessed in great measure, you should not seek abundance; there must be modesty and decrease. For this reason after (the hexagram) 'Possession in Great Measure' comes (the hexagram) 'Modesty'."(其有旣大, 不可至於盈滿, 必在謙損, 故大有之後, 受之以謙也.)

From this day forward Tu Ch'ŏnbok stopped preparing for the civil examination.

A Poem Written as a Child

Yuhandang's younger sister-in-law asked her to write something for her, so Yuhandang replied, "When my eldest brother gathered all his younger brothers to read, I listened or studied beside them, but as my writing skill is dull, how could I have written anything? And even if I was skilled in writing, as it is not a woman's responsibility, I have really never written anything."

Her younger sister-in-law always complained that she was not telling her the truth, so one day on the 7th day of the seventh lunar month when Yuhandang was taking out clothes and laying them out in the sun, the younger sister-in-law came to watch and discovered between the clothing chests a piece of paper that had been written on. When the younger sister spread it out, she found the following eight-line poem (K. *yulsi*; C. *lüshi* 律詩).

As the daughter of a Confucian scholar,

(*A si yuga nyŏ* 我是儒家女)

In the year when I studied the *Elementary Learning*.

(*Yŏn pang Sohak si* 年方小學時)

The *Book of Odes* and *Book of History* were originally a family task handed down from generation to generation.

(*Sisŏ wŏn se ŏp* 詩書元世業)

Tairen (太妊)[76] and Taisi (太姒)[77] are my teachers.

(*Im [Ren] Sa [Si] chŭk o sa* 任姒卽吾師)

In cultivating oneself there are three types of self-examination[78] that are appropriate.

(*Su ki ŭi sam sŏng* 修己宜三省)

In governing one's mind there are nine considerations.

(*Ch'i sim chae ku sa* 治心在九思)

The young and ignorant must be raised properly,

(*Tong mong su yang chŏng* 童蒙須養正)

---

76 Tairen (太妊) was the mother of King Wen of Zhou.

77 Taisi (太姒) was the wife of King Wen of Zhou.

78 'Xue'er', *Analects*. "Zengzi said, 'Every day I examine myself in three ways. In doing things for others, have I been disloyal? In my relationships with friends, have I been untrustworthy? Have I transmitted knowledge that I have not mastered myself?'" (曾子曰, 吾日三省吾身. 爲人謀而不忠乎? 與朋友交而不信乎? 傳不習乎?)

So every day memorize the poetry of Huian (Zhu Xi).

(*Il song Hoeam si* 日誦晦庵詩)

Holding this poem, the younger sister-in-law said with admiration, "At last I have got hold of Yuhandang's writing!"

And she took the writing to Lady Wŏn and showing it to her said, "Yuhandang said that she had not written anything, but at last I have got hold of something she wrote."

Her mother looked at it and said, "Indeed, it looks as though she started her academic studies early."

"How do you know that?"

"From the words 'The young and ignorant must be raised properly' (*Tong mong su yang chŏng* 童蒙須養正), I know it was when she was a child, and from the phrase 'In the year when I studied the *Elementary Learning*' (*Yŏn pang Sohak si* 年方小學時), I know it was written when she was eight or nine years old."

"There is only one poem sent by Nanhai Nüzi (南海女子) to her brother when she was seven years old,[79] and the wife of Baili Xi (百里奚) only left

79 'Taking Farewell of Brother' (Songxiong 送兄), *Tangyin* (唐音). "On the way to parting, the clouds have just gathered, and at the pavilion where we will part, the leaves are all flying away. Lamentations, unlike geese people cannot fly in a straight line." (别路雲初起, 離亭葉正飛. 所嗟人異雁, 不作一行歸.) This poem was written by an eleven-year-old girl known as 'Nanhai Nüzi'

behind one poem, 'Song of the Gate Bolt' (*Yanyi ge* 扊扅歌).[80] Just by looking at this single poem by Yuhandang, I know that she began her academic studies when she was eight or nine years old. What could she have done if she had written many poems?"

And she recited it from memory continuously.

Visiting Parents after Three Years

Three years had passed since Yuhandang had left her parents' care. She missed her parents desperately as they were several days' journey away, and since arriving at the home of her parents-in-law, she had not been able to leave even for a single moment as she prepared meals for her parents-in-law, sacrificial rites for their ancestors, and served countless guests. When her

(South China Sea Girl).

80 Baili Xi was a person who lived during the Spring and Autumn period, and when he was captured by Chu (楚), Duke Mu of Qin (Qin Mugong 秦穆公) redeemed him with five black sheepskins and made him his prime minister. When he was setting off as a wanderer, his wife caught a chicken and roasted it using the door latch to make a fire. Later after Baili Xi had become a prime minister, an elderly laundry maid came to see him, and when she sang about this incident, he realized that she was his wife.

younger brother was getting married, she asked her parents-in-law if she could visit her parents, Minister Tu and his wife gave their permission but asked her to return quickly. Yuhandang took her leave, and when she arrived at her parents' home, her parents and brothers were overjoyed and shared their affection for each other as they met again after three years of separation. Her mother embraced her grandchildren and patted them affectionately as she said to Yuhandang, "It is said, 'when a woman gets married, she becomes distant from her parents and brothers',[81] but why after you left has it been so difficult for you to come back?"

"Even though I am lacking courtesy, after leaving my parents and brothers, is it not like the thoughts of the spring water flowing to the River Qi (泉源淇水之懷)?[82] Although there are many women in the household of my parents-in-law who are all assigned to different tasks, my parents-in-law like the food and clothing that I make with my hands, so without a good reason, I was unable to leave."

---

81 'Spring Water' (Quanshui 泉水), *Book of Odes*. "When a woman gets married, she becomes distant from her parents and brothers." (女子有行, 遠父母兄弟.)

82 'Spring Water', *Book of Odes*. "How the water bubbles up from that spring and flows to the River Qi. My heart is in Wei and there is not a day I do not think of it." (毖彼泉水, 亦流于淇. 有懷于衛, 靡日不思.) 'Spring Water' in the *Book of Odes* is about a daughter from Wei marrying into the family of another feudal lord and missing her parental family in Wei. After her mother quotes the question from 'Spring Water' in the *Book of Odes*, Yuhandang responds with another phrase from the same poem.

Cleanliness Is the Most Important Thing for Ritual Food

Yuhandang was entrusted with preparing the ancestral rites. She chose the day before each ancestral rite to clean the house, wash the clothing, as well as to ensure that the male and female servants were all neatly dressed. She also spoke quietly in a low voice to tell them to wash and clean each of the ritual vessels and implements.

"For a banquet the food should be clean; the taste should be valued; there should be numerous different types of food, and they should be plentiful. This is not so in the case of food for the ancestral rites, as in this case cleanliness is of the greatest importance."

So she carried everything out with the utmost devotion, and only after the ancestral rite was over did she feel at ease. As a consequence, all the family members and relatives followed her example.

The Way of Managing Servants

When Yuhandang's mother-in-law Lady Wŏn's paternal niece Miss (*sojŏ* 小姐) Wŏn came, she saw Yuhandang and asked, "My lady's many benevolent deeds are due to the fact that you are innately a gentlewoman, but for someone like me, because I am not good at studying, there is no way for me to learn. Nevertheless, how can one manage male and female servants so that even servants, who are like animals in the mountains and fields, can become loyal retainers?"

"There is no special method for managing servants. Even though they are lowly, first of all we should teach them the duties of filial piety towards their parents and fraternal affection for their siblings, and if we gently persuade them again and again, even though they are ignorant, they will trust and obey words that are in accord with righteousness, and only after that will they make up their mind to obey their master. If they want to do something for their parents, grant them permission, and if you take care of servants without parents with all your heart, there will naturally be no conflict between the minds of superiors and inferiors. If you concern yourself sufficiently about whether they are cold or hot, hungry or full, as they are not made of wood or stone, how could they not be moved? If one grants favor first and stands on dignity later, is sparing with blame and generous in treatment, this is the same way that past kings treated their subjects, and generals treated their troops, which was all in accordance with the same principle. How could the way of treating private servants in an individual household not be the same as this?

In this way, because ensuring that people were not cold or hungry was the most important thing, people in former times reported to the king, 'A top-level monarch knows if others are hungry even if he is full, and he knows if others are cold even if he is warm. A monarch on the next level down knows that other people are hungry when he himself is hungry, and knows that other people are cold when his own body is cold, but the monarch on the level below that does not realize that other people are hungry and cold even when he himself is hungry and cold.'[83] These words are indeed extremely accurate. They are not only relevant to being concerned about servants in one's household who might be cold and

---

83 'Remonstration I' (Jianshang diyi 諫上第一) *Yanzi Chunqiu* (晏子春秋). "Yan Ying (晏嬰) said, 'I heard it said that benevolent kings of old knew whether other people were hungry even if they themselves were full, and even if they were warm whether others were cold, and even if they were at rest whether others were working hard, but our present monarch is not aware of this.'" (晏子曰, '嬰聞古之賢君, 飽而知人之饑, 温而知人之寒, 逸而知人之勞, 今君不知也.')

hungry, but this is also how the superior person deals with all people and things. Also, in a letter that Tao Yuanming of Jin (晉) sent with a servant to the son of his elder brother he warned, 'As he is also someone's child, please treat him well.'[84] No matter how lowly servants might be, treating them with humanity is to emulate the attitude of a benevolent sovereign. Even though Tao Yuanming was a talented teacher who was very learned, he defined the way of treating other people with just two characters 'good treatment' (*sŏn u* 善遇). Could there be any better way of defining how a woman should deal with the servants in her household than with the two characters '*sŏn u*' (善遇: good treatment)?"

Miss Wŏn praised her good words.

---

84 'Good Conduct', *Elementary Learning*. "When Tao Yuanming (陶淵明) became Governor of Pengze (Pengze ling 彭澤令), he did not go together with his family but sent a servant to his son with a letter that said, 'As you are having difficulty preparing the morning and evening meals on your own, I am now sending you this servant, and he will help you to draw water and gather firewood. As he is also someone's child, please treat him well.'" (陶淵明爲彭澤令, 不以家累自隨, 送一力, 給其子, 書曰, '汝旦夕之費, 自給爲難, 今遣此力, 助汝薪水之勞. 此亦人子也, 可善遇之.') In the original source it is Tao Yuanming's son not 'the son of his elder brother'.

Study Hard

Yuhandang taught all her sons from a young age to exert themselves in their studies saying, "“The character for 'study' (*hak* 學) is first mentioned in the 'Charge to Yue' (Yueming 說命)[85] chapter of the *Book of History* (*Shujing* 書經). Among the moral laws, filial piety, respect, loyalty and trust (*hyo je ch'ung sin* 孝悌忠信) are simply doing what one is supposed to do, so if anyone's conduct goes against the principles of filial piety, respect, loyalty and trust, how could they have the face to stand between heaven and earth? As the character '*hak*' means study (學: *paeul hak*), and as the study of scholarship is people studying something that they don't know about and then finding out about it, studying is not something that just superior people do. All the countless skills for making things (*paekki ch'ŏn'gong* 百技千工) under heaven were originally unknown, and learning them was the scholarship of "the countless skills for making things." Even the talent for making arrows or wheel spokes is study that came from learning from a teacher; even a craftsman who makes angular bowls and round bowls also learned from a teacher, and this is

85 The *Book of History* records early Chinese history in the following order, Yu (虞), Xia (夏), Yin (殷) and Zhou (周). 'Charge to Yue' (Yueming 說命) records the dialogue between the 22nd king of Yin Gaozong (高宗) and his minister Fu Yue (傅說), and is divided into Parts 1, 2 and 3. Scholarship (*hak*) is discussed in Part 3.

studying. Even the learning of artisans requires diligence day and night to achieve skillfulness, so how much more do you have to study diligently to learn filial piety, fraternity, loyalty and trust as a superior person.

People of this secular world who raise their children, doting on them but not educating them, cannot achieve anything; and even families that do teach (their children), if they have a talent for writing or teaching composition, they think it admirable and are proud of it but do not understand the importance of the study of righteousness. Also, there is no household in the world where learning is not respected because of greed for wealth and fame even when it is done by an especially eccentric person who has knowledge but does not control himself and instead makes foolish compositions that become famous all over the world. Because every home is like this, the way of the world is gradually getting baser and baser, and the way to restore governance through courtesy and righteousness (*yeŭi chi ch'i* 禮義之治) of the Three Earliest Dynasties (Sandai: Xia, Yin and Zhou 三代: 夏·殷·周) is disappearing. Concern about the state of the world is not something a woman would know about, but even in the past, the woman of Qishi (漆室) concerned herself about the nation.[86] Even now in the world if there

86 'Lu Qishi nü' (魯漆室女), *Biographies of Women*. At the time of Duke Mu of Lu (Lu Mugong 魯穆公), the ruler was old and the crown prince was a child. Because of this a young unmarried

are educated women, would it be in any way presumptuous for them to be concerned with the state of the world? This means as I have brought up you my many sons, I am liable for blame in this household, and I am also liable for blame in the world at large. As the scholarship of a superior person concerns the moral principles of filial piety, fraternity, loyalty and trust, it is natural that if you want to know how to do the right thing, you first have to know righteousness. If you want to know righteousness, you first have to read many of the sages' classics. Only after understanding each word and putting them into practice, can you say that you are on the point of engaging in scholarship."

The fifth son Obong knelt down and said, "Mother has admonished us day and night solely about moral conduct. As you wish to make us unworthy inferior persons into outstandingly high-level superior persons, even though we inferior persons are so unworthy, how can we not take your words to heart? In the past we inferior persons have heard this teaching countless times, and today's words are even more earnest, so I will write them down."

And he picked up a writing brush and wrote them down.

---

woman of the Qishi region was concerned for the country.

The Great Significance of the *Doctrine of the Mean* and the *Great Learning*

Obong also said, "If you intend to study you have to have a solid understanding of the *Doctrine of the Mean* (*Zhongyong* 中庸) and the *Great Learning* (*Daxue* 大學), so I will ask you about the meaning of the *Doctrine of the Mean* and the *Great Learning*. When the *Doctrine of the Mean* speaks about 'character' (*sŏng* 性), the Chinese character for 'original nature' (*ponsŏng sŏng*) is mainly used, and when the *Great Learning* mentions 'mind' (*sim* 心) the Chinese character *sim* is used (*maŭm sim*). As Zengzi wrote the *Great Learning* and Zisi (子思) wrote the *Doctrine of the Mean*, both these sages wrote them for the sake of future scholars. But even if they talk about character (*sŏng*) but not about mind (*sim*) or discuss about original nature (*ponsŏng*) but not about mind (*sim*), or if they talk about mind but not about character, or in talking about mind, character was not mentioned, how can the words of a sage incline only to one side?"

"What I am trying to say is that if one does that, rather it will have no true taste. If you want to know, go and ask your eldest brother or go and ask your father."

Obong quickly went to ask his eldest brother, so Ilbong said, "Knowing by asking is not as good as understanding by finding out for yourself, so try thinking about it carefully yourself."

Obong also went to ask his father, and his father said, "You always ask your mother or your elder brothers, so why is it that you are coming to ask me today?"

Obong told him what his mother and eldest brother had said, so his father smiled and said, "Your mother knows the answer to this, but she did not tell you. Everyone has studied the phrase 'preserve the mind, cultivate character' (*chonsim yangsŏng* 存心養性), so which one would you leave out. Think about this and ask again."

Obong went back to his mother and told her what his eldest brother and father had said and asked her again, so Yuhandang smiled and said, "Your father's words are indeed correct. How could either mind or character be omitted? For this reason Master Zhu, in writing the preface to the *Great Learning* mentioned the character '*sŏng*',[87] and in both the *Doctrine of the Mean* and in the *Great Learning*, both mind and character are mentioned."

---

87 As the original text of the *Great Learning* focuses on 'mind' (*maŭm sim*), in Zhu Xi's '*Daxue* zhangju xu' (大學章句序), Zhu mentions 'original nature' (*ponsŏng sŏng*), and as the *Doctrine of the Mean* focuses on 'original nature', in Zhu Xi's '*Zhongyong* zhangju xu' (中庸章句序), he mentions 'mind' (*maŭm sim*).

Obong was overjoyed, "Indeed that is so."

As he was speaking, the eldest son Ilbong came in and hearing him said to his mother, "When children are frustrated because they do not understand the meaning of a text, because it is beneficial for them to understand and realize the meaning for themselves, I did not tell him the answer when he asked before, but now mother has told him."

"There is a saying 'Cause them to become possessors of themselves' (*sa cha tŭk chi* 使自得之),[88] so as it is good to help someone understand, and the child was going around busily wanting to know, I taught him."

The Reason for Particularly Liking the *Book of Changes*

Yuhandang was diligently spinning yarn, and next to her the *Book of Changes* was open on a table, so her eldest son Ilbong asked, "Mother likes books, but why is it that the *Book of Changes* particularly is always near at hand?"

---

88 'Teng Wengong I' (Tengwengong shang 滕文公上), *Mencius*. "Emperor Yao said, 'Encourage them and lead them, rectify them and straighten them, help them and give them wings, thus causing them to become possessors of themselves. Also, follow this up by stimulating them and conferring benefits on them.'" (放勳曰, 勞之來之, 匡之直之, 輔之翼之, 使自得之, 又從而振德之.)

"Which classical text do you like?"

"Concerning academic studies, in the *Doctrine of the Mean* the Chinese character for 'sincerity' (*sŏng* 誠) is mentioned, in the *Great Learning* the character 'reverence' (*kyŏng* 敬) is mentioned, so if one wants to study the classic texts of the sages, are not the *Doctrine of the Mean* and the *Great Learning* the most essential? As the *Book of Changes* discusses the principle of the harmonization of heaven and earth, its scope is large, but it is not as essential and relevant as the *Doctrine of the Mean* and the *Great Learning*."

"What you say is right. But the reason why I like the *Book of Changes* is not because as a woman I want to know the law of the harmonization of heaven and earth or the principle of '*yin* and *yang*' (*ŭmyang* 陰陽) and 'decrease and increase' (*sojang* 消長). But rather because all the admonishments of the Classics may be seen in parts of the *Book of Changes*, so I value the *Book of Changes*. Even though the character 'sincerity' (*sŏng* 誠) is mentioned in the *Doctrine of the Mean*, the meaning of the character 'sincerity' (*sŏng*) is in the 'Creative hexagram' (Qiangua 乾卦) in the *Book of Changes*.[89] The character 'reverence' (*kyŏng* 敬) is mentioned in the *Great Learning*, and in the *Book of*

89 'Creative hexagram' (Qiangua 乾卦), *Book of Changes*: "Heaven, in its motion, (gives the idea of) strength. The superior man, in accordance with this, nerves himself to ceaseless activity." (天行健, 君子以自彊不息.)

Changes the character 'reverence' is in the 'Receptive hexagram' (Kungua 坤卦),[90] so the content of the *Doctrine of the Mean* and the *Great Learning* is in two hexagrams in the *Book of Changes*. Not only this, the 'hatred of wine' of Xia Yu-*shi* (夏禹氏)[91] and Confucius's admonition of 'not eating to excess'[92] are contained in the three characters "*chŏl ŭm sik*" (moderation in eating) in the *Book of Changes*, and 'his mouth was kept quiet and composed'[93] and 'not many words'[94] in the *Book of Rites* are contained in the phrase 'watchfulness over our words'[95] in the *Book of Changes*, and the sayings of people of old,

---

90 'Receptive hexagram' (Kungua 坤卦), *Book of Changes*: "Complete is the 'great and originating (capacity)' indicated by Kun! All things owe to it their birth; it receives obediently the influences of Heaven." (彖曰, 至哉, 坤元. 萬物資生, 乃順承天.)

91 The 'hatred of wine' of Xia Yu-*shi* (夏禹氏): These words are spoken by the monarch of Lu in 'Liang wang Wei ying shang zhu hou yu fan tai' (梁王魏嬰觴諸侯於范臺), 'Strategy of Wei' (Wei ce 魏策), *Strategies of the Warring States* (*Zhanguo ce*). "In the past the daughter of the Celestial Emperor (Tiandi 天帝) had Yidi (儀狄) make alcohol, and the taste was so good that she offered it to King Yu. King Yu drank it and found it to be delicious, but he banished Yidi and stopped drinking alcohol saying, 'Among my future descendants there will certainly be someone who brings the country to ruin because of alcohol.'" (昔者, 帝女令儀狄作酒而美, 進之禹, 禹飲而甘之, 遂疏儀狄, 絶旨酒曰, '後世必有以酒亡其國者.')

92 Confucius's admonition of 'not eating to excess' (K. *pu tasik*; C. *bu duoshi* 不多食): 'Xiangdang', *Analects*. "(Confucius) did not eat to excess." (不多食.)

93 'The Jade Bead Pendants of the Rotal Cap' (Yuzao 玉藻), *Book of Rites*. "The carriage of a man of rank was easy, but somewhat slow; grave and reserved, when he saw any one whom he wished to honor. He did not move his feet lightly, nor his hands irreverently. His eyes looked straightforward and his mouth was quiet and composed. No sound from him broke the stillness, and his head was upright. His breath came without panting or stoppage, and his standing gave (the beholder) an impression of virtue. His looks were grave, and he sat like a personator of the dead. When at leisure and at ease, and in conversation, he looked mild and bland." (君子之容舒遲, 見所尊者齊遬. 足容重, 手容恭, 目容端, 口容止, 聲容靜, 頭容直, 氣容肅, 立容德, 色容莊, 坐如尸, 燕居告溫溫.)

94 There is no phrase in the *Book of Rites* that matches this phrase 'not many words' (*K. pu taŏn*; *C. bu duoyan* 不多言). However, there is a similar phrase in 'Zihan', *Analects*, "Confucius did not speak about profit (*li* 利), fate (*ming* 命) and benevolence (*ren* 仁)." (子罕言利與命與仁.)

95 'Lower Jaw Hexagram' (Yigua 頤卦), *Book of Changes*. "(The trigram representing) a mountain

'illness enters in at the mouth' and 'disaster comes out of the mouth'[96] are also included in the phrases 'watchfulness over our words' and 'temperate regulation of our eating and drinking' in the *Book of Changes*.

None of the innumerable words of the sages and admonitions of the kings are not mentioned in the *Book of Changes*, so for this reason only I like the *Book of Changes*. 'If one is sincere and respectful there will be peace under heaven'[97] in the *Doctrine of the Mean* and 'Their States being rightly governed, the whole kingdom was made tranquil and happy'[98] in the *Great Learning* are of great efficacy for the study of the sages' classic texts. But the phrase 'all under heaven (begins to be) adorned and brightened'[99] in the *Book of Changes* does not go against those writings."

---

and under it that for thunder form Yi. The superior man, in accordance with this, (enjoins) watchfulness over our words, and the temperate regulation of our eating and drinking." (象曰. 山下有雷, 君子以愼言語, 節飮食.)

96 'Illness enters in at the mouth' (K. *pyŏng chong ku ip*; C. *bing cong kou ru* 病從口入) and 'disaster comes out of the mouth' (K. *hwa chong ku ch'ul*; C. *huo cong kou chu* 禍從口出): 'Kou ming' (口銘) by Fu Xuan (傅玄, 217–278) a literatus in the Wei and Jin dynasties era. "Illness enters in at the mouth; disaster comes out of the mouth." (病從口入, 禍從口出.)

97 'Chapter 32', *Doctrine of the Mean* (*Zhongyong*). "For this reason if the superior person is sincere and respectful there will be peace under heaven." (是故, 君子篤恭而天下平.)

98 *Great Learning*. "Things being investigated, knowledge became complete. Their knowledge being complete, their thoughts were sincere. Their thoughts being sincere, their hearts were then rectified. Their hearts being rectified, their persons were cultivated. Their persons being cultivated, their families were regulated, their states were rightly governed. Their states being rightly governed, the whole kingdom was made tranquil and happy." (物格而后知至, 知至而后意誠, 意誠而后心正, 心正而后身修, 身修而后家齊, 家齊而后國治, 國治而后天下平.)

99 "Commentaries" (Wenyan zhuan 文言傳), 'Creative hexagram' (Qiangua), *Book of Changes*. "'The dragon appears in the field', all under heaven (begins to be) adorned and brightened." (見龍在田, 天下文明.)

'Seventh Lunar Month' (Qiyue), *Book of Odes*

After reading the 'Seventh Lunar Month' (Qiyue) chapter of the *Book of Odes*, Yuhandang's third and fourth sons asked, "It says 'in the seventh lunar month the Fire Star passes the meridian' (Qiyue liuhuo 七月流火),[100] but what kind of star is the 'Fire Star' and what does it mean by 'passes the meridian'?"

"It is right for you two to read the text to find out about the constellations and the star degree numbers (*tosu*), but it is better to think about absorbing the text into your own body and putting it into practice."

Sambong said, "How can we put into practice the passage 'in the seventh lunar month the Fire Star passes the meridian' with our own body?"

"Even if you just say that one phrase, how can you not put it into practice? When the people of Bin (豳) saw the appearance of the Fire Star passing the meridian, they understood how swiftly the seasons change

---

100 'Seventh Lunar Month' (Qiyue), *Book of Odes*. "In the seventh month, the Fire Star passes the meridian; / In the ninth month, clothes are given out. / In the days of [our] first month, the wind blows cold; / In the days of [our] second, the air is cold; / Without the clothes and garments of hair, / How could we get to the end of the year?" (七月流火, 九月授衣. 一之日觱發, 二之日栗烈, 無衣無褐, 何以卒歲.)

and worried about the clothes they would wear in the ninth lunar month, and this means that they were worrying about the season two months ahead of time. They said, "then get up quickly on our roofs" (亟其乘屋) and "we shall have to recommence our sowing" (其始播百穀),[101] so in the tenth lunar month, they were sitting worrying about ploughing the field in the second lunar month of the following year, so how can it not be part of the academic study of a superior person to be anxious about everything he says and does? A person of old said, '*In pul hŭng* (寅不興) *p'ye il il chi mu* (廢一日之務), *ch'un pul kyŏng* (春不耕) *p'ye il nyŏn chi sik* (廢一年之食), *yu pul hak* (幼不學) *p'ye p'yŏngsaeng chi ŏp* (廢平生之業).' This means 'if you do not get up at 3–5 am, you will fail at your work during the day; if you do not do farming in the spring, you will fail to grow the food required for one year; if you fail to study when you are young, you will fail in your work throughout your life'; so are not these words extremely appropriate? For this reason Master Zhu was worried and wrote a letter to his friend saying, 'It is easy

---

101 'Seventh Lunar Month' (Qiyue), *Book of Odes*. "In the ninth month, they prepare the vegetable gardens for their stacks, and in the tenth they convey the sheaves to them; the millets, both the early sown and the late, with other grain, the hemp, the pulse, and the wheat. 'O my husbandmen, our harvest is all collected. Let us go to the town, and be at work on our houses. In the day time collect the grass, and at night twist it into ropes; then get up quickly on our roofs; —We shall have to recommence our sowing.'" (九月築場圃, 十月納禾稼, 黍稷重穋, 禾麻菽麥. 嗟我農夫, 我稼既同, 上入執宮功, 晝爾于茅, 宵爾索綯, 亟其乘屋, 其始播百穀.)

to stop studying and it is difficult to find righteousness; the seasons flow like water so I am extremely anxious and afraid.'[102] With this being the case how can you students be lazy about your studies even for a moment. The people of Bin, who just did farming, worried about the future when they saw the Fire Star pass the meridian. As men, the affairs of the world are your responsibility, so shouldn't you be anxious to study hard when you are young? It is right to apply even ordinary passages from the Classics to oneself and keep them in mind."

'Reverence Study Exhortation' and 'Exhortation on Rising Early and Sleeping Late'

One day Yuhandang was standing next to the balustrade, when she heard the sound of Yukpong sitting alone reading in the thatched annex. This

102 'Letter answering Lü Baigong' (Da Lü Baigong 答呂伯公), *Collected Works of Zhu Xi* (*Huian ji* 晦菴集). "It is easy to stop in the middle of studying, and it is difficult to find righteousness, and as the seasons flow like water, I am extremely anxious. But perhaps this is a good thing to say." (功夫易間斷, 義理難推尋, 而歲月如流, 甚可憂懼. 奈何奈何.) Baigong was the courtesy name of Zhu Xi's friend Lü Zuqian (呂祖謙, 1137–1181).

gladdened Yuhandang's heart, so she entered the thatched annex, sat down and said, "It is said that the sound of one's son studying is better than all the sounds of nature. Today, upon hearing the sound of you reading, I know that this saying is true! It has made me happy to hear you reading, so please read to me."

Yukpong read 'Reverence Study Exhortation' (Jingzhai zhen 敬齋箴)[103] and 'Exhortation on Rising Early and Sleeping Late' (Suxing yemei zhen 夙興夜寐箴)[104] out loud and Yuhandang said,

"Do you know the meaning of these two texts as you read them?"

"I just know that they are words of admonishment and persuasion as I read them, but I do not know their deep meaning."

"'Exhortation on Rising Early and Sleeping Late' concerns studying during the 'periods of time' (*sibun* 時分), 'Reverence Study Exhortation' concerns the 'location' (*chidu* 地頭) for studying."

---

103 'Reverence Study Exhortation' (Jingzhai zhen 敬齋箴) is Zhu Xi's exhortation (*zhen* 箴) on the way of cultivating reverence (*jing* 敬) in forty lines of four characters each, which is included in *Huianji*, *Xinjing* and other works.

104 'Exhortation on Rising Early and Sleeping Late' (Suxing yemei zhen 夙興夜寐箴) is an exhortation about exerting oneself from early morning until late at night and the determination needed for that written in four characters and forty-eight lines by the Song dynasty scholar Chen Bai (陳栢). It is included in such works as *Eight Treatises on Following the Principles of Life* (*Zun sheng bajian* 遵生八牋) and *Dushu fennian richeng* (讀書分年日程), Vol. 1.

"What do 'periods of time' and 'location' mean?"

"The words 'periods of time' refer to the different times of day for scholars to study, namely, dawn, morning, daytime, evening, and nighttime. The word 'location' refers to the study of location, namely, east, south, west and north. Sitting down in a place where you could sit or stand, and taking a look at the place where you are likely to stand is the study of 'location'. If we discuss 'Exhortation on Rising Early and Sleeping Late' and 'Reverence Study Exhortations' that you are reading now, 'Exhortation on Rising Early and Sleeping Late', which speaks of studying in periods from the moment the cock crows through the morning, daytime until the night, is studying in 'periods of time'. '*Ze di er ta*' (擇地而踏)[105] means 'tread lightly on the ground', and the words '*chu men ru bin*' (出門如賓)[106] mean act as though you are going out of the door to meet a valued guest and warn you to pay attention to the ground, so this is studying location in 'Exhortation on Rising Early and Sleeping Late'. A scholar of old said about reading a text without

---

105 'Reverence Study Exhortation' (Jingzhai zhen 敬齋箴), *Annotated Classic of Mind-and-Heart* (*Xinjing fuzhu* 心經附註). "You must be careful with your feet; you must be modest with your hands; tread lightly on the ground, and if there is an anthill, go back." (足容必重, 手容必恭, 擇地而踏, 折旋蟻封.)

106 'Reverence Study Exhortation' (Jingzhai zhen 敬齋箴), *Annotated Classic of Mind-and-Heart* (*Xinjing fuzhu* 心經附註). "When you walk out of a door to greet people behave as though you are receiving a noble guest; when you do your work, behave as though you are performing a sacrifice. Be fearful and careful. Whatever you do, do not take things lightly." (出門如賓, 承事如祭, 戰戰兢兢, 罔敢或易.)

understanding its meaning, 'A book is a book and I am I.'[107] So how could the words have any benefit to oneself?"

"Now that I hear the meaning of the text, I understand. The words 'periods of time' and 'locations' are not just in these two texts; also in the phrase 'four times and four directions' (*sasi sabang* 四時四方), the four times refers to the 'periods of time', and the four directions refers to the 'locations'. Also, the phrase 'a transitory moment' (K. *sunsik chi kyŏng*, C. *shunxi zhi qing* 瞬息之頃) pertains to 'periods of time', and the phrase 'very close between' (K. *chich'ŏk chi kan*; C. *zhichi zhi jian* 咫尺之間) pertains to 'locations'."

"You have indeed reasoned and understood well. Your talent is also not inferior to that of your brothers."

---

107 'Way of Reading the *Great Learning*' (Du *Daxue* fa 讀大學法), *Great Learning*. "How can you just see the words when reading the *Great Learning*? You must sincerely want to know how to control your own mind. Is it possible to test one's mind so that one loves good just like one loves beautiful women and hates evil just like one hates a bad smell? Is there really no goodness in leisure? In this way, if you fail to achieve even one thing, you must be courageous and persevering, and you will surely achieve great progress. If you do not know such things then a book is a book and I am I, what benefit can there be in that?" (讀大學, 豈在看他言語. 正欲驗之於心如何. 如好好色, 惡惡臭, 試驗之吾心, 果能好善惡惡如此乎? 閒居爲不善, 是果有此乎? 一有不至, 則勇猛奮躍不已, 必有長進. 今不知如此, 則書自書, 我自我, 何益之有.)

Fascicle 2

Righteous Storehouse Anecdote I

It was a day in which rain and snow were falling alternately, and the wind and cold made people's bodies shiver. A guest wearing a tattered hat (*kat*) and threadbare hemp clothes bowed down to Minister Tu in the courtyard and then went inside to see him and said, "Although this is the first time we have met, having missed breakfast, it is difficult for me to continue along my way on such a cold day when the snow is falling."

Minister Tu ordered wine to be warmed up quickly and given to him and that an evening meal be prepared in haste so that he could eat. On the following day, Tu Ch'ŏnbok reported to Minister Tu saying, "The guest is someone we have only met for the first time, but his living conditions are very poor, so I would like to give him some money from the righteous storehouse when we send him on his way."

"Give him a mid-level amount."

"Giving him a mid-level amount is appropriate, but when I looked at that person's head, I saw that he is a white-haired elderly gentleman, who is unable to work so that he can eat and live. It is extremely cold now, so if we want to prevent that person from being hungry and cold after he has returned home, we should give him the highest-level amount."

"That is true. According to what that person said, he has an elderly mother, so the highest-level amount is more appropriate."

Tu Ch'ŏnbok listened to his father's words and gave him the highest-level amount, so the guest thanked him and said, "I encountered snow in the middle of my journey and came in here. Thank you for giving me so much beyond my expectation."

After he gave thanks again, Minister Tu said, "Even though this wealth came from the righteous storehouse in my home, it is the world's wealth, and as you are also a person of this world, why should you not be able to take the world's wealth and use it for rites."

The fourth son Sabong told Yuhandang, "The clothes of the guest who came from outside look old and thin, and the road looks arduous, so I am going to take off my clothes and send them to him."

"What was the guest's physique?"

Ibong said, "Sabong's intention is benevolent and virtuous, but he is young and does not know what he is doing. Sabong is short in stature, and the guest is extremely tall, so I think even if he gives him his clothing, it would not be practical. As I have clothes that I can take off, what if I send them?"

Yuhandang said, "Your words are indeed good, so please do that."

When Ibong asked his wife to bring him his clothes she replied,

"The clothes you have taken off are thin and threadbare and will easily wear out with time. Your new set of clothing is thick, so if we send it, not only will it keep out the cold this year but also next year, so wouldn't that be good."

Yuhandang sent a female servant to present the clothing when a male servant came in and said, "The guest already departed a long time ago."

Ibong said, "Even though he has gone, I have already made up my mind to give the clothes so how can I stop now? Quickly take them and give them to him."

So carrying the clothing, the male servant quickly went more than ten *li* and caught up with the guest. After he conveyed Ibong's words to him, the guest was embarrassed and deeply moved. He unpacked his luggage to get some of the money he had received from the righteous storehouse and gave him four or five strings of cash in appreciation for his hard work and for coming so quickly in such cold weather. The male servant politely refused them saying, "The reason the master of our house created the righteous storehouse was for this kind of purpose. As a servant I am just carrying out this intention, so how could I receive this money and injure the benevolent heart of my master?"

When he strongly refused, the guest was even more deeply moved, so he turned around and went back to express his gratitude to Minister Tu.

"In one household, old and young without exception are all superior persons, so I am lost for words—even the lowliest servants are all superior persons."

Righteous Storehouse Anecdote II

One day a visitor from a nearby village, stood outside the gate and calling a male servant, said to Minister Tu, "I come from a nearby village and my family is poor, and it is difficult for us to make ends meet. Please provide me with plenty of money from your righteous storehouse."

Minister Tu called Tu Ch'ŏnbok to discuss this and Tu Ch'ŏnbok replied, "This is someone who has been living here for a long time, and now he is a strong young man. Even if he just ploughed a field, he could eat; even if he read books, he could eat; or even if he worked as an artisan or a merchant, he would be able to eat. As he has failed in the four occupations of scholarship, farming, artisanship and trade (*sa nong kong sang* 士農工商) and just wanders around for his food and clothing (*yuŭi yusik* 遊衣遊食), how can he help but be poor? He has not encountered any particular misfortune at this time, so how can you give money from the righteous storehouse just because he says that his family is poor."

"I have also made up my mind not to give anything to him."

And he had a male servant convey this message and say, "The itemized purposes (*chŏlmok* 節目) for which the righteous storehouse is intended include marriages or funerals, or if one's parents become sick, or for emergencies such as if someone gets into difficulties on a journey. We cannot give anything simply because someone claims to be poor."

After the servant had told him this, Tu Ch'ŏnbok went inside and told Yuhandang, who said, "It is right that money from the righteous storehouse cannot be used in such a case. However, even if that guest became a beggar because he did not engage in scholarship, farming, artisanship or trade, and even though that is his mistake, on hearing this, I feel sorry for him. Long ago someone called Yi Yin (伊尹)[108] said, 'if even one person cannot find a way to earn a living (C. *pifu bu huo* 匹夫不獲), I feel ashamed in my heart (C. *qi xin chi zhi* 其心恥之) as if I were beaten in the market place (C. *ruo ta yu shi* 若撻于市).'[109] If such a person as Yi Yin was alive today, he would rather feel ashamed of himself to see such a person. In the 'Western Inscription' (Xi ming 西銘)[110] written by Zhang Hengqu, it states, 'All under Heaven who are tired, crippled, exhausted, sick, without brothers, childless, widows or widowers—all are my siblings who are helpless and have no one else to appeal to.'[111] So he what he was saying was that all under heaven who are enduring difficulties are our brothers and must be treated like helpless people who are wandering aimlessly without being able to speak. Nowadays, if you wish to become a person of great purpose like Master Zhang Hengqu, should you

---

108 Yi Yin (伊尹) was a famous prime minister of the Yin (Shang) dynasty who helped King Tang (湯) to overthrow Xia and governed the nation well.

109 'Charge to Yue III' (Yueming xia), *Book of History*. "Formerly, there was the first premier of our dynasty, Bao Heng, who raised up and formed its royal founder. He said, 'If I cannot make my sovereign like Yao or Shun, I shall feel ashamed in my heart, as if I were beaten in the market place.' If any common man did not get (all he should desire), he said, 'It is my fault.'" (昔先正保衡, 作我先王, 乃曰, '予弗克俾厥后惟堯舜, 其心愧恥, 若撻于市, 一夫不獲, 則曰時予之辜.')

110 Zhang Hengqu: Zhang Zai (張載, 1020–1077). A Northern Song Neo-Confucian scholar who wrote *Rectifying the Ignorant* (*Zhengmeng* 正蒙).

111 'Western Inscription' (Xi ming 西銘), *Complete Writings of Master Zhang* (*Zhangzi quanshu* 張子全書). "All under Heaven who are tired, crippled, exhausted, sick, without brothers, childless, widows or widowers—all are my siblings who are helpless and have no one else to appeal to." (凡天下, 疲癃殘疾, 惸獨鰥寡, 皆吾兄弟之顚連而無告者也.)

not also have such an attitude? If the speech and behavior or temperament of the guest outside are not very rough and aggressive, then it is clear that that person lost his parents when he was young and has been wandering aimlessly without learning to read when he was young. If anyone comes along and teaches him, and he chooses from among scholarship, farming, artisanship and trade according to what suits his ability and strength, and then works hard every day, and if he works hard every year to achieve success in at least one occupation, he can become an example to people of how to become a superior person of benevolence (K. *inin kunja* 仁人君子)."

Tu Ch'ŏnbok praised his wife, "If one makes up one's mind to live in accordance with Master Zhang Hengqu's 'Western Inscription' (Xi ming) is there anything in the world that is not a man's responsibility? If the teaching is done diligently, no one will remain unmoved, so I will call him and teach him."

With Yuhandang's eldest granddaughter at his side, he said to Yuhandang, "Hearing the story of that person, I felt sympathy, so I would like to teach him to start a family business and avoid becoming a beggar, but as people's hearts and minds are different from what they were in the past, how shall I know how to inspire him? It would be right to teach him the duties of a superior man but ..."

"How can the hearts and minds of people in the past and present differ? Even if you look at the medicinal herbs in the medical textbooks, what used to be sweet in the past is still sweet, and what used to be bitter in the past is still bitter. If even ignorant things like trees and plants taste no differently from how they tasted in the past, how could the character of people, who are the most divine of all created beings, be different now from how it was in the past? If you teach, it will be like the sweet taste of trees and plants that has not changed. If you fail to teach and preserve the fundamental nature, even if the taste of trees and plants is sweet, it is the same as if you make a mistake while preparing food. Its good taste will change. Is there anything that cannot be taught?"

"Your words are truly correct. For this reason, Mencius said, 'Everyone can become a sage like Yao or Shun.'"[112]

Tu Ch'ŏnbok went outside, sat down, and ordered the male servant to call the guest. He then had him sit down on the wooden floor of the external living area, and admonished him saying, "If people try to live without working, not only will hunger and cold pierce their bones, but it

---

112 'Gaozi xia' (告子下), *Mencius*. "Cao Jiao (曹交) asked, 'You said that everyone can become a Yao or Shun, is that true?' Mencius said, 'That is true.'" (曹交問日, '人皆可以爲堯舜, 有諸?' 孟子日, '然.')

is also easy for them to lose their human nature. You have to choose one occupation among scholarship, farming, artisanship and trade and then work hard night and day and provide for your family day after day and avoid going around as a beggar. As this is your task, I hope that from today you will strengthen your resolve to succeed in one of these occupations."

As he persuaded him gently and taught him over and over, the guest expressed his gratitude saying, "I lost my parents when I was young and could not study, and as my family was poor, I could not engage in farming. Because I could not endure the hunger and cold, I came here, but my original mind is not like that. Hearing this today, I feel sorry that I was indolent for a while."

Then he repented of his mistake, admitted his own fault and went back to his home.

Three years later a guest appeared in smart clothing, riding on a horse. He arrived outside the door, called the male servant and sent in a request to Tu Ch'ŏnbok, "As you are the person I saw before, I would like to see you." Tu Ch'ŏnbok called him to come in, but he could not recognize the person's face.

The guest said to Tu Ch'ŏnbok, "I came here three years ago when I was wandering aimlessly, and after hearing the admonishments and teachings of Tu Ch'ŏnbok, I went back and started farming from that day. As I worked so diligently that even if I slept, I did not sleep throughout the night, my family's economic circumstances improved. Now that I am earning a living for my family, we can avoid hunger and cold. These are all merits taught to me by Tu Ch'ŏnbok, so at home even when we lift a spoon of rice to eat, we praise the kindness of Tu Ch'ŏnbok."

"If we could make all beggars like you repent of your past mistakes and do good deeds (*hoegwa ch'ŏnsŏn* 悔過遷善), we would be able to see the world of Yao and Shun once again."

Then after giving him alcohol to drink and praising him, Tu Ch'ŏnbok went into the inner quarters and said to Yuhandang, "The guest who came as a beggar several years ago has now come in splendid clothing and on an ornate saddle, and his appearance is quite different from before. He says that through farming his family's economic situation has improved, which is quite astounding."

"Human nature is inherently good, so is there anyone in the world who cannot be taught and become better?"

The Story of Zhou Ji of Qi

One day early in the morning Ch'ŏnbok straightened up his clothes and looking in the mirror, said to Yuhandang, "Yesterday a guest from next door came and told me that my face looked better than before, but looking at it today, I am not sure if it is better."

"He sounds like the guest of Zhou Ji (鄒忌) of Qi who praised Zhou Ji's face."[113]

"If a wife does not praise because of her personal affection, wouldn't that be different from Zhou Ji's case?"

And as they laughed, their niece Miss Tu, after attending to them, asked, "Listening to both of you talking, it sounds as though the story about Zhou Ji of Qi is an amusing one, so I would like to hear it."

Tu Ch'ŏnbok replied, "As it is in *Strategies of the Warring States* (*Zhanguo ce* 戰國策), just look for it in *Strategies of the Warring States*."

113 'Strategy of Qi' (Qi ce 齊策), *Strategies of the Warring States* (*Zhanguo ce* 戰國策). Yuhandang appears to be referring to a passage in this work that states, 'Zhou Ji's height was more than eight feet' (鄒忌脩八尺有餘).

As Miss Tu wanted to know about it quickly, she asked Yuhandang, and Yuhandang said, "In the past Zhou Ji was a person from Qi. His height was eight feet and his face was handsome. One morning he straightened his clothes and looking in the mirror asked his wife, 'Who is more handsome, me or Xugong (徐公), who lives in the northern part of the city?' And his wife replied, 'How could Xugong compare with you?' As Xugong, who lived in the northern part of the city, was renowned as a handsome man in Qi, Zhou Ji did not believe her, and so he asked his concubine, 'Who is more handsome, me or Xugong, who lives in the northern part of the city?' The concubine replied, 'How could Xugong compare with you?' A guest came in from outside, and as he also asked him, the guest said, 'You are more handsome. How could Xugong compare with you?' The next day Xugong visited, and after looking at him closely, in Zhou's own opinion his appearance was inferior to Xu's.

After sleeping in the evening, he awoke and said, 'My wife said I was handsome because of her personal affection for me; my concubine said I was handsome because she is afraid of me; and the guest said I was handsome because he wanted to get something from me.' And when he went to court, he said to King Wei of Qi (齊威王), 'I truly know that I am not as handsome as Xugong; my wife said that I was because of her personal affection; my concubine said that I was because she was afraid of me; and my guest said I was handsome because he wanted to get something from me. As Qi now measures 1,000 *li* in all four directions, and it has 100 cities, the palace women have personal affection for the king, the court ministers all fear the king, and in all four directions there are people who want to get things from the king. Looked at it in this way, the king is being severely blocked (from seeing the truth).'

Agreeing with him, the king said, 'Give the highest level of reward to those who remonstrate with me about my faults when they meet me face to face; give a mid-level reward to those who submit a written memorial of remonstration; and give a low-level reward to anyone who discusses (my faults) in the street and the words reach my ears.' So when this order was first given, the doorways were packed with crowds of ministers intending to remonstrate with the king. After one year, even if they wanted to say something, there was nothing more to say. When the Yan, Zhao, and Wei dynasties heard of it, they came to Qi to pay tribute, so in the *Strategies of the Warring States*, this is referred to as 'winning the battle in the court' (C. *zhan sheng yu chaoting* 戰勝於朝廷).

The words of Zhou Ji to King Wei of Qi were a remonstration about his situation, and in general if the king did not like to hear about his faults, it would have been difficult even for his wife and concubines to remonstrate with him about them. Not only is this the case for men, but also if women do not like to hear about their faults, it is difficult even for their servants to remonstrate with them. If you see such writings or hear such words, it is only right that you should apply them to yourself and gladly listen to what others have to say."

Weaving Should Also Be Done Like Studying

Yuhandang was sitting at the loom weaving, so her younger sister-in-law came to watch and said to Yuhandang, "Now that Yuhandang is elderly, it looks as though weaving is hard work."

"In the past the mother of Gongfu Wenbo (公父文伯)[114] engaged in weaving as the mother of the prime minister, so how could I cease to

---

114 'Learning from the Ancients' (Jigu 稽古), *Elementary Learning*. "Gongfu Wenbo came out of the court to see his mother, who was engaged in weaving at that moment. When Wenbo said, 'As a senior member of our household is there any reason for my mother to be weaving?' His mother sighed and replied, 'The country of Lu will fall! You were given this official position as such a young person, and you still do not know this!'" (公父文伯退朝, 朝其母, 其母方績. 文伯曰, 以歜之家, 而主猶績乎! 其母歎曰, 魯其亡乎! 使僮子備官而未之聞耶!)

perform my womanly duties?"

"Yuhandang has always told us to apply all matters to our own selves, to understand them and to put them into practice. Speaking about this loom today, how shall I put it into practice?"

Yuhandang smiled and said, "Yes, whenever the children read a text, in order to teach them not to read thoughtlessly but to learn it through experience and put it into practice, I say that, and speaking of this loom, how can there be nothing to learn from it and put into practice? The warp threads (*nalchul*)[115] are placed lengthwise, and these are called 'heavenly warp' (*ch'ŏn'gyŏng* 天經). The woof threads (*ssijul*)[116] are placed horizontally, and these are called 'earthly woof' (*chiwi* 地緯). So the greatness of 'heavenly warp and earthly woof' (*ch'ŏn'gyŏng chiwi* 天經地緯)[117] can indeed be learned from this small loom. If we discuss the flying of the shuttle (*puk*), going once this way and once that way, continuously and without ceasing, it is like the coming and going of the sun and the moon in the sky and the rising and ebbing of the tide in the sea. If a man wants to teach about the harmonization of heaven and earth, even this should not be looked at with indifference.

---

115 Warp threads (*nalchul* or *nalsil*) are the threads that run lengthwise when weaving cloth.
116 Woof threads (*ssijul* or *ssisil*) are the threads that run crosswise when weaving cloth.
117 The heavenly lengthwise threads and earthly crosswise threads symbolize the eternally unchanging and righteous principle.

In the past there were persons who cut up the cloth they had made after weaving it. For example, Mencius's mother cut up the cloth in order to teach her son a lesson.[118] The wife of Yue Yang was worried about her husband's studying so she cut up her cloth.[119] Afterwards Mencius became someone who was close to being a sage and a teacher of the people, and afterwards Yue Yang became a famous general who conquered Zhongshan (中山). It is right for those who are mothers of men and those who become wives of men to take notice of their looms when they see them. Zeng Shen's mother, upon hearing three times that Zeng Shen had committed

---

118 'The Mother of Mencius of Zou' (Zou Meng Ke mu 鄒孟軻母), *Biographies of Women*. "When Mencius was a child he left off studying and returned home. Mencius' mother, who was weaving cloth, asked him, 'How much progress did you make with your studies?' Mencius said, 'There is not much difference (from before).' Mencius' mother cut up the cloth (she had woven) with a knife. Mencius was shocked, and when he asked her the reason for this, Mencius' mother said, 'You giving up on your studies is the same as me cutting up this cloth.' … This alarmed Mencius, so he exerted himself diligently in his studies from morning until night. Making Zisi his teacher, he eventually became a famous Confucian scholar." (孟子之少也, 既學而歸. 孟母方績, 問曰, '學何所至矣?' 孟子曰, '自若也.' 孟母以刀斷其織. 孟子懼而問其故. 孟母曰, '子之廢學, 若吾斷斯織也.' … 孟子懼, 旦夕勤學不息. 師事子思, 遂成天下之名儒.)

119 'Yue Yang's wife' (Yue Yangzi qi 樂羊子妻), *History of Later Han* (*Hou Han Shu*). "When Yue Yang returned home after one year, his wife knelt down before him and asked him the reason why. When Yue Yang replied, 'I have been away for a long time and there was no other reason than that the thought came to me', his wife cut the cloth with a knife and said, 'This cloth is born from a silkworm's cocoon and is completed on the loom. By connecting each thread, each inch of cloth is made, and to finally complete a bolt of cloth, you have to keep working on making the cloth inch by inch. If I cut up this cloth now, I am losing all the effort and time that I put into it. … How is your coming home midway (through your studies), any different from me cutting up this cloth?' Yue Yang, who was moved by these words, returned to complete his studies, and did not come back home again for seven years." (一年來歸, 妻跪問其故, 羊子曰, '久行懷思, 無它異也.' 妻乃引刀趨機而言曰, '此織生自蠶繭, 成於機杼. 一絲而累, 以至於寸, 累寸不已, 遂成丈匹. 今若斷斯織也, 則捐失成功, 稽廢時日. … 若中道而歸, 何異斷斯織乎?' 羊子感其言, 復還終業, 遂七年不返.)

murder, threw away her shuttle.[120] People in the past, therefore, likened this event to when a person reports to the king and makes a false accusation. As the king and his minsters should be admonished simply by seeing a shuttle, should not women, who might too easily believe the words of others, also take this to heart?"

The Way of Teaching Children

One day, Lady Chu came and conversed with Yuhandang all day.

"Every time the children listen to Yuhandang, when they return, they say that each word is generous and imbued with a blessed spirit. Listening to today's words, there was not a single word spoken with the intention of

---

120 'King Wu of Qin Addresses Gan Mao' (Qin Wuwang wei Gan Mao 秦武王謂甘茂), 'Strategy of Qin' (Qin ce 秦策), *Strategies of the Warring States*. "In the past Zeng Shen lived in the township of Fei. In Fei there lived someone with the same name as Zengzi who committed a murder. Someone said to Zengzi's mother, 'Zengzi has committed a murder.' Zengzi's mother said, 'My son is not a person who would commit a murder' and continued weaving with composure at the loom. A little later another person also said, 'Zengzi has committed a murder.' As before Zengzi's mother composedly kept on weaving. Sometime later when yet another person said 'Zengzi has committed a murder', Zengzi's mother became alarmed, threw away her shuttle, scrambled over a wall and ran away." (昔者, 曾子處費. 費人有與曾子同名族者而殺人. 人告曾子母曰, '曾參殺人', 曾子之母曰, '吾子不殺人'. 織自若. 有頃焉, 人又曰, '曾參殺人'. 其母尚織自若也. 頃之, 一人又告之曰, '曾參殺人'. 其母懼, 投杼踰墻而走.)

hurting anyone or harming anything. Not only does your physiognomy show that you will have many sons and many blessings (*tanam tabok* 多男多福), but if we first discuss the physiognomic principles of temperament (*simsang* 心相), it is stated that 'physiognomy is not the same as temperament',[121] and today I have indeed experienced this."

"There has been no other study all my life, and although I make the children listen, I never make them listen to frivolous or vulgar words."

"In general you speak abundantly, as even passing words are not something to be spoken lightly."

"That is truly correct. Long ago Emperor Wu of Han (漢武帝) heard that Dong Fangshuo (東方朔) was good at interpreting dreams, so he called him and said, 'In a dream in the night, two roof tiles fell off and became birds, so please interpret this dream.' Dong Fangshuo replied, 'Two palace ladies will die today.' Emperor Wu laughed out loud and said, 'I did not dream what I told you, but in order to test you, I lied and asked you about the dream, and without knowing that you interpreted it.' But as he laughed, Dong Fangshuo replied with a serious look on his face, 'Even though dreams are vain things, nevertheless they are true; and words that come from a person's

---

121 'Refutation of Physiognomy' (Fexiang 非相), *Xunzi* (荀子). "Examining physiognomy is not the same as discussing the mind." (相形不如論心.)

mouth, unlike vain dreams, are even more likely to be correct.' Thereupon, the sound of crying could be heard from the rear garden. Emperor Wu urgently asked what had happened and was told that two palace ladies had been fighting one another and had fallen over a balustrade and died instantly. Emperor Wu considered Dong Fangshuo's words to be miraculous and recorded them in an unofficial history (*yasa* 野史) as a warning to people to be careful in what they say, so subsequent generations of scholars would take this to heart, and women would be even more restrained."

"By citing these words as a basis for action, you have indeed made me desperate to speak with care."

Lady Chu asked Yuhandang another question, "Daughters-in-law who first enter the house of another family, all learn scholarship and one by one put the words into practice, so scholarship is a wonderful thing to learn and put into practice."

"There is nothing difficult about teaching scholarship to men and women but having them put it into practice is difficult."

"For this reason in the *Book of History* it states, 'It is not the knowing that is difficult but the doing that is difficult.'"[122]

---

122 'Charge to Yue II' (Yueming zhong), *Book of History*. "Yue did obeisance with his head to the ground, and said, 'It is not the knowing that is difficult, but the doing.'" (說拜稽首曰, '非

"To just speak words with your mouth and not put them into practice is truly the same as the saying, 'the parrot can speak, and yet it is nothing more than a bird'.[123] This saying is indeed correct. The way to teach is with writings and spoken words, but to teach by your own living example is more effective. To not tread on the threshold in order to teach children not to tread on the threshold by showing them your example is better than reading the words 'Do not tread on the threshold'[124] to them one hundred times. When you eat rice, showing them not to overeat by your own example is better than reading the saying, 'in his food he does not seek to gratify his appetite'[125] to them a thousand times. If not a single word or single action sets a bad example, it will be natural for children to trust the teachings of their elders, listen to them, and put them into practice for their own benefit."

"As that is the way to teach children, how can everyone in the

---

知之難, 行之惟艱.')

123 'Summary of the Rules of Propriety I' (Quli shang 曲禮上), *Book of Rites*. "The parrot can speak, and yet it is nothing more than a bird; the ape can speak, yet it is nothing more than a beast. Here now is a man who observes no rules of propriety; is not his heart that of a beast?" (鸚鵡能言, 不離飛鳥, 猩猩能言, 不離禽獸. 今人而無禮, 雖能言, 不亦禽獸之心乎?)

124 See footnote 14.

125 'Xue'er', *Analects*. "Confucius said, 'He who aims to be a man of complete virtue in his food does not seek to gratify his appetite, nor in his dwelling place does he seek the appliances of ease; he is earnest in what he is doing, and careful in his speech; he frequents the company of men of principle that he may be rectified—such a person may be said indeed to love to learn.'" (子曰, 君子食無求飽, 居無求安, 敏於事而愼於言, 就有道而正焉, 可謂好學也已.)

household not learn? This way of teaching children is a wonderful method, but except for Yuhandang, it does not seem as though there are many people who can put it into practice."

Zhu Zhifan's Departure as an Envoy to Chosŏn

In the 34th year of the reign of the Wanli Emperor in the Pyŏngo Year (C. Bingwu nian 丙午年, 1606)[126] Hanlin Academician Zhu Zhifan (朱之蕃)[127] sent a letter to Lord Minister Tu saying, "Having received the imperial command, I will be going to Chosŏn as an envoy, and my friends have sent me many letters of farewell, so if I receive a wonderful letter from my greatly blessed senior Lord Minister Tu, when I experience suffering along the journey of tens of thousands of *li*, sometimes I will read it, and at least it will give me a little comfort in the midst of all the anxieties of being on the road."

---

126 In the original text it states, "In the 44th year of the reign of the Wanli Emperor in the Pyŏngo Year" (Mallyŏk sasipsa'nyŏn Pyŏngo). This error has been corrected here.

127 Zhu Zhifan (朱之蕃, 1558–1624) was a Ming dynasty literatus. In 1606 he came to Chosŏn as an envoy and exchanged many poems with Chosŏn literati. His visit is recorded in *Notes of an Envoy to Chosŏn* (*Fengshi Chaoxian gao* 奉使朝鮮稿).

Lord Minister Tu read this and said to Tu Ch'ŏnbok, "I do not think it is really necessary to exchange these kinds of letters at my advanced age."

"It is a common thing to write and present a poem of farewell when someone is going on a long journey, and as Hanlin Academician Zhu has received a command from the state, it is different from a private journey. Also Chosŏn's scenery and customs are famous in all the world. It has established a civilization of rites and music and is a nation known as "Small China" (So Chunghwa 小中華). Hanlin Academician Zhu's writing style is wonderful, so if he goes to Chosŏn, he will be able to carry out the responsibilities assigned to him (*chŏndae chi im* 專對之任)[128] well, and as he will return in honor, it seems to me it would be good to write to this person as well."

"Indeed that is true. As he sent this letter to me from afar requesting a letter from me, I will have to write one and send it."

Finally, he ordered a writing brush and paper to be brought. His eldest grandson Ilbong came with the inkstone; his great grandchild Wŏnsŏng

---

128 The term *chŏndae chi im* (專對之任) refers to the duties an envoy abroad was expected to carry out at his own discretion. 'Zilu' (子路), *Analects*. "Though a man may be able to recite the three hundred odes, yet if, when entrusted with a governmental charge, he knows not how to act, or if when sent to any quarter on a mission, he cannot give his replies unassisted, notwithstanding the extent of his learning, of what practical use is it?" (子曰, '誦詩三百, 授之以政, 不達, 使於四方, 不能專對, 雖多, 亦奚以爲?')

brought the writing brush and ink; Yuhandang brought the water dropper (*yŏnjŏk* 硯滴), and after she had added water to the ink stone to make the ink, Minister Tu picked up the writing brush and wrote as follows:

> The destiny of Chosŏn (Haedong) is similar to that of China (Hwangjo). (海東邦運似皇朝)
>
> Long ago Tan'gun established the nation alongside Yao. (伊昔檀君亦幷堯).
>
> As in the past and present it took twenty-five years, (二十五年今古事)
>
> So you will deservedly hear once again the songs of the Blue Hills (Chosŏn). (君行應復靑丘謠)

After Lord Minister Tu had finished writing, his son and grandsons told everyone to look, and all his descendants said, "This composition that you wrote in a brief moment is indeed good."

Minister Tu asked Yuhandang, "Do you understand the meaning of the first phrase?"

"I understand it. Because our China and Chosŏn are both in the region of the astronomical body known as Jiweixing (箕尾星), if the culture of

China encounters the fortune of advancement, Chosŏn will also encounter the fortune of advancement. Because of this, twenty-five years after Emperor Yao ascended the throne in the Kapchin Year (C. Jiachen nian 甲辰年, BC 2357), Tan'gun appeared in Chosŏn.[129] Emperor Yao is a sage, and Tan'gun is also a sage, so both together accomplished civilized reigns. Also, twenty-five years after Taizu of the Ming dynasty (Ming Taizu 明太祖) founded the nation in the Musin Year (C. Wushen nian 戊申年, 1368), Chosŏn's Great King Kanghŏn (Kanghŏn Taewang 康獻大王)[130] founded the nation. Because Emperor Taizu was a sage and Great King Kanghŏn was a sage, China and Chosŏn established civilized rule together, so it is wondrous that both in the ancient past and in recent times in this world, there were twenty-five years between the transformations of each nation's destiny.[131] The two verses of your composition include all these meanings, so not only is the

---

129 'Tan'gun Chosŏn' (檀君朝鮮), *Comprehensive Mirror of the Eastern Kingdom* (*Tongguk t'onggam* 東國通鑑). "Originally there were no rulers (*kunjang* 君長) in the East, but a deity (*sinin* 神人) descended to the base of a birch tree, and the people of the country made him their king, and that person was none other than Tan'gun. They called the country Chosŏn, and this happened in the Mujin Year of Emperor Yao of China." (東方初無君長, 有神人降于檀木下, 國人立爲君, 是爲檀君. 國號朝鮮, 是唐堯戊辰歲也.)" In an annotation to this passage it states, "Emperor Yao ascended the throne in the Kapchin Year (甲辰年, BC 2357), and Tan'gun ascended the throne twenty-five years later in the Mujin Year (戊辰年, BC 2333); it is not true that he founded the nation at the same time as Yao." (堯之立, 在上元甲子甲辰之歲, 而檀君之立, 在後二十五年戊辰, 則曰, '與堯並立'者, 非也.)

130 Kanghŏn Taewang (康獻大王): T'aejo Yi Sŏnggye (太祖 李成桂, 1335–1408, r. 1392–1398).

131 This means that in the history of China and Korea, whenever China underwent a major dynastic change, after a gap of twenty-five years, Korea also underwent a dynastic change.

quality of your writing good, it is also extremely good because the meaning of your composition is appropriate for one that is addressed to an envoy to Chosŏn."

Minister Tu laughed and said, "It is rare even for men to know about the fortunes of successive rulers and the historical records of China and foreign lands, but as a woman you know those things clearly, so every time I see the outstanding brilliance of my grandchildren, I say they inherited it from you."

"As a woman I have not read many books, so what could I know? I just replied to what you asked based on words I have heard, but hearing your teaching I feel ashamed. The children are brilliant as a result of their father's teaching, but I feel sorry that they might learn my shortcomings."

Minister Tu sent the composition to Hanlin Academician Zhu, and when he returned from being an envoy, Hanlin Academician Zhu sent him a letter saying, "I went to Chosŏn this time, examined everything thoroughly and found that its rites, music and customs were wonderful; everything was developed, and it was not in the slightest bit different from our China. Its raised pavilions here and there by its rivers and lakes seemed to be competing for superiority with ours in China, so it is justly called 'Small China'. I took thousands of pages of 'poems of parting' with me, so many Chosŏn literati saw them, and I was glad that they greatly praised Lord Minister Tu's writing, saying that it was as though it had been written before the era of Qin and Han (秦漢)."

Furthermore, he sent a painting of Yŏn'gwang Pavilion (練光亭)[132] and a poem engraved on Hoeran Rock (廻瀾石)[133] in Kŭmch'ŏn (金川). Lord Minister Tu took his grandchildren and unfolded the painting and poem.

Yuhandang sat down next to them and read out loud, "P'yŏngyang is the place where Kija (Jizi 箕子) established his capital when he rode out on his white horse at the time of King Wu of Zhou[134] and is the place where he established Chŏngjŏn (井田), so it would have been better if I had drawn the site of Chŏngjŏn rather than the natural scenery around Yŏn'gwang Pavilion. At that time, too, King Wu arose as a sage in China, and in Chosŏn Kija, who was also a sage, founded the nation. In this, too, we can see that the cosmological destiny of the two nations is the same. Chosŏn

---

132 Yŏn'gwang Pavilion (Yŏn'gwangjŏng 練光亭): This is a raised pavilion by the banks of the Taedong River in P'yŏngyang.

133 Hoeran Rock (Hoeransŏk 廻瀾石): This is a stone inscription that was erected in 1567 at the bank of the stream Ojoch'ŏn in Kŭmch'ŏn-ŭp, Kŭmch'ŏn-gun, North Hwanghae Province. The name 'Hoeransŏk' (廻瀾石) is carved in large characters on one side, and on the other side a poem describing the scenery of the area is engraved.

134 This reference to P'yŏngyang is mentioned in the story of Kija's arrival in the East (Jizi donglai shuo 箕子東來說). 'Song Weizi shijia' (宋微子世家), *Records of the Grand Historian*. "After this King Wu of Zhou enfeoffed Jizi as ruler of Chaoxian (Chosŏn), but he (Jizi) was not his vassal." (於是, 武王乃封箕子於朝鮮, 而不臣也.)

received edification from Kija and was greatly enlightened by the teaching of the Five Cardinal Human Relationships, and the chastity of its women became the best of all the nations of the world, while its mountains and rivers are obstacles along the way for ten thousand *li*, and I seem to always be seeing them."

The Way to Bring Up Children

One day, Lady Yang the daughter-in-law of the nephew of Yuhandang's mother-in-law asked Yuhandang, "When teaching children, as Yuhandang mentioned, adults should not show wrong behavior and do wrong things, so if you learn and practice the saying that adults should take the initiative in teaching, you will naturally not go against the rules of ancient times. However, even though it is difficult to raise young children from the moment they are born, the children of Yuhandang's family have been raised well from as soon as they were born, so what is your secret?"

"In the words of a famous doctor of old, 'the treatment of one woman is more difficult than the treatment of ten men, and the treatment of one child is more difficult than the treatment of ten women.'[135] That saying means that it is easier to cure ten men of a disease than one woman, and that it is more difficult to cure one child of a disease than it is to cure ten women; and that saying is indeed true. Unlike adults, children do not have hardened bones; they do not have much energy and blood; they cannot speak because they are wrapped in a carrying cloth (*p'odaegi*); and as it is difficult to know when they are sick, it is hard to use medical treatments and medicine. Furthermore, the fact that adults get sick in midsummer or due to their food is their own fault because they did not take care of their physical body, but if children get sick it is not their own fault, but rather because adults did not take care of them; so shouldn't a parent's heart be even more careful? If we discuss the method of taking care of children, only after you have clearly understood the principles of the harmonization of heaven and earth and people's sleeping and eating, will you know the way of raising children. How can there be any clever methods for people like us who are lacking in scholarship?"

---

135 'Children' (Soa 小兒), *Exemplar of Korean Medicine*. "There is an old saying, 'It is more difficult to cure one woman of a disease than it is to cure ten men, and it is more difficult to cure one child of a disease than it is to cure ten women. It is even more difficult to cure a child because it is difficult to ask a child about its symptoms, and it is difficult to take its pulse." (古語曰, 寧醫十丈夫, 難醫一婦人, 寧醫十婦人, 難醫一小兒. 蓋小兒難問證, 難察脉, 治之尤難故也.) The original source is *Introduction to Medicine* (*Yixue rumen* 醫學入門) by the renowned Ming dynasty physician Li Chan (李梴).

"Even if we cannot discuss the principles of the harmony of heaven and earth, I would like to hear about the etiquette of Yuhandang's family."

Yuhandang laughed, "In our home we do not have any particularly wise method except that I admonish the young children with the single character '*kwa*' (過) meaning 'excess'. Even when a child is being breastfed, it should not be fed to satiety; even when it cries, you should not let it cry excessively; also it should not get excessively hungry; it should not be exposed to excessive wind, or excessive heat, or excessive cold. You should not give excessive love to a child to make it laugh; a baby should not be embraced or carried in people's hands; it should be left alone and allowed to do things by itself, and you should not force it to sit up; it should also stand up of its own accord, and adults should not force it to stand up. A good method is to let them do things on their own in accordance with the principles of heaven and earth and nature; forcing children to sit down or stand up, even if it is done out of love for the child, will rather cause harm. Therefore, in the words of Mencius, "There was a person from Song who pulled up his seedlings so that the grain would grow faster."[136] Mencius'

---

136 'Gongsun Chou I' (公孫丑上), *Mencius*. "There was a man of Song, who was grieved that his growing corn was not longer, and so he pulled it up. Having done this, he returned home, looking very stupid, and said to his people, 'I am tired today. I have been helping the corn to grow long.' His son ran to look at it, and found the corn all withered." (宋人有閔其苗之不長而

words can also be applied in this case. Raising young children is like nurturing young seedlings, so if you try to sit them up or make them stand up, it is the same as pulling up seedlings."

"These are truly words that make one realize the principles of heaven and earth. What kind of clothing do you put on a baby as soon as it is born?"

"As soon as they are born, they are wrapped in swaddling clothes. Is there any particular reason to dress them up? There is an old saying by a famous physician that 'if you wrap a baby in the sweat-soaked clothing of a seventy- or eighty-year-old man, it will live long and gain wealth and honor',[137] so that kind of clothing or swaddling cloth are fine."

"Why did this famous doctor say such a thing?"

"Since a young child lacks its own *ki* (C. *qi* 氣) energy and blood, it is clear that it would be beneficial to wrap its body with the old man's essence (*chinaek* 津液) and energy."

揠之者, 芒芒然歸, 謂其人曰, '今日病矣. 予助苗長矣.' 其子趨而往視之, 苗則槁矣.)

137 'Children', *Exemplar of Korean Medicine*. "If you make clothes out of the old knee breeches or outer wear of an old man of seventy or eighty years and dress your child in them, by nurturing this essence (*chin'gi* 眞氣) the child will have a long life." (宜用七八十歲老人舊裩舊襖, 改作小兒衣衫, 眞氣相滋, 令兒有壽.) The original source is *Recovery from All Ailments* (*Wanbing huichun* 萬病回春) by the Ming dynasty physician Gong Tingxian (龔廷賢).

"I heard these words carelessly in the past, but today I realize what they mean. Is it correct to say that it is good to wash a child thoroughly once every three days?"

"Some people who live near water say that it is better to wash their children in cold water, so some put them in water to wash them and then take them out. There are many people who have failed abjectly because their way of washing their children was such that they were unable to heed the admonishment of the character *kwa* (excess).[138] In my house even if I want to wash a child, I believe it is better not to wash it because I worry that the wind will enter its navel."[139]

"It is said that if you do not wash your child, its face will turn black after it has grown up, is that true?"

"Even if your face becomes dark, it is better than over-washing and contracting a disease. Much less does it matter if a child's face is dark or pale

---

138 'Children', *Exemplar of Korean Medicine*. "In the world at large, people think that children have heat (*yŏl* 熱) in their bodies, so when they bathe them, they leave them sitting in the water for a long time. If you do this, the cold will damage the exterior, and the energy of the water will penetrate inside; and because of the wind, the limbs can tremble, so should we not be cautioned against this?" (世俗, 以爲小兒體熱, 或遇澡浴, 卽與久坐湯水之中, 風冷外傷, 水濕內滲, 變成風搐, 可不戒之?) The original source is *Straightforward Prescriptions for Young Children* (*Zhizhi xiaoer fang* 直指小兒方) by the Song dynasty physician Yang Shiying (楊士瀛).

139 'Children', *Exemplar of Korean Medicine*. "Ten ways of raising children. First, keep the back warm. … Ten, concerning bathing, avoid it as much as possible." (養子十法, 一要背煖. …… 十少洗浴.) The original source is *Introduction to Medicine* (*Yixue rumen* 醫學入門) by the renowned Ming dynasty physician Li Chan (李梴).

when it is born as the skin will be shed, so why should it matter if it is dark at first? Quickly whitening a child's skin to show it off to other people is also like the farmer who pulled up shoots to make them grow more quickly."

"Everyone in Yuhandang's house says that they have never had smallpox (*yŏkchil* 疫疾), so what was your secret?"

"Smallpox first appeared from the late Zhou (周) dynasty to the early Qin (秦) dynasty, and it is indeed the most difficult disease in the world to cure. What secret method could I have as an ignorant woman? My father-in-law got an ancient prescription and made every effort to feed the children with black sesame oil when they were young. Because of the efficacy of this, half of my father-in-law's many descendants did not contract smallpox and the other half who did contract smallpox only had it lightly."

"I have learned a lot while listening to these words. Is there any way to know a child's fortune as soon as it is born?"

"It is said in a medical book, 'You can know a child's fortune by the sound of its crying' and 'If a child's wrist bones do not protrude when it crawls, it is not fortunate, and if its heel bones do not stick out when it walks, it is not fortunate'."[140]

---

140 'Children', *Exemplar of Korean Medicine*. "If the bones of the palm of the hand are not all formed, even if it can crawl, it will die. If all the heel bones are not formed, even though it

"The way of raising children is very different from what it was in the past, so there are many people who have become ill because they were raised in accordance with the ways of antiquity (*sanggo sidae* 上古時代)."[141]

"That is true. In antiquity people lived in caves. They wore clothes made of grass, and they picked and ate fruit from trees, so from the time they were in the womb, young children did not avoid wind, cold, heat and damp (*p'ung han sŏ sŭp* 風寒暑濕). They did not suffer harm during pregnancy or after being born even if they were not careful about wind, cold, heat and damp. Nowadays, because people feed their children to the point of satiety and keep them warmly clothed (*p'osik nanŭi* 飽食暖衣), and live in a deep room with a folding screen and oiled-paper screen against the north wall, even after becoming pregnant, they live like this for ten months, so it is natural that if you care for a child in the same way as a child that was conceived when the ancient people wore grass clothing and ate fruit from trees, it will come to harm."

can walk, it will die." (掌骨不成, 能匍匐而死. 踵骨不成, 能行而死.) The original source is *Effective Formulae from Generations of Physicians* (*Shiyi dexiao fang* 世醫得效方) by the Yuan dynasty physician Wei Yilin (危亦林).

141 *Sanggo sidae* (上古時代) refers to the time before Xia, Yin (Shang) and Zhou (i.e. prehistoric times).

"These words are indeed correct. I can't raise my children as they did in ancient times when people wore grass clothes and ate fruit from trees, but even if I also always leave them next to the northern wall in an inner room, it seems that they will be harmed."

"Even if you place a child next to the northern wall of a deep room, do not leave it there for an excessively long time. Rather, the right way to raise it is to gradually take it out after 100 days to expose it to the sunlight and wind in moderation."[142]

"These words are indeed true. I just heard Mencius' admonition concerning pulling up new shoots (C. *yamiao* 揠苗), but Mencius also said 'let not the mind forget its work, but let there be no assisting the growth of nature'[143]—meaning do not forget but do not assist to grow—these are indeed apposite words on the way of raising children."

---

142 'Children', *Exemplar of Korean Medicine.* "If the weather is warm, hold the baby and let the wind and sunlight shine on it, by doing this its *ki* and blood will be strengthened so that it can withstand the wind and cold and disease does not occur. These days, people hold children in their arms and do not let them touch the ground, which weakens their muscles and makes diseases easier to contract. This is not the way to love and protect children." (凡嬰兒 … 若天氣和暖, 抱之使見風日, 則氣血堅剛, 可耐風寒, 不致疾病. 今人懷抱小兒, 不着地氣, 致令筋骨緩弱, 疾病易生, 非愛護之道.) The original source is *Effective Formulae from Generations of Physicians* (*Shiyi dexiao fang* 世醫得效方) by the Yuan dynasty physician Wei Yilin (危亦林).

143 'Gongsun Chou I', *Mencius.* "There must be the constant practice of this righteousness, but without the object of thereby nourishing the passion-nature. Let not the mind forget its work but let there be no assisting the growth of that nature. Let us not be like the man of Song." (必有事焉而勿正, 心勿忘, 勿助長也, 無若宋人然.)

"Even a single word of the sages makes so much sense, so to what could they not be applicable? Taking care of children is extremely difficult, which is why people of old said, 'Serve your elderly parents as if you were taking care of a child',[144] and 'when a woman raises silkworms, she should go back to look at them often as though she was raising a child',[145] so this is the same as Mencius' admonition 'not to forget'. Setting children down and sitting them up before they are able to do so on their own is a violation of Mencius' admonitions not to 'pull up shoots' and not to 'assist the growth of nature'. When a baby cries, do not rush to soothe them by hurriedly breastfeeding them, but after they have stopped crying, breastfeed them sufficiently; when the adult is feeling frustrated do not breastfeed (the baby); wash away the breast milk occasionally; after a person has given off a bad smell, they should not hurriedly embrace (a child); don't be excessively angry near a child, and don't shout too loudly. Even if women are not ignorant about these things and know about all of them, nevertheless, it is still difficult to refrain from doing them one by one."

"After the birth of a child, I generally understand the way of raising a child. Is there any way to tell the difference between a boy and a girl when the child is still in the womb?"

---

144 Source unknown.
145 Source unknown.

"These words are in the medical books, but it is difficult to distinguish between them. Someone in the past said, 'It would be better to be without the *Book of History* than give entire credit to it.'[146] If you wait ten months after conceiving a baby, you will know, so why do you need to know in advance?"

"I heard that father has some prescription, so he knows; and that father has taught his grandsons, so that they can all conceive male children. Are these words true?"

"Because father is familiar with astronomical geography, human affairs and physics (*insa mulli* 人事物理) is that not why people say that? If father's grandchildren conceive ten children, seven or eight of them will be male, so don't other people say that that is a wonderful thing."

"I intend to study from father."

"Father always says concerning those words that if a person conceives ten children and all ten are boys then such a method exists, but if out of those ten children two or three are girls, then that method does not exist. It is difficult for an ordinary woman in the world to put into practice the method to conceive a male child and to raise it well."

---

146 'Jinxin II' (盡心下), *Mencius*, "Mencius said, 'It would be better to be without the *Book of History* than to give entire credit to it.'" (孟子曰, '盡信書, 不如無書.')

"What method is there?"

"Having many children is considered the most important of the five blessings. Hua Fengren blessed Emperor Yao with many sons,[147] at the time of Zhou a poet presented an ode to King Wen (文王) with the words, 'And from her came a hundred sons';[148] Confucius' mother prayed at Mt. Niqiu (尼丘山)[149] and gave birth to Confucius and his brothers. However, from ancient times has not giving birth to sons been an extremely essential and important (*kwanjŭng* 款重) blessing? If they want to obtain the blessing of having many sons, how could parents wish for such a blessing without investing all their heart and virtue? If you harbor even the slightest malevolence (*salgi* 殺氣) in your heart, or if you speak even the slightest malevolence with your mouth, disasters and tribulations will come to your own self. For this reason 'on the good-doer he sends down all blessings', and 'on the evil-doer he sends down all miseries'.[150] It is said that 'if you do good deeds, you will bring about a hundred auspicious

---

147 See footnote 53.

148 'Pure and Reverent' (Sizhai 思齊), *Book of Odes*. "Pure and reverent was Tairen, / The mother of King Wen, / Loving was she to Zhou Jiang—A wife becoming the House of Zhou. / Taisi inherited her excellent frame, / And from her came a hundred sons." (思齊大(太)任, 文王之母, 思媚周姜, 京室之婦, 太姒嗣徽音, 則百斯男.)

149 Mt. Niqiu (尼丘山): 'Confucius' family' (Kongzi shijia 孔子世家), *Records of the Grand Historian*. It is said that Confucius' father Shuliang He (叔梁紇) and his mother An Zhengzai (安徵在) prayed at this mountain in Qufu (曲阜) in Shandong (山東) Province, and Confucius was born.

150 'Instructions of Yi' (伊訓), *Book of History*. "The ways of God are not invariable: on the good-doer he sends down all blessings, and on the evil-doer he sends down all miseries." (惟上帝不常, 作善, 降之百祥, 作不善, 降之百殃.)

things; if you do bad deeds, you will bring about a hundred kinds of bad things.' Looking at it in this way, if I hurt someone else's child, won't the other person also hurt my child? According to the words of Mencius, 'treat with the kindness due to youth the young in your own family (幼吳幼) so that the young in the families of others shall be similarly treated.'[151] That is to say, if I love the children in my own family, that love will reach the children of other families.' When I hear women say that they know what to do as women, I feel deep regret for being born as a woman."

The Human Mind and Moral Mind

Yuhandang said, "What arises from the 'private nature of form-and-energy' is called the 'human mind' and what arises from the 'rectification of life' is called the 'moral mind'."[152]

---

151 'Liang Huiwang I' (梁惠王上), *Mencius*. Treat with the reverence to age the elders of your own family, so that the elders in the families of others shall be similarly treated; treat with the kindness due to youth the young in your own family, so that the young in the families of others shall be similarly treated – do this and the kingdom may be made to go round in your palm." (老吾老, 以及人之老, 幼吾幼, 以及人之幼, 天下可運於掌上.)

152 'Chapter on the Human Mind and the Moral Mind' (Renxin dioxin zhang 人心道心章),

Her granddaughter replied, "If it arises from the 'private nature of form-and-energy', is it human greed?"

"According to the words of Master Zhu, 'the human mind is certainly not human greed.' How can you ask if we have two minds? The human mind and the moral mind are not separate. It is called by many names such as the 'original mind' (*ponsim* 本心), the 'conscience' (*yangsim* 良心), the 'mind of a newborn baby' (*chŏkchasim* 赤子心), and it is also called the 'great human mind' (*taeinsim* 大人心), so please read the *Classic of Mind-and-Heart* (*Xinjing*) carefully."

"If the human mind arises from the private nature of 'form-and-energy' and the moral mind arises from the 'rectification of life', when Yao and Shun passed on their way of using the mind in the *Book of History* (*Shujing*), why did they not mention the moral mind that arises from the rectification of life but first mentioned the human mind that arises from the private nature of form-and-energy?"[153]

Classic of the Mind-and-Heart (*Xinjing*). "Master Zhu said, 'There is only one vague perception of the mind; the fact that it is said that there is a difference between the human mind and the moral mind is because some things arise out of the private nature of 'form-and-energy' (*xingqi* 形氣), and some things stem from the 'rectification of life', as perceptions are not the same." (朱子曰, '心之虛靈知覺, 一而已矣, 而以爲有人心道心之異者, 以其或生於形氣之私, 或原於性命之正, 而所以爲知覺者不同.')

153 'Counsels of the Great Yu' (Da Yu mo 大禹謨), *Book of History*. "The mind of man is restless, prone (to err); its affinity to what is right is small. Be discriminating, be uniform (in the pursuit of what is right), that you may sincerely hold fast the Mean." (人心惟危, 道心惟微, 惟精惟一, 允執厥中.)

"Generally in language, lighter matters are mentioned first and serious matters are mentioned later, but also sometimes important things are mentioned first and lighter things later. The sequential order of the human mind and the moral mind does not necessarily have any bearing on their relative importance. I think it was because there is more in the human mind to be wary of. In the deliberations of previous Confucian scholars, we cannot see any discussion about the sequential order of the human mind and the moral mind. When people read texts, they have to diligently put into practice their 'admonitions about the rectification of the heart-mind' (*chŏngsim chi hun* 正心之訓) and their 'admonitions about the existence of the mind' (*chonsim chi hun* 存心之訓). Whether it is the moral mind or the human mind, if we only memorize passages from the classics by reciting them how can they benefit our physical being?"

"Grandmother's teaching is indeed like that."

Cases of Long Pregnancies

Yuhandang's eldest granddaughter asked, "There is no difference in the principle of the conception of a child between people in the past and people in the present, and there is no difference between sages and ordinary people, yet there are some who give birth as they approach the tenth month of pregnancy, and there are those who give birth several months after the tenth month, so is that not an extraordinary thing?"

"It is normal to give birth within ten months, and as the harmony of heaven and earth is infinite (*mugung mujin*), there are those who give birth several months after (ten months), and there are those who give birth after several years (of gestation), so it is not necessarily an extraordinary thing. There is the account of Emperor Yao being born after fourteen months in the *History of Han*;[154] there is the account of King Yu (禹) of

---

154 'Biographies of Empresses and Imperial Affines I' (Waiqi zhuan shang 外戚傳上), *History of Han* (*Hanshu* 漢書). "Lady Quan became a *jieyu* (婕妤) (Han dynasty concubine's title) and took up residence in Gouyi Palace (鉤弋宮). She was greatly favored, and in the 3rd Year of Taishi (太始), she gave birth to Emperor Zhao (昭帝) and called him Gouyizi (鉤弋子). As she gave birth to the child after fourteen months of pregnancy, the king said, 'I heard that Emperor Yao in the past was born after fourteen months of pregnancy, and Gouyi is the same.'" (拳夫人進爲婕妤, 居鉤弋宮. 大有寵, 太始三年生昭帝, 號鉤弋子. 任身十四月乃生, 上曰, '聞昔堯十四月而生, 今鉤弋亦然.')

Xia (夏) being born after fourteen months in the book called *The Dunjia Illustrations of the Opening of the Mountain*;[155] the account of Xie (契) being born after fourteen months is in *Record of Heretofore Lost Works*;[156] the account of Emperor Zhao of Han (漢昭帝) being born after fourteen months is in *Spring and Autumn Annals of the Sixteen Kingdoms*;[157] and the account of Wang Yangming (王陽明) being born after fourteen months is in his 'Chronicle' (Nianpu 年譜).[158] The account of Ju Gyuri being born after fifteen months is in *Shizuan zuobian*;[159] the account of Guo Tan (郭坦) being born after twenty-two months is in a book called *Pearl Boat*;[160] the

---

155 *Shuofu* (說郛). "*In Dunjia Illustrations of the Opening of the Mountain* (*Dunjia kaishan tu* 遁甲開山圖) it states, 'In the evening Nüdi (女狄) drew water at the foot of Mt. Shiniu (石紐山), in the spring water she caught the essence of the moon (*yuejing* 月精) like an egg, and liking it, she placed it in her mouth and swallowed it without realizing it. Finally she became pregnant, and fourteen months later she gave birth to Yu (禹)." (遁甲開山圖. '女狄暮汲石紐山下, 泉水中得月精如鷄子, 愛而含之, 不覺而呑, 遂有娠, 十四月生夏禹.)

156 'Yin Tang' (殷湯), *Record of Heretofore Lost Works* (*Shiyi ji* 拾遺記). "One year after Di (狄) incubated the egg, she became pregnant, and fourteen months later she gave birth to Xie (契)." (狄乃懷卵, 一年而有娠, 經十四月而生契.)

157 *Spring and Autumn Annals of the Sixteen Kingdoms* (*Shiliuguo chunqiu* 十六國春秋) was compiled by the official historian Cui Hong (崔鴻, 478–525), but no records about Emperor Zhao of Han can be found in it. In the *History of Han* (*Hanshu* 漢書) it states that Gouyi furen Zhaoshi (鉤弋夫人趙氏) gave birth to Emperor Zhao after fourteen months.

158 'Chronicle of Wang Shouren (Wang Yangming)' (Wang Shouren nianpu 王守仁年譜), *Complete Works of Wang Yangming* (*Wang Yangming quanji* 王陽明全集). "His mother Zheng was in the fourteenth month of pregnancy. In his grandmother's dream, a divine being wearing silk clothes and a jade crown appeared from a cloud with the sound of music and handed her a child. His grandmother who had received the child was shocked and awoke, and already she could hear the crying of the (newborn) baby." (太夫人鄭娠十四月. 祖母岑夢神人衣緋玉雲中鼓吹, 送兒授岑, 岑警寤, 已聞啼聲.)

159 *Shizuan zuobian* (史纂左編) is a reference to *Lidai shizuan zuobian* (歷代史纂左編) by Tang Shunzhi (唐順之, 1507–1560). Ju Gyuri is unknown.

160 Chen Jiru (陳繼儒, 1558–1639), *Pearl Boat* (*Zhenzhu chuan* 珍珠船). "Sacrificial official (*gongfeng*

account of the Yellow Emperor Xuanyuan-*shi* (黃帝軒轅氏) is in *In Search of the Supernatural*;[161] and the account of Wang Jie being born after twenty-four months is in *Shizuan zuobian*. The account of Yi P'il being born after three years is in *Ŏ□oejŏn*,[162] and the account of Peng Zu (彭祖) being born after three years (pregnancy) is in *Records of Ritual Matters by Dai the Elder*;[163] the account of Wen Panshi (溫盤石) being born after three years is in *Garden of Marvels* by Liu Jingshu (劉敬叔),[164] and the account of Yuanzhuo being born after three years is in *Collected Works of Dongpo* (東坡集). The account

---

guan 供奉官) Guo Tan (郭坦) did not come out of his mother's womb after over a year. A person who was adept at acupuncture inserted over 100 acupuncture needles, but in the end there was still no movement, and it was only after twenty-two months that he was born. Both the mother who gave birth and the child were unharmed, except that Guo Tan had several tens of black spots on his chest, which were traces of the acupuncture that had been administered." (供奉官郭坦, 在母胎餘年不育. 有善針人百餘針, 竟亦不動, 至二十二月生. 子母俱安. 唯胸臆中有黑點數十處, 乃當日針痕也.) The same content can also be found in *Forest of Flagons* (*Zhilin* 巵林) and *Categorized Tales* (*Leishuo* 類說).

161 'The Birth of the Yellow Emperor' (Huangdi zhi sheng 黃帝之生), *In Search of the Supernatural* (*Soushen ji* 搜神記). "When Shen Nong reached the end of his life Shaodian-*shi* (少典氏) took Fu Bao (附寶) to be his wife. Fu Bao saw a large rainbow of light enveloping the central star of the Big Dipper and illuminating the outskirts of the city, and after a pregnancy of twenty-five months, she gave birth to the Yellow Emperor in Shouqiu (壽丘)." (及神農之末, 少典氏又娶附寶. 見大霓光繞北斗樞星, 照郊野. 附寶孕二十五月, 生黃帝於壽丘.)

162 Unknown source.

163 'Dixi' (帝繫), *Records of Ritual Matters by Dai the Elder* (*Dadai Liji* 大戴禮記). "Luzhong-*shi* (陸終氏) married Nütui-*shi* (女隤氏) the younger sister of Guifang-*shi* (鬼方氏). Nütui-*shi* gave birth to six sons. As no child emerged three years after conception, an incision was made in her left side, and six children came out. The first was Fan (樊), who became Kunwu (昆吾). The second was Huilian (惠連), who became Shenhu (參胡). The third was Jian (籛), who became Pengzu (彭祖)." (陸終氏娶于鬼方氏, 鬼方氏之妹謂之女隤氏, 產六子. 孕而不粥, 三年, 啟其左脅, 六人出焉. 其一曰樊, 是爲昆吾. 其二曰惠連, 是爲參胡. 其三曰籛, 是爲彭祖.)

164 *Garden of Marvels* (Yiyuan 異苑). "Wen Panshi, a native of Taiyuan, was born three years after his mother became pregnant. As soon as he was born, he sat up and smiled, his hair covered his face, and his molars were all in place." (太原温盤石, 母懷身三年然後生, 墮地便坐而笑, 髮覆面, 牙齒皆具.)

of Hyerŭng (C. Huileng 慧棱) being born after six years is in *Pangyŏng sŏ*;[165] the account of Xie Zunzhe (脇尊者) being born after sixty years is in *Record of the Transmission of the Lamp*.[166] The account of Laozi (老子) being born after seventy-two years is in *Biographies of Divine Immortals*,[167] and in *Jingtian Left Compilation*, it states that Laozi was born after eighty years.[168] Even if these people were born one month late, or the pregnancy lasted a little more than a year, there was no harm done; and among them are holy men, sages, kings, virtuous ministers, as well as people who lived to the age of eight hundred and people who lived to the age of five hundred. Even

---

165 Source unknown.

166 *Jingde Record of the Transmission of the Lamp* (*Jingde Chuandeng lu* 景德傳燈錄). *Chuandeng lu* is a record of Indian Buddhist patriarchs (*zushi* 祖師) and Chinese Buddhist patriarchs (*chuandeng faxi* 傳燈法系). The ninth Indian Buddhist patriarch Buddhamitra (a Buddhist nun) was born after sixty years: she "was born after sixty years in the womb, so it is said she was called 'difficult birth' (*nansaeng* 難生)." The tenth patriarch Xie Zunzhe, originally had the name 'difficult birth' (*nansaeng*), but when he attended the ninth Indian patriarch Buddhamitra, he never slept lying on his side, so he came to be called 'Xie Zunzhe' (lit. Venerable Ribs). The account of Xie Zunzhe being born after a sixty-year gestation in *Yuhandang Sa-ssi ŏnhaengnok* is different from the truth, but in 'Shenxian xingming' (神仙姓名), *Shizu bokao* (氏族博攷), compiled by the renowned physician Ling Dizhi (凌廸知), it mentions, "Laozi was in his mother's womb for eighty years and was called Lao Dan (老聃) because his ears were long, and Xie Zunzhe was called Nansheng (difficult birth) because he was in his mother's womb for sixty years." (李耳在母胎八十年, 耳有聃, 故一名老聃, 脅尊者在母胎六十年, 故號難生.)

167 There is no mention of Laozi in *Biographies of Divine Immortals* (*Shenxian zhuan* 神仙傳) by Ge Hong (葛洪). 'Laozi', *Extensive Records of the Taiping Era* (*Taiping Guangji* 太平廣記). "Some people say that Laozi's mother gave birth to him after a seventy-two-year pregnancy, and that when he was born, he was ripped out of his mother's left armpit, and it is said that because his hair was white from the moment he was born, he was called Laozi (Master Old)." (或云, 母懷之七十二年乃生, 生時剖母左腋而出, 生而白首, 故謂之老子.)

168 *Jingtian Left Compilation* (*Jingtian zuobian* 荊天左編) refers to *Successive Dynasties Jingtian Left Compilation* (*Lidai shizuan zuobian* 歷代史纂左編) by Tang Shunzhi.

though some were heterodox in their views, they were still good people. It is said that being born after a long pregnancy is auspicious because you have spent a long time inheriting your innate character."

Questions and Answers on the *Book of Rites*

When Yuhandang's great-granddaughter was eleven years old, after reading the *Book of Rites*, she asked Yuhandang, "In the *Book of Rites* it says, 'When walking a man should walk on the right and a woman should walk on the left',[169] so this seems to be saying that men and women should take different paths. The left of a person coming will be the right of a person going, and the right of a person going will be the left of a person coming. In that case the man coming and the woman going will be on one side, and the man going and the woman coming will be on the other side, so how can we say that the paths of men and women are different?"

"It is not talking about the left and right side of people, but it is talking

---

169 'Royal Regulations' (Wangzhi 王制), *Book of Rites*. "On the roads, men took the right side and women the left, carriages kept in the middle." (道路男子由右, 婦人由左, 車從中央.)

about the left and right side of the road."

"Is it a discussion of Confucian scholars of old?"

"It is not clear that this is something that Han Yu (韓愈) ever spoke about,[170] and although this phrase is in the *Elementary Learning*, it is not explained in the annotations."[171]

The great-granddaughter asked again, "For men and women not to allow their hands to touch when giving and receiving[172] is the general rule, but it is difficult to put this rule into practice when helping one another to wrap a baby in a carrying cloth (*p'odaegi*)."

"It is not difficult. As stated in the *Elementary Learning*, 'When giving and receiving a vessel, (one person should) put it down first and then (the other person) should pick it up',[173] likewise, when handing a child over to another person, once the child has been laid down on a mat, the other person can

---

170 Unknown source.

171 'Minglun', *Elementary Learning*. "Liu-*shi* said, 'The ancient law is that men go on the right side of the road, and women go on the left side.'" (劉氏曰, 道路之法, 其右以行男子, 其左以行女子, 古之道也.)

172 'Li Lou I' (離婁上), *Mencius*. "For men and women not to allow their hands to touch in giving and receiving is the general rule; when a sister-in-law is drowning, to rescue her with the hand is a peculiar exigency." (男女授受不親, 禮也, 嫂溺援之以手, 權也.)

173 'Minglun', *Elementary Learning*. "Except at sacrifices and funeral rites, they should not hand vessels to one another. In all other cases when they have occasion to give and receive anything, the woman should receive it in a basket. If she (should) have no basket, they should both sit down, and the other should put the thing on the ground, and she should then take it up." (非祭非喪, 不相授器. 其相授, 則女受以篚, 其無則皆坐奠之而後取之.) The original source is 'Pattern of the Family' (Neize 內則), *Book of Rites*.

embrace it. For adults to hand over a child to one another while standing up is extremely dangerous. If you make a mistake and drop it, its life might be at risk, or it might easily become disabled, so it is only right to be extremely cautious."

As she was saying this the great-granddaughter's eldest sibling came in, heard this, and laughing said, "In an ancient text it states, 'There never has been a girl who learned to bring up a child, that she might afterwards marry',[174] so are you studying how to raise a child before getting married?"

"As women in the past read 'Pattern of the Family' (Neize 內則) and *Biographies of Women*, I did not hear that they read them after deleting the main text '(Son's) wives should serve their parents-in-law'[175] and the original text, 'Wives conceive children.'[176] The daughter of Fan Chunfu (范淳夫) read Mencius when she was a child,[177] so would her father, who was a teacher of

---

174 *Great Learning*. "In the 'Announcement to Kang' (Kanggao 康誥) it is said, 'Act as if you were watching over an infant.' If (a mother) is really anxious about it, though she may not hit exactly the wants of her infant, she will not be far from doing so. There never has been a girl who learned to bring up a child that she might afterwards marry." (康誥曰, '如保赤子'.心誠求之, 雖不中, 不遠矣. 未有學養子而后嫁者也.)

175 'Pattern of the Family' (Neize 內則), *Book of Rites*. "(Son's) wives should serve their parents-in-law as they served their own." (婦事舅姑, 如事父母.)

176 'Wives conceive children.' (*furen ren zi* 婦人妊子): See footnote 12.

177 'Chapter on the Trees of Mt. Niu' (Niushan zhi mu zhang 牛山之木章), *Annotated Classic of Mind-and-Heart* (*Xinjing fuzhu*). "After reading 'Chapter on preserving and holding (one's heart-and-mind)' (Cao cun zhang 操存章) in Mencius, Fan Chunfu's daughter said, 'Mencius did not know about the mind. How can the mind go in and out?' Cheng Yi (程頤) heard this and said, 'Even if we do not know Mencius' original intention, nevertheless, he knew about the mind'." Fan Chunfu was a Song dynasty scholar, and his given name is Zuyu (祖禹,

academic studies, make her read it after removing the sentence 'treat with the kindness due to youth the young in your own family, so that the young in the families of others shall be similarly treated"'[178]

The eldest sibling laughed and said, "Every question you asked was detailed and deep so I considered it extraordinary and laughed as I spoke. Furthermore, your words conform so well to reason that it is astonishing."

Yuhandang said, "In an ancient text it states, 'a young child (K. *yuja*; C. *youzi* 幼子) should never be allowed to see an instance of deceit' (K. *sang si mu kwang*; C. *chang shi wu kuang* 常視無誑).[179] You are looking at a child, so how could you make fun of her?"

And she laughed out loud.

1041–1098).

178 See footnote 151.

179 'Summary of the Rules of Propriety I' (Quli shang), *Book of Rites*. "A young child should never be allowed to see an instance of deceit." (幼子常視無誑.)

Questions and Answers on 'Learning from the Ancients', *Elementary Learning*

After reading 'Learning from the Ancients' in *Elementary Learning*, Yuhandang's third granddaughter asked, "In the first topic of 'Learning from the Ancients', it presents the words of Tairen and then the words of Confucius. As this changes the order of the eras in which they lived, how can this be?"[180]

"Because this chapter is the one that elucidates 'Entering Instruction',[181] it records the prenatal education of Tairen when she was bearing King Wen in her womb. It then records the words of instruction that Mencius' mother gave to Mencius when he was a child, and then it records the words of Confucius with which he taught Boyu (伯魚).[182] Confucius was a sage

---

180 'Learning from the Ancients' (Jigu 稽古) tells of the prenatal education of Tairen, the mother of King Wen of Zhou. This is followed by an anecdote about what Mencius's mother taught Mencius when he was young, and then an anecdote about what Confucius taught his son. The anecdotes are arranged in the order of the ages of the subjects being taught, not in the order of the eras in which the personages lived.

181 The contents of 'Entering Instruction' (Rujiao 入敎), which precedes 'Learning from the Ancients' in *Elementary Learning*, as well as 'Illustrating the Cardinal Principles' (Minglun 明倫) and 'Respecting the Body' (Jingshen 敬身), were considered evidence based on past events. The anecdotes of Tairen, Mencius' mother and Confucius that comprise the first part are related to the contents of 'Entering Instruction'.

182 Boyu (伯魚) was the courtesy name of Confucius' son Kong Li (孔鯉).

who lived before Mencius, but in order of teaching, it was like this because these words of instruction were given to Boyu after he had grown up."

"Looking at this again, it is indeed like that."

Questions and Answers on the 'Four Pillars'

One day Yukpong's eldest son Kyusŏng asked Yuhandang, "Daoist Master Chang's son came to the outer quarters and examined the 'Four Pillars' (year, month, day and hour of birth) of all the fathers (in our family) and discussing them exclaimed, 'All your Four Pillars are remarkable!'"

"He said your father's elder brother's Four Pillars are *Ch'ŏn'gan ilgi kyŏk* (天干一氣格),[183] and your father's second eldest brother's Four Pillars are *Chiji sangdŭng kyŏk* (地支上等格),[184] didn't he?"

---

183 *Ch'ŏn'gan ilgi kyŏk* (天干一氣格): This means that the Heavenly Stem (Ch'ŏngan 天干) character (*cha* 字) is the same in each of the four sets of four characters designating the hour, day, month and year of birth (*Saju*, meaning Four Pillars). The Ten Heavenly Stem characters are as follows: *kap* (甲), *ŭl* (乙), *pyŏng* (丙), *chŏng* (丁), *mu* (戊), *ki* (己), *kyŏng* (庚), *sin* (辛), *im* (壬) and *kye* (癸).

184 *Chiji sangdŭng kyŏk* (地支上等格): This means that the Earthly Branch (Chiji 地支) character (*cha* 字) is the same in each of the four sets of four characters designating the hour, day, month and year of birth (*Saju*, meaning Four Pillars), and this combination is in the upper level of auspicious character combinations. The twelve Earthly Branch characters are as follows: *cha*

Kyusŏng was overjoyed and said, "Indeed that is so. Grandmother even though you knew that all along, why have you never spoken about it?"

"I have seen a few books on such fortunetelling techniques in the past, but because they are just 'miscellaneous techniques' (*chapsul* 雜術), I haven't talked about them all my life."

"What '*kyŏk*' is called '*Ch'ŏn'gan ilgi kyŏk*'?"

"Your father's elder brother was born at the Imin Hour (壬寅時) on the Imo Day (壬午日) in the Imja Month (壬子月) in the Imsul Year (壬戌年), so because the Heavenly Stem (Ch'ŏn'gan) 'Im' (壬) occurs four times, it is called *Chŏn'gan ilgi kyŏk*. Your second eldest paternal uncle (*sukpu*) was born at the Pyŏngja Hour (丙子時) on the Kyŏngja Day (庚子日) in the Pyŏngja Month (丙子月) in the Kapcha Year (甲子年), so because the Earthly Branch 'Cha' (子) occurs four times, it is called *Chiji sangdŭng kyŏk*."

"If there is the same single character in all the Four Pillars of other people is that also *Chŏn'gan ilgi kyŏk*?"

"It is the same for everyone, and there are countless ways of forming a *kyŏk*."

(子), *ch'uk* (丑), *in* (寅), *myo* (卯), *chin* (辰), *sa* (巳), *o* (午), *mi* (未), *sin* (申), *yu* (酉), *sul* (戌) and *hae* (亥).

"What are the *kyŏk* of our third and fourth paternal uncles?"

"The third was born at the Pyŏngsin Hour (丙申時), on the Pyŏngjin Day (丙辰日) in the Kyŏngin Month (庚寅月) in the Pyŏngin Year (丙寅年), so because for the Heavenly Stem there are three 'Pyŏng' (丙) characters with a different character between them and different Earthly Branches, it is called *Kyŏkkan sambong kyŏk* (隔間三峰格). The fourth was born at the Kapcha Hour (甲子時) on the Mujin Day (戊辰日), in the Kapcha Month (甲子月) in the Mujin Year (戊辰年), so because there are two Mujin characters and two Kapcha characters, both the Heavenly Stem characters and the Earthly Branch characters are twinned, so it is called the *Ssangbi hojŏp kyŏk*."[185]

"Why is it called *hojŏp kyŏk*?"

"Butterflies join together and go around in pairs, and this expression is based on their spirit."

"What are the *kyŏk* for our fifth paternal uncle, our father and our seventh paternal uncle?"

"(The fifth paternal uncle) was born at the Kyŏngo Hour (庚午時), on the Kapsin Day (甲申日) in the Kapsin Month (甲申月) in the Kyŏngo Year (庚午年), so this is also called *Ssangbi kyŏk*, and because the year and hour are the same, and the month

---

185 *Ssangbi hojŏp kyŏk*: See footnote 44.

and the day are the same, it is called *So ssangbi kyŏk* (小雙飛格). Your father was born at the Ŭlsa Hour (乙巳時) on the Chŏngsa Day (丁巳日) in the Chŏnghae Month (丁亥月) in the Ŭlhae Year (乙亥年), which is the *Ch'ŏn'gi pihwa kyŏk* (天氣比和格).[186] Ch'ilbong was born at the Chŏngmi Hour (丁未時) on the Chŏngch'uk Day (丁丑日) in the Kiyu Month (己酉月) in the Chŏngch'uk Year (丁丑年), which is the *Kyŏkkan sambong kyŏk*."

Kyusŏng said, "Now I understand."

And as he liked it (too much), Yuhandang said, "As this is hindering your studies, knowing about it is not essential."

Medicinal Plants, Trees, Birds and Animals

One day Yuhandang went to Wanshu Garden (萬樹園) and was picking wild vegetables and medicinal herbs, when her twenty-fifth grandson Chasŏng dug up a *ch'angch'ul root* (C. *cangzhu* 蒼朮: *Atractylodes japonica*)[187] and holding it asked

---

186 *Ch'ŏn'gi pihwa kyŏk* (天氣比和格): In this case there are two matching Heavenly Stems and two matching Earthly Branches in the four sets of four characters (*Saju*). Yuhandang's husband, the sixth son's Heavenly Stems pairs are '乙-乙' and '丁-丁'.

187 *Ch'angch'ul* (C. *cangzhu* 蒼朮: *Atractylodes japonica*): This is the root of the *Atractylodes japonica* (*sapchu*) and is used for medicinal purposes. *Atractylodes japonica* is a grass of the Asteraceae family

Yuhandang, "Why is a *ch'angch'ul* called *ch'ul* (朮)?"

"Is it important to study in order to know the names of those plants and trees? But according to Confucius 'From them we become largely acquainted with the names of birds, beasts, and plants.'[188] Go to Liuyi Pavilions (六藝樓: Six Confucian Arts Pavilions) and look at a book that deals with the study of Chinese characters (*chahak* 字學). It is probably because the form of the character '*ch'ul*' in *ch'angch'ul* when it is written as a seal script character (*chŏnja* 篆字)[189] looks like a *ch'angch'ul* when it first appears."[190]

Chasŏng said, "Are the names of the other medicinal herbs all like that?"

"The names of medicinal herbs are also categorized based on their color, so *hwangbaek* (黃柏: *Phellodendron amurense*)[191] and *hyŏnsam* (玄蔘: *Scrophularia*

---

188 'Yang Huo' (陽貨), *Analects*. "Confucius said, 'My children, why do you not study the *Book of Odes*? The Odes serve to stimulate the mind. They may be used for purposes of self-contemplation. They teach the art of sociability. They show how to regulate feelings of resentment. From them you learn the more immediate duty of serving one's father, and the remoter one of serving one's prince. From them we become largely acquainted with the names of birds, beasts, and plants.'" (子曰, 小子何莫學夫詩? 詩可以興, 可以觀, 可以群, 可以怨, 邇之事父, 遠之事君, 多識於鳥獸草木之名.)

189 Seal script is the style of Chinese character that is said to have been created by Cang Jie (蒼頡), the court recorder (*shiguan* 史官) of the Yellow Emperor (Huangdi 黃帝).

190 '*Zhu*' (K. *ch'ul* 朮), *Compendium of Materia Medica* (*Bencao gangmu* 本草綱目). "The seal script version of the Chinese character '*zhu*' (K. *ch'ul*) has the same appearance as (the plant's) roots, tendrils, stems and leaves." (朮字篆文, 象其根幹枝葉之形.)

191 *Hwangbaek* (黃柏: Phellodendron amurense): An Oriental medicine made from the dried bark of the *hwanggyŏngp'i namu* (*Phellodendron amurense*).

buergeriana)[192] have been given those names because they are yellow (*hwang*) and black (*hyŏn*). Also there are those named because of their taste such as *kamch'o* (甘草: *Glycyrrhiza uralensis*) and *kosam* (苦蔘: *Sophora flavescens*), as one is sweet (*kam*) and one is bitter (*ko*), and among those named because of their shape, there is *insam* (人蔘: *Panax ginseng*) because it is shaped like a person (*in* 人), and because *kudŭng* (鉤藤 *Uncaria rhynchophylla*)[193] is bent like a fish hook (*ku* 鉤), it was called *kudŭng*, meaning '*kalgori tŭngnamu*' ('hook wisteria'). There are also those that just came by their names of themselves, so in the case of *panha* (半夏: *Pinellia ternata*), it first appears in the fifth lunar month, which is halfway through the summer, so it was given the name *panha*, which means 'half summer'.[194] There are also those named after their medicinal properties (*sŏngmi* 性味), so because *tanggwi* (當歸: *Angelica gigas*) has the medicinal effect of promoting the circulation of the blood, its name contains the character *kwi* (歸) meaning 'return'.[195] Or there are those named after physical locations,

---

192 *Hyŏnsam* (玄蔘: Scrophularia buergeriana): An Oriental medicine made from *Scrophularia buergeriana* or its dried root.

193 *Kudŭng* (鉤藤: *Uncaria rhynchophylla*): An Oriental medicine. Its sprigs are shaped like fish hooks and are covered with thorns.

194 *Panha* (半夏): In the Fifth Lunar Month (*Zhongxia zhi yue* 仲夏之月) in 'Proceedings of Government in the Different Months' (Yueling 月令) in the *Book of Rites*, it states 'the midsummer herb grows' (K. *panha saeng*; C. *banxia sheng* 半夏生).

195 *Tanggwi* (當歸: *Angelica gigas*): *Compendium of Materia Medica* (*Bencao gangmu* 本草綱目). "*Danggui* (K. *tanggwi: Angelica gigas*) has a rapid effect in treating the symptoms of bad blood rising after childbirth in pregnant women. If someone whose *qi* and blood is out of order takes it, they will calm down immediately. Because it can provide both *qi* and blood with a place to

so *ch'ŏn'gung* (C. chuanxiong 川芎: Cnidium officinale) was given its name because Ch'ŏn'gung is the place where good *kunggung* (C. *xiongqiong* 芎藭: *Cnidium officinale*) grows."[196]

"Is *min'gang* (C. *minjiang* 閩薑)[197] ginger (*saenggang*) that comes from the Minjiang (閩江) region?"

"It is called *min'gang* because ginger that grows in the Min (Fujian Province) region is good. Master Zhu was born in Minzhong (閩中), so whenever I see *min'gang*, I cherish it because it makes me think of where Master Zhu was."

"Has *hwangnyŏn* (C. *Huanglian* 黃連: *Coptis chinensis*) been given its name due to its color?"

"Hwangnyŏn is named due to both its color and its appearance. Because *hwangnyŏn*'s color is deep yellow, and its appearance is supple and like threaded beads, it is called *hwangnyŏn*, and there are also ones named

---

return to; it is clear that its name *danggui* probably originates from this." (當歸治妊婦産後惡血上沖, 倉卒取效. 氣血昏亂者, 服之卽定. 能使氣血各有所歸, 恐當歸之名必因此出也.)

196 *Ch'ŏn'gung* (C. *chuanxiong* 川芎: *Cnidium officinale*): 'Cnidium officinale' (C. *Fuxiong* 撫芎), *Revised Compendium of Materia Medica* (*Bencao gangmu shiyi* 本草綱目拾遺). "Generally speaking *xiongqiong* from the Sichuan (四川) region of Shu (蜀) is considered best, and its taste is spicy and sweet. *Xiongqiong* from other regions has a taste that is spicy and intense, but the efficacy is greatly inferior." (蓋芎藭以蜀産爲上, 味辛而甘. 他產氣味辛烈, 遠不逮矣.) There is no mention of the efficacy of *xiongqiong* in *Compendium of Materia Medica* (*Bencao gangmu* 本草綱目), but there is a similar explanation to Yuhandang's in *Revised Compendium of Materia Medica* (*Bencao gangmu shiyi* 本草綱目拾遺) by the Qing dynasty physician Zhao Xuemin (趙學敏).

197 *Min'gang* (C. *minjiang* 閩薑): *Min'gang* generally refers to a dish made of thinly sliced ginger simmered with sugar. The source of Yuhandang's explanation about *min'gang* being ginger from the Min region is unknown.

due to their appearance and taste. Because *sesin* (C. *xixin* 細辛: Manchurian wild ginseng)[198] has thin thread-like roots and tastes spicy, it is called *sesin* (lit. slender-bitter)."

"I know plants and trees can be used as medicines, but I would like to know whether insects and birds and animals can also be used as medicines."

"Yes, they can."

"What kind of bird is a *ch'anggyŏng* (C. *canggeng* 鶬鶊: Oriolus chinensis) and is it true that when women are jealous (K. *tugi*; C. *duji* 妬忌), if they eat it in a medicine, their jealousy will cease?"

"Those words are in the *Classic of Mountains and Seas*."[199]

"There are a lot of amusing stories in books about jealousy, so I would like to hear them."

"In ancient times Liu-*shi* (劉氏)[200] the wife of Taifu (太傅) Xie An (謝安) was extremely jealous. Taifu was worried because she could not tolerate his concubine (K. *kich'ŏp*; C. *jiqie* 妓妾), so his nephews said to his wife, 'The poems

---

198 *Sesin* (C. *xixin* 細辛: Manchurian wild ginseng): This is an Oriental medicine and is also called '*chokturip'ul* in Korea.

199 'Mt. Xuanyuan' (軒轅山), *Classic of Mountains and Seas* (Shanhaijing 山海經). "There is a bird there that looks like an owl, but its head is white. It is called an oriole (*huangniao* 黃鳥). Its call sounds like its name, and if you eat the flesh of this bird, it will stop you feeling jealous." (有鳥焉, 其狀如梟而白首. 其名曰黃鳥. 其鳴自詨, 食之不妒.)

200 'Delusion and Infatuation' (Huoni 惑溺), *Revised New Account of the Tales of the World* (*Shishuo xinyu bu* 世說新語補). As the content is the same as that recounted by Yuhandang, it is not repeated here.

'Ospreys' (Guanju 關雎)[201] and 'Locusts' (Zhongsi 螽斯)[202] are famous to later generations because they are about the virtue of not being jealous.' Lady Yu, who knew that they were consoling her, said, 'Who wrote 'Ospreys' and 'Locusts'?'

'The Duke of Zhou (Zhougong 周公) wrote them.'

'The Duke of Zhou wrote them because he was a man, but if King Wen's consort Taisi had written them, there would definitely be no such words.'

She responded in this way, so it was difficult to conciliate the wife's intolerant character.

Not only that, but when in ancient times Ren Gui (任瓌) was promoted to the position of Minister of War (Bingbu shangshu 兵部尙書), Emperor Taizong of Tang bestowed two beautiful concubines upon him, so his wife Liu-*shi* (柳氏)[203] cut off their hair out of jealousy. Taizong poured wine

---

201 'Ospreys' (Guanju 關雎), *Book of Odes*. In Zhu Xi's annotation it states, "(The couple in 'Ospreys') enjoy one another while also respecting one another just as the ospreys have a close affection while also maintaining distinction." (言其相與和樂而恭敬, 亦若雎鳩之情摯而有別也.)

202 'Locusts' (Zhongsi 螽斯), *Book of Odes*. In Zhu Xi's annotation it states, "The reason the queen consort (*bi* 妃) (in 'Locusts') is not jealous and has many offspring, is because even though concubines are swarming like locusts, she likens it to having many children, so with this kind of virtue, it is only right that it should be accompanied with this kind of blessing." (后妃不妬忌而子孫衆多, 故衆妾以螽斯之群處和集而子孫衆多比之, 言其有是德而宜有是福也)

203 Liu-*shi* (柳氏) the wife of Ren Gui (任瓌): 'Rather Die because of Jealousy' (Ning si yi du 寧死亦妬), *Draft Notes from the Court and Country* (*Chaoye qian zai* 朝野僉載). As the content is the

into a bottle made of gold and sent it to her saying, 'If you drink this wine you will die because it is poisoned. So drink it and die. If you will not be jealous from now on then do not drink it.' Lady Liu bowed before the court document, and receiving it, said in reply, 'My husband and I both came from humble stock, but now he has obtained high rank, my husband has many concubines, so truly I would rather die than live. I will drink the wine in the golden bottle.' Taizong heard this and said to his minister, 'This person is not afraid to die, so you cannot make her (do something) out of the fear death. Put them in separate quarters.' Even if the wife of Minister Ren was fed a lot of oriole meat, it would be difficult to cure her illness."

Yuhandang's second granddaughter responded, "Neither Ren nor Xie were able to prevent their wives from feeling jealous, since they achieved the positions of minister (K. *sangsŏ*; C. *shangshu*) and grand mentor (K. *taebu*; C. *taifu*), they would certainly have known the principles adhered to by the people of their country. If a superior man is afflicted by the temptations of women, it is not unusual to admonish him, and superior men in the positions of minister and grand mentor who especially provoke jealousy (in their wives) will be ridiculed at court, so this is an even greater reason why this should not happen."

---

same as that recounted by Yuhandang, it is not repeated here.

"Women are sitting in the inner quarters, and for better or worse, this kind of thing can happen. Naturally, it is easy for gossip about it to be spread out to the outside world. This not only spreads to the outside world but is then handed down to a million generations of descendants, so how can we not be cautious?"

A Virtuous Daughter-in-Law Who Is Also an Intimate Friend

Yuhandang always served her parents-in-law with respect and devotion, and was careful day and night, never being lazy. When her father-in-law entered the inner quarters, Yuhandang prepared the bed cushions and pillows with her own hands, checked each book, and stacked them up in front of him, so that they remained in their original order, and none of the objects were placed carelessly. When her father-in-law came in, the daughters-in-law, granddaughters and grandsons' wives would enter in turn and attend to his needs, but Yuhandang was always by his side, ensuring that every word and every action was carried out in accordance with his commands, and none of the women could keep up with her.

Minister Tu said to Lady Wŏn, "My wife, because you always clean my books and utensils and ease my troubles, I call you my 'intimate friend and wife' (*chigi puin* 知己婦人). Lately, our eldest daughter-in-law is also like this, so I call her 'a virtuous daughter-in-law (*hyŏnbu* 賢婦) who is also an intimate friend (*chigi* 知己).'"

"I am old and was ill recently, but I am glad that our eldest daughter-in-law is wise enough to take my place. Our eldest daughter-in-law will also grow old in turn, but our grandson's wives and great-grandchildren will all be wise and gradually step forward (to take her place), so I will hear them called 'grandsons' wives (*chŭngsonbu* 曾孫婦) who are also intimate friends'."

Nokhamhwa (*Pyrola japonica*) and *Aenghamdo* (Cherry)

Minister Tu entered the inner quarters at sunset, so several of his daughters and daughters-in-law followed Yuhandang and came out of the inner quarters to welcome him. As Lord Minister Tu came in, he asked Yuhandang, "Since when has the *moranhwa* (牡丹花: tree peony) been called *nokhamhwa* (鹿衔花: *Pyrola japonica*)?"

"In Tang dynasty times when the *moranhwa* was blooming, deer plucked the blossoms and carried them away in their mouths, so it came to be called *nokhamhwa* ('deer-holding in the mouth-flower')."

"Find that book and bring it to me."

"I already put it on your writing desk (*sŏan* 書案)."

Minister Tu was surprised and responded, "How did you know I wanted to find out about the *moranhwa*?"

"Yesterday the children said that many *moranhwa* had bloomed behind Shuiyue Pavilion, and today as father went to Shuiyue Pavilion in the morning, it seemed that words would be spoken and lines written about *moranhwa*. As I thought this to be likely, I found the book about *moranhwa* in advance."

Minister Tu turned around to look at his various daughters and granddaughters and said, "If you, too, get married and do everything as intelligently as this, how could your parents-in-law not love you?"

Lord Minister Tu asked again, "You knew about *nokhamhwa*, but there is a fruit that has the same Chinese character '*ham*', meaning 'to hold in the mouth' as in *nokhamhwa*. Do you know what that is, too?"

"It is *aenghamdo* (鶯含桃: 'oriole-holding in the mouth-peach')."[204]

"That is indeed true. Is there another woman in the whole world who has read so many books as thoroughly as you?"

As her younger sisters-in-law and all the young girls asked for an explanation about *aenghamdo,* Yuhandang said, "It is called '*aenghamdo*' because long ago an oriole plucked cherries and flew away holding them in its beak."

Yuhandang's great-grandchildren asked Yuhandang, "It says in a poem from Tang dynasty times, "they are not what was left after the birds had eaten (their fill) in the imperial gardens."[205]

"He did not write the character '*cho*' (鳥), meaning 'bird', but '*aeng*' (鶯), meaning 'oriole', so the poem says '*aenghamchan*' (鶯含殘: oriole-hold in the mouth-spoil). When you write poetry, too, the correct way is to see where to place the emphasis (K. *kojŏ*; C. *gaodi* 高低) in your writing."

"Indeed, that is true."

---

204 In 'Rhapsody on Mt. Yeting' (Yetingshan fu 掖庭山賦) by the Tang literatus Xu Jingzong (許敬宗, 592–672), there are the lines, "A foal is fed on bean leaves in the courtyard, and an oriole flies through the valley holding cherries in its beak." (駒食藿而馴場, 鶯含桃而出谷.)

205 In the poem 'Bestowing Cherries on the Government Officials at the Emperor's Command' (勅賜百官櫻桃) by the Tang dynasty poet Wang Wei (王維), there is the passage, "These cherries were all offered at the imperial tombs for the spring ancestral rites; they are not what was left after the birds had eaten (their fill) in the imperial gardens." (摠是寢園春薦後, 非關御苑鳥含殘.)

When Attending Her Mother-in-Law

When Yuhandang attended her mother-in-law, she stayed nearby in an adjacent room (*hyŏpsil*), and she watched over her mother-in-law's daily life whether she was sleeping or awake. When answering her questions, even though they were separated by a sliding door, she always sat up to answer. Her mother-in-law felt embarrassed and thought her requests might be troublesome, so one day when asking a question, she added, 'as it is a cold day and the fire has gone out remain lying down when you answer.'

Yuhandang said, "According to an ancient saying, '(Loyal ministers and filial children) do not show their respect because it is a bright place, and they do not neglect their conduct because it is a dark place',[206] so how could I dare to answer while remaining lying down?"

---

206 'Learning from the Ancients', *Elementary Learning*. Lord Wei Ling (衛靈公) was together with his wife one night when he heard the sound of a carriage reaching the palace gate and stopping and then going again. At that moment his wife said that the person was definitely Qu Baiyu (蘧伯玉), adding, "In general loyal ministers and filial children do not show their respect because it is a bright place, and they do not neglect their conduct because it is a dark place." (夫忠臣與孝子, 不爲昭昭信節, 不爲冥冥惰行.) Lord Wei Ling sent someone to find out who it was, and as expected, it was Qu Baiyu.

The Way of Preparing Food

One day, Lady Chu visited, and Yuhandang came out with some food she had prepared. After eating Lady Chu asked Yuhandang, "Whenever our relatives visit Yuhandang and eat food, upon returning they always say, even though the food was good, the vessels and the wine tables were extremely frugal rather than extravagant, and after sitting down to a meal and being served until it gets dark, they do not easily feel like taking their leave, so what kind of method do you have to achieve this?"

"How could I have any special method? It is just that even when relatives visit this house, as they are treated no differently from guests, they are served with respect. And without discussing the way of treating people in accordance with their social rank, when serving food, how could one dare to serve food in vessels that are not clean? I am always careful to follow this principle regardless of the guest's social status."

"When making food, adding ginger and cinnamon enhances the taste, but there are many foods that it is forbidden to combine, so it is easy to violate this if one does not know household affairs (*in'ga* 人家) and daily expenditure (*ilyong* 日用). I always ask and learn from you, and as I want to teach other women, this time I want to ask you a lot."

"A person familiar with medical arts would know these things, so how would a mere woman like myself know?"

"I will listen to as much as you know yourself."

"It is right to be aware of the fact that if the women of the household do not know the taboos when making food and violate them, those who eat may easily become ill. Once in the past there was a man who wanted to borrow a servant to dig for medicine at the house of Chengzi (程子) who said, 'I'm trying to dig up mulberry root bark (*sangbaekp'i* 桑白皮), but it is poisonous when exposed to sunlight, so then I cannot use it; as it is easy for a servant from another house to deceive me, that is why I asked to borrow one of yours, as your servant will not deceive me.'[207] Even lowly servants are extremely careful if someone might get hurt, so how much

---

207 'Family Matters' (Jiashi jiushi 家世舊事), *Collected Writings of the Cheng Brothers* (*Er Cheng wenji* 二程文集). When Cheng Mingdao was an official registrar (*zhubu* 主簿) and Xie Shizhi (謝師直) was the administrative assistant to the transport commissioner of Jiangdong (Jiangdong zhuanyun panguan 江東轉運判官), Xie Shizhi asked if he could borrow a servant to dig up mulberry root bark (K. *sangbaekp'i*; C. *sangbaipi* 桑白皮). When Cheng Mingdao mentioned that there were many official servants attached to the transport commission and asked why he did not use them, Xie Shizhi said, "In the *Materia Medica* (*Bencao*), it states that if mulberry root bark is dug up from the ground and exposed to sunlight, it can kill people. Because the people you employ would not deceive you, I asked to borrow from you and that is all." (本草說, 桑白皮出土見日者, 殺人. 以伯淳所使人不欺, 故假之耳.) In *Annotated Shennong's Materia Medica Classic* (*Shennong bencaojing shu* 神農本草經疏) it states, "Things taken out of the earth kill people." (出土上者, 殺人.)

more must educated people be careful. There is no special way to cook food. Since Shennong-*shi* (神農氏) taught people the way to cook food with fire, there has been no food that is not cooked, so when you adjust the level of heat, the taste is good. The way of adjusting the level is through the 'civil and military fire method' (*munmu hwabŏp* 文武火法). 'Civil fire' burns gently, and 'military fire' burns strongly. The taste of the food becomes good when it is first heated with a 'civil fire' and then with a 'military fire'.

Bamboo shoots are like mulberry root bark, so if you break them off in the sunlight, you cannot eat them; if you eat a lot of crab apples, you will get an eye disease; if you feed gingko to young children, they will get convulsions (*kyŏngp'ung* 驚風);[208] if you eat too many aubergines, you will get dysentery (*ijil* 痢疾); if you eat a lot of shoots, you will get ill. Garlic, green onion, and leek cannot be eaten together with honey;[209] melons that have been soaked in water for a long time should not be eaten; and you cannot eat melons with two stalks or two blossom scars. Mushrooms cannot be

---

208 Gingko (Ŭnhaeng 銀杏): 'Fruit Category' (果部), *Exemplar of Korean Medicine*. "When eaten raw, it irritates the throat, and when eaten by children, it causes shock." (生則戟人喉, 小兒食之發驚.) The original source is *Riyong bencao* (日用本草) by the Yuan dynasty physician Wu Rui (吳瑞).

209 *Concise Manual from the Golden Chamber with Commentary* (*Jinkui yaolüe lunzhu* 金匱要略論註). "If you eat green onions and honey together, you can die. Garlic should be avoided even more. … If you eat raw green onions or leeks within four days of eating honey, you will experience chest pain." (生葱不可共蜜, 食之殺人. 獨顆蒜彌忌. … 食糖蜜後四日内食生葱·韭, 令人心痛.)

eaten with alcohol; the white part of chickens' feet cannot be eaten, and they must not be eaten together with perilla; eggs cannot be eaten with chili pepper. The head and tail of the terrapin contain a lot of poison, so they cannot be eaten, also, they cannot be eaten together with purslane (*pirŭm namul*).[210] Rat meat cannot be eaten with apricots (*haengin* 杏仁); red-nosed dogs cannot be eaten.[211] Milk cannot be eaten with vinegar and fish;[212] soju cannot be drunk with apricots. As puffer fish and scorched-rice water for drinking at bedtime (*sungnyung charikki*) must never be eaten, you must refrain from serving them when entertaining guests in your house.

You need to make sure that the taste of the food is not bad, but you have to be especially careful about avoiding luxurious things. During the Tang dynasty an office holder filled his belly while living a life of luxury (K. *gŭmŭi oksik*; C. *jinyi yushi* 錦衣玉食: 'brocade garments and jade meals') and said to a monk with whom he was familiar, 'I have to cook rice over charcoal to

---

210 *Concise Manual from the Golden Chamber with Commentary*. "You cannot eat the meat of turtles and terrapins with purslane (*pirŭm namul*)." (龜鱉肉不可合莧菜食之.)

211 *Invaluable Prescriptions for Ready Reference* (*Beiji qianjin yaofang* 備急千金要方). "The Yellow Emperor (Huangdi 黃帝) said, 'If you eat a white dog and shrimps (*haiyou* 海鮋) you will get a bad illness, and if a white dog dies by itself but does not stick out its tongue, eating it will harm people. Many dogs go mad in the spring, and a dog with a red and dry nose is about to go mad, so its meat cannot be eaten.'" (黃帝云, '白犬合海鮋食之, 必得惡病, 白犬自死不出舌者, 食之, 害人. 犬春月多狂, 若鼻赤起而燥者, 此欲狂, 其肉不任食.')

212 'Contraindicated Foods' (Yinshi jinji 飲食禁忌), *Compendium of Materia Medica* (*Bencao gangmu*). "Milk with fish and vinegar should be avoided." (牛乳忌生魚酸物.)

eat; if I don't do that it is difficult for me, and I cannot eat it.' Later, after squandering his fortune, he was walking down the street, and while he was passing a bridge over a river, he obtained millet and cooked it in an earthenware pot (*chilsot*). He ate it with greater relish than if it had been unctuous rice and meat. The monk laughed and said, 'Is this also food cooked over charcoal?'

When he asked him, the person said that he could not answer because he was ashamed. Wealth and honor does not mean being extravagant; eating or not eating food because it is of low quality is not good at all.'"[213]

How to Consult Almanacs

On the Winter Solstice (K. Tongji; C. Dongzhi 冬至) Yuhandang's twenty-seventh grandson Iksŏng, who was eleven years old, brought in the new calendar and was considering the speed and slowness of the 'junctures' (*chŏlgi* 節氣).

---

213 'No leisure to select delicacies' (*Bu xia ze meishi* 不暇擇美食), *Ancient and Modern Collection of Matters from the Past and Present*. As the content is the same as Yuhandang's account, it is not included here. The original source is *Record of Dramatic Tales* (*Jutan lu* 劇談錄) by Kang Pian (康駢).

Yuhandang asked, "Do you know how to consult an almanac (*ch'aengnyŏk* 册曆) or not?"

"I am just looking at the speed and slowness of the solar terms that's all; is there anything especially worth looking for?"

"Even if you read a line or half a line of any text, if you understand it, you will know the principles of heaven and earth and all things as well as the methods of statecraft required for governing families and nations. If you do not understand it, how can it be of any benefit at all to memorize the classics of the sages as if they were your own words? Just like any other book, an almanac is the continuous operation of the heaven, earth, sun and moon, and contains all the changes of vegetation and insects. How could you wish to just read it carelessly?"

"The movement of heaven and earth and the changes of the hot and cold seasons are in the almanac, but are there also words about plants and insects in the almanac?"

"In the first lunar month (*chŏngwŏl*) it is said dormant insects (K. *ch'ipch'ung*; C. *zhechong* 蟄蟲) 'begin to move' (K. *si chin*; C. *shi zhen* 始振) and 'otters sacrifice fish' (K. *tal che ŏ*; C. *ta ji yu* 獺祭魚).[214] In the second lunar month it is said 'hawks are

---

214 'Proceedings of Government in the Different Months', *Book of Rites*. First lunar month. "The east winds resolve the cold. Creatures that have been torpid during the winter begin to

transformed into doves' (K. *ŭng hwa wi ku*; C. *ying hua wei jiu* 鷹化爲鳩), 'the swallow makes its appearance' (K. *hyŏnjo chi*; C. *xuanniao zhi* 玄鳥至) and 'the peach starts to blossom' (K. *to si hwa*; C. *tao shi hua* 桃始華).[215] In the third lunar month it is said 'the Eurasian hoopoe descends' (K. *tae sŭng*; C. *dai sheng* 戴勝) and 'lands on the mulberry trees' (K. *k'ang u sang*; C. *jiang yu sang* 降于桑);[216] in the fourth lunar month it is said 'it is the harvest time of the barley' (K. *maekch'u chi*; C. *maiqiu zhi* 麥秋至);[217] in the sixth lunar month it is said 'decaying grass becomes fire-flies' (K. *puch'o wi hyŏng*; C. *fucao wei ying* 腐草爲螢);[218] in the seventh lunar month it is said 'hawks at this time sacrifice birds' (K. *ŭng nae che cho*; C. *ying nai ji niao* 鷹乃祭鳥);[219] in the eighth lunar month it is said 'the swallows return' (K. *hyŏnjo kwi*; C. *xuanniao gui* 玄鳥歸);[220]

---

move. The fishes rise up to the ice. Otters sacrifice fish." (東風解凍, 蟄蟲始振. 魚上冰, 獺祭魚.)

215 'Proceedings of Government in the Different Months', *Book of Rites*. Second lunar month. "The rain begins to fall; the peach tree begins to blossom; the oriole sings. Hawks are transformed into doves… In this month the swallow makes its appearance." (始雨水, 桃始華. 倉庚鳴, 鷹化爲鳩. …… 是月也, 玄鳥至.)

216 'Proceedings of Government in the Different Months', *Book of Rites*. Third lunar month. "The cooing doves clap their wings, and the crested birds (Eurasian hoopoe) light on them (mulberry trees)." (鳴鳩拂其羽, 戴勝降于桑.)

217 'Proceedings of Government in the Different Months', *Book of Rites*. Fourth lunar month. "Delicate herbs (now) die; it is the harvest time (even) of the wheat [barley]." (靡草死, 麥秋至.)

218 'Proceedings of Government in the Different Months', *Book of Rites*. Sixth lunar month. "(Young) hawks learn to practice (the ways of their parents). Decaying grass becomes fire-flies." (鷹乃學習, 腐草爲螢.)

219 'Proceedings of Government in the Different Months', *Book of Rites*. Seventh lunar month. "Cool winds come; the white dew descends; the cicada of the cold chirps. (Young) hawks at this time sacrifice birds." (涼風至, 白露降, 寒蟬鳴, 鷹乃祭鳥.)

220 'Proceedings of Government in the Different Months', *Book of Rites*. Eighth lunar month. "Sudden and violent winds come; the wild geese arrive; the swallows return (whence they came). Tribes of birds store up provisions (for the future)." (盲風至, 鴻鴈來, 玄鳥歸, 群鳥養羞.)

in the ninth lunar month it is said 'the wild geese come, (and abide) like guests' (K. *hongan laebin*; C. *hong'an laibin* 鴻鴈來賓), 'the *chai* (wild dogs) sacrifice larger animals' (K. *si nae che su*; C. *chai nai ji shou* 豺乃祭獸), and 'chrysanthemums show their yellow flowers' (K. *kuk yu hwanghwa*; C. *ju you huanghua* 鞠有黃華);[221] so there are countless varied records like this. If you don't understand this when you consult the almanac, how can it be of any benefit to engage in the superior person's study of the investigation of things?"

"Are these records all from 'Proceedings of Government in the Different Months' in the *Book of Rites*?"

"Some of the contents of the almanacs of later generations are from the 'Proceedings of Government in the Different Months', and some are from other sources, too."

Iksŏng hurriedly called for his elder brother Yesŏng and his younger brother Chinsŏng, and took them to inform their wives, "Today we are going to learn all about the almanac's plants and trees and birds and animals."

---

221 'Proceedings of Government in the Different Months', *Book of Rites*. Ninth lunar month. "The wild geese come, (and abide) like guests. Small birds enter the great water and become mollusks. Chrysanthemums show their yellow flowers. The *chai* (wild dogs) sacrifice larger animals, and kill (and devour) the smaller." (鴻鴈來賓, 爵入大水爲蛤. 鞠有黃華, 豺乃祭獸戮禽.)

"Carefully examine 'Proceedings of Government in the Different Months' in the *Book of Rites*."

Chinsŏng said, "As some things are better to see with your eyes, and some are better to listen to with your ears, I want to listen more carefully."

"As we are pleading with you, please tell us a little. In the first lunar month, the words '*ch'ipch'ung sijin*' mean, 'all winter insects build houses and live there, but in the spring they scatter and fly', so in the *Book of History* it states, 'the people (*kwŏlmin* 厥民) are dispersed (*sŏk* 析)'.[222] '*Tal che ŏ*' means 'the otters catch fish and offer sacrifices'; in the seventh lunar month '*ŭng nae che cho*' means 'the hawks catch birds and offer sacrifices'; in the seventh lunar month '*si nae che su*' means 'the wild dogs catch animals and offer sacrifices'. Even these beasts are able to perform sacrifices at the right time, so how can people be careless about following the natural order (*ch'ŏnsi* 天時) and offering sacrifices of the products of the land as they become available?

In the second lunar month '*ŭng hwa wi ku*' means 'hawks are transformed into doves', and the words '*chak ip tae su wi hap*' (爵入大水爲蛤) in the ninth lunar month mean that 'the sparrows enter the great water

---

222 'Canon of Yao' (Yaodian 堯典), *Book of History*. "The day is of the medium length, and the star is in Niao—you may thus exactly determine mid-spring. The people are dispersed (in the fields), and birds and beasts breed and copulate." (日中星鳥, 以殷仲春, 厥民析, 鳥獸孶尾.)

and become mollusks'. But just because sparrows become mollusks, nevertheless, mollusks cannot become sparrows. Therefore, the *Book of Rites* did not use the character '*hwa*' (化: transform) concerning the sparrows, but because it states that the 'hawks transformed into doves' and then became hawks again, it used the term '*hwa*' (化: transform) for the hawks when it stated '*ŭng hwa wi ku*' ('hawks are transformed into doves'). Even looking at this kind of thing, we have to notice that not a single character concerning the transformations of birds and beasts has been carelessly omitted in the Classics.

In the third lunar month, the words '*taesŭng kang u sang*' mean 'the hoopoe lands on the mulberry tree', so the hoopoe is a bird that comes when it is time to feed mulberry leaves to silkworms in the spring."

Chinsŏng asked, "Just now you said that not even a single character has been used carelessly in the Classics. Is there a special meaning for the character *kang* (降: to land) to be placed here?"

"What you are asking is stupid. The special reason why the character *kang* is used in the *Book of Rites* is because when the hoopoe arrives it is time for people to raise silkworms, and so it seems that heaven sent the hoopoe down to make people realize this; as they used the character '*kang*', the sages' mindful intention was deep.

In the fourth lunar month '*maekch'u chi*' means 'it is the harvest time of the barley', so because all (other) grains ripen in the autumn, but barley ripens in the fourth lunar month, it is called 'barley autumn' (*pori kaŭl*). Households have completely run out of grain from the previous year, and when there is still no new grain, if one gathers in the barley, it seems to be just like the harvest. Therefore, sages of the past considered barley to be important. In the *Book of Odes* the words '*yi a nae mo*' (C. *yi wo lai mou* 貽我來牟)[223] mean that 'heaven gave us wheat and barley'.

In the ninth lunar month '*kuk yu hwanghwa*', means 'the chrysanthemums show their yellow flowers'. The peach blossoms in the second lunar month and the paulownia flowers in the third lunar month are not referred to by their color, but the chrysanthemum is referred to by its yellow color. Therefore, because when the frost descends the chrysanthemums are yellow and all the five colors (*chŏngsaek* 正色),[224] the sages consider them to be noble and wrote about them. So even if you just have a single almanac, you will be able to deliberate on the principles of heaven

223 'Thinking of culture' (Siwen 思文), *Book of Odes* (*Shijing*). "Thou didst confer on us the wheat and the barley, / Which God appointed for the nourishment of all." (貽我來牟, 帝命率育.)

224 The word *chŏngsaek* (正色) refers to the 'five colors' (*osaek* 五色), namely, blue, yellow, red, white and black.

and earth, the sun and the moon, the heavenly bodies, insects, plants and trees, and birds and beasts. Even without doing that, if we just refer to the large moons and small moons of the almanac, won't we be able to generally perceive these things?"

Yesŏng asked, "We didn't pay attention to this, so today we have learned a lot. In 'Proceedings of Government in the Different Months' in the *Book of Rites*, it stated that the wild geese come in spring, and it said that the wild geese also come in autumn. If they came in spring, is it saying that they came back again in autumn; if it states that they came in autumn, wouldn't they be going back in spring, what does it mean by using the word 'come' in both the spring and the autumn?"

"You are skeptical, and your question is worth asking. When the wild geese go to the north from the south in the spring, they pass through China on their way to the north; in the winter when they go south because of the cold in the northern regions, they pass through China on their way to the south. They just recorded their coming and stated that they came both in the spring and in the autumn. They wrote this because all things under heaven seem to come for the sake of China."

"I see. What are and how should one understand the principles of governing (*kyŏngnyun* 經綸) a country and a household in the almanac?"

"If we just take a single almanac and discuss it, all the vast knowledge and experience under heaven may be found within it. When the fire is vigorously agitated by the spring wind, it is like the spirit of Master Yan (Yanzi 顏子).[225] When the autumn frosts are clear and high, and the harvest is gathered in solemnly, it is like the spirit of Mencius. Because Confucius is a great sage, all four seasons are expressions of his spirit, so if scholars come to examine the seasonal divisions of all twelve months, they will think they are studying the spirit of various sages.

If they examine the appearance of the plants and trees sprouting (*maengdong* 萌動) in the spring, sage kings will carry out benevolent affairs of state; if they examine the maturation of vegetation and insects in the autumn, the accumulation of the state affairs of the sage king will be revered. With the first emergence of *yang qi* in the spring, the words 'love the young and weak children' are included in 'Proceedings of Government in the Different Months'.[226] In the autumn when the *yang qi* is weakening, the words 'take care of the elderly and weak' are included in 'Proceedings

---

225 Master Yan (Yanzi 顏子) refers to Yan Hui (顏回), Confucius' favorite disciple, who died when he was just thirty-two years old.

226 'Proceedings of Government in the Different Months', *Book of Rites*. Second lunar month. "In this month they keep both the young buds and those more advanced from being disturbed; they nourish both the young animals and those not fully grown; they especially watch over all orphans." (是月也, 安萌牙, 養幼少, 存諸孤.)

of Government in the Different Months'.[227] Concerning the Spring Equinox (Ch'unbun), in the Spring Equinox, there are the words 'the weight of 30 catties, the steelyard, and the weight of 120 catties'[228] and 'equalize the measures of length and capacity',[229] which mean to correct the length of yardsticks. The spring equinox and the autumn equinox are when the cold and heat are very even between heaven and earth, so it states that the measures of length and capacity and such like items of all the nations of the world should all be evenly aligned, so that they do not diverge. If we discuss this, we can refine people, vegetation, insects, offering hospitality, utensils and such like, so will not all affairs whether great or small be aligned with the seasonal order of heaven and earth?"

Iksŏng said, "Grandmother always says even small things are connected to large things, so grandmother has mastered righteousness. As we have also enjoyed listening, we have realized a lot, too."

---

227 'Proceedings of Government in the Different Months', *Book of Rites*. Eighth lunar month. "In this month they take special care of the decaying and old; give them stools and slaves, and distribute supplies of congee for food." (是月也, 養衰老, 授几杖, 行糜粥飲食.)

228 'Proceedings of Government in the Different Months', *Book of Rites*. Second lunar month. "At the equinox they make uniform the measures of length and capacity; the weight of 30 catties, the steelyard, and the weight of 120 catties. They correct the peck and bushel, the steelyard weights and the bushel-scraper." (日夜分, 則同度量. 鈞衡石, 角斗甬, 正權槪.)

229 'Proceedings of Government in the Different Months', *Book of Rites*. Eighth lunar month. "At the (autumn) equinox, they make uniform the measures of length and capacity; equalize the steel-yards and their weights; rectify the weights of 30 and 120 catties; and adjust the pecks and bushels." (日夜分, 則同度量. 平權衡, 正鈞石, 角斗甬.)

The Origins of Holidays and Seasonal Customs I

Several of Yuhandang's grandchildren gathered together and asked, "We heard your words about the transformations of grass, trees, and beasts in the twelve months. The first day of the first lunar month, the third day of the third lunar month, the fifth day of the fifth lunar month, the seventh day of the seventh lunar month, and the ninth day of the ninth lunar month are all designated as holidays (*myŏngjŏl* 名節), but why are the second day of the second lunar month, fourth day of the fourth lunar month, the sixth day of the sixth lunar month, and the eighth day of the eighth lunar month not designated as holidays?"

"In the past the sages considered *yang* (陽) to be noble, and they considered *yin* (陰) to be base. Because in the case of the first day of the first lunar month, the third day of the third month, the fifth day of the fifth month, the seventh day of the seventh month, and the ninth day of the ninth month, both the days and the months are *yang*, they are called holidays; but because in the case of the second day of the second month, the fourth day of the fourth month, the sixth day of the sixth month, and the eighth day of the eighth month both the months and the days are *yin*, they are considered base and so are not designated as holidays. *Yang* is considered noble and is likened to superior persons (*kunja*). In the tenth lunar month *yin* is flourishing extremely and *yang* has disappeared, during the Winter Solstice (during the eleventh lunar month), because the *yang* number 'one' reappears for the first time, the Winter Solstice is also considered an important holiday. These words are in the poem 'Winter Solstice' by Shao Kangjie (邵康節).[230]

> Midnight on the Winter Solstice (冬至子之半)
> The center of heaven has not changed. (天心無改移)
> It is the place one *yang* is moving to for the first time. (一陽初起處)
> This is the time when nothing can be born. (萬物未生時)
> The taste of the clear water is mild. (玄酒味方淡)
> The sound of great music is rare. (太音聲正希)
> If you cannot believe these words, (此言如不信)
> Inquire of Paoxi once more. (更請問庖犧)

---

230 'Winter Solstice Poem' (K. Tongji ŭm; C. Dongzhi yin 冬至吟), *Beating Earth Collection* (*Jirang ji* 擊壤集) by Shao Kangjie (邵康節). In the Han'gŭl version in *Yuhandang Sa-ssi ŏnhaengnok* the character '*ki*' (起) is written as the character '*tong*' (動), but here it is written as in the original poem in *Beating Earth Collection.*

According to an ancient custom, on the Winter Solstice women made socks and offered them to their parents-in-law while wishing them a long life. The meaning behind this is because the *yang* energy of the number one arises from the ground, so they should respond to this by treading (on the ground) in new socks. Therefore, a person called Cui Yin (崔駰) wrote the following poem called 'Sock Inscription' (K. Mal myŏng; C. Wa ming 襪銘).[231]

The *yanggi* arises from below. (陽升於下)
The sun is forever in the sky. (日永於天)
Forever tread on great blessings (長履景福)
For a billion years. (至于億年)

All the grandsons asked again, "The third day of the third lunar month, the fifth day of the fifth lunar month, and the seventh day of the seventh lunar month all have double *yang* numbers, so why is the ninth day of the ninth lunar month especially called 'double *yang*' (Chungyang 重陽)?"[232]

---

231 Cui Yin wrote the poem 'Sock Inscription' (Wa ming 襪銘) in the Later Han (後漢) period. It can be found in such works as *Collection of Literature Arranged by Categories* (*Yiwen leiju* 藝文類聚) and *Records from Mt. Tianzhong* (*Tianzhong ji* 天中記).

232 The ninth day of the ninth lunar month is called 'Double Yang Holiday' (Chungyangjŏl 重陽節). 'Chungyang' means 'double *yang*'.

"In the numerals in the Lo Shu Square (K. *naksŏ*; C. *luoshu* 洛書) 2, 4, 6, and 8 are *yin* (numbers), and 1, 3, 5, 7 and 9 are *yang* (numbers). As the number 9 is the foremost among the *yang* numbers, the ninth day of the ninth lunar month is called 'Double Yang Holiday' (Chungyangjŏl 重陽節)."

"Why is it that different foods are prepared for the various different holidays, and also different games are played on each of the days?"

"The making of kites out of silk and calling them 'spring banners' (K. *ch'unbŏn*; C. *chunfan* 春幡) at the 'Beginning of Spring' (K. Ipch'un; C. Lichun 立春) is a custom from the Han dynasty times;[233] the making of flowers out of silk and calling them 'multi-colored silk flowers' (*ch'aehwa* 綵花) and 'multi-colored silk beauties' (*ch'aesŭng* 綵勝) is a custom from Tang dynasty times,[234] and the making of swallows out of multi-colored silk and calling them 'multi-colored silk swallows' (K. *ch'aeyŏn*; C. *caiyan* 綵鷰) is a custom from the

---

233 *Supplemented History of the Later Han* (*Hou Hanshu buyi* 後漢書補逸). 'Spring Banners' (Ch'unbŏn 春幡). "At the beginning of spring, 'spring banners' are made. Oxen and farmers made of clay are placed outside doors." (立春之日, 竪春旛, 施土牛耕人於門外.) In 'Etiquette' (Liyi zhi 禮儀志), *History of the Later Han* (*Hou Hanshu*), they are called 'green banners' (K. *ch'ŏngbŏn*; C. *qingfan* 靑幡).

234 'Beginning of Spring' (Lichun 立春), *New Book of the Literati Garden* (*Hanyuan xinshu* 翰苑新書), "'multi-colored silk beauties' (K. *ch'aesŭng*; C. *caisheng* 綵勝). At the 'Beginning of Spring' (Lichun 立春) in the homes of the nobility, they cut up silk to make small flags and call them 'spring banners' (K. *ch'unbŏn*; C. *chunfan*). Or they put them on the heads of women, or tie them under branches of blossoms. Also, they cut up silk to make spring butterflies, spring swallows, and spring decorations and use them as playthings." (立春之日, 士夫之家, 剪綵爲小幡, 謂之春幡. 或懸於佳人之頭, 或綴於花枝之下. 又剪爲春蝶, 春燕, 春勝, 以爲戱.)

state of Chu (K. Hyŏngch'o; C. Jingchu 荊楚).[235] The preparing of five kinds of spicy herbs, arranging them in a bowl, and calling them 'five bitter dishes' (K. *osinban*; C. *wuxinpan* 五辛盤) flourished even more during the Song dynasty.[236] Because of the making and drinking of wine made from tangerines, there are the words from the poem by Su Dongpo, 'the green onions of the bitter herb dishes (K. *sinban*; C. *xinpan* 辛盤) and the yellow tangerines (K. *hwanggam*; C. *huanggan* 黃柑) of the 'twelfth lunar month wine' (K. *napchu*; C. *lajiu* 臘酒).[237]

On New Year's Eve, bamboo is burned to make a noise to scare away all manner of evil spirits,[238] branches of peach trees are hung on doorways

---

235 'First Lunar Month' (Zhengyue 正月), *Record of the Seasons of Jingchu* (*Jingchu suishi ji* 荊楚歲時記). "When the 'Beginning of Spring' arrives everyone cuts up silk to make swallows as accessories for their head, and they write the two characters '*yichun*' (K. *ŭich'un* 宜春: 'proper spring') and paste them on their doors." (立春之日, 悉剪綵爲鷰以戴之, 貼宜春二字.)

236 'First Lunar Month', *Record of the Seasons of Jingchu*. "According to *Record of Local Conditions* (*Fengtu ji* 風土記) by Zhou Chu (周處), he stated, 'Making 'five bitter dishes' (*wuxinpan*) with five types of spicy vegetables on the first day of the first lunar month cleanses the Dao of the body.' The annotation states, 'The five different spicy tastes stimulate the energy of the five organs (C. *wuzang*; K. *ojang* 五臟), namely, garlic, wild chives, chives, canola and coriander."' (周處風土記曰, '元日造五辛盤, 正月元日, 五薰鍊形.' 注: '五辛所以發五臟之氣, 即大蒜·小蒜·韭菜·雲臺·胡荽是也.')

237 'Lichunri xiaoji cheng Li Duanshu' (立春日小集呈李端叔), *The Complete Works of Su Dongpo* (*Dongpo quanji* 東坡全集). "In the 'five bitter herbs' there are green chives; in the 'twelfth lunar month wine' (*lajiu*) there are tangerines." (辛盤得青韭, 臘酒是黃柑.)

238 'First Lunar Month', *Record of the Seasons of Jingchu*. "Upon examination, it states in *Classic of the Deities and the Extraordinary* (*Shenyijing* 神異經), 'In the western mountains there are people over one foot tall and with only one leg; they are not afraid of people, and people who come into contact with them get chills and a fever. They are called *shansao* (山臊). People set bamboo on fire which makes a sound like firecrackers so the *shansao* are shocked and run far away in fear. In *Black Yellow Classic* (*Xuanhuangjing* 玄黃經) it states, 'They are called *shanzhaogui* (山獟鬼).'" (按神異經云, '西方山中有人焉, 其長尺餘, 一足, 性不畏人, 犯之則令人寒熱. 名曰山臊. 人以竹著火中烞熚有聲, 而山臊驚憚遠去. 玄黃經所謂山獟鬼也.')

and are called 'peach talismans' (K. *tobu*; C. *taofu* 桃符) to repel ghosts,[239] and the making and drinking of *toso* wine (C. *tusujiu* 屠蘇酒)[240] is also a custom from the state of Chu. As there is a book called *Record of the Seasons of Jingchu* (*Jingchu suishi ji* 荊楚歲時記) all of you read it carefully. Every year, the seventh day of the first lunar month is called 'Inil' (人日: 'human day'). The first day of each lunar month belongs to the rooster (astrological sign), so it is called 'Kyeil' (雞日: 'rooster day'), the second day is called 'Kuil' (狗日: 'dog day'), the third day 'Chŏil (猪日: 'pig day'), the fourth day 'Yangil' (羊日: 'sheep day'), the fifth day 'Uil' (牛日: 'ox day'), the sixth day 'Mail' (馬日: 'horse day'), and the seventh day 'Inil' (人日: 'human day'), and it is said that if when you examine the clearness and cloudiness of the weather, it is clear, the animals belonging to that day will flourish.[241] The preparing and eating of seven types of wild vegetables and calling them 'seven types of vegetables' (*ch'ilchongch'ae* 七種菜)[242] is found in *Record of the Seasons of Jingchu.*

---

239 'First Lunar Month', *Record of the Seasons of Jingchu.* "Upon examination Zhuanzi (莊子) said, 'If you tie a chicken on your door, and above it hang a rope made of reeds and next to it attach a peach tree amulet, all kinds of ghosts will be afraid of it.'" (按莊周云, '有掛雞於户, 懸葦索於其上, 插桃符於旁, 百鬼畏之.')

240 *Toso* wine (C. *tusujiu* 屠蘇酒): As a wine that was said to ward off infectious diseases and negative energy if it was drunk on Lunar New Year's Day, there was a custom of people drinking *toso* wine even from a young age.

241 'First Lunar Month', *Record of the Seasons of Jingchu.* "Upon examination, in *Questions of Etiquette and Customs* (*Wen lishu* 問禮俗) by Dong Xun (董勛), it states, 'The first day of the first lunar month a chicken, the second day a dog, the third day a sheep, the fourth day a pig, the fifth day an ox, and the seventh day a human being, and the cloudiness and brightness of those days is a prognostication of whether the harvest will be good or not." (按董勛問禮俗云, '正月一日爲雞, 二日爲狗, 三日爲羊, 四日爲猪, 五日爲牛, 六日爲馬, 七日爲人, 以陰晴, 占豐耗.')

242 'First Lunar Month', *Record of the Seasons of Jingchu.* "The seventh day of the first lunar

Sangwŏn (C. Shangyuan 上元)[243] marks the arrival of the first full moon of the new year, and because people went out to view the moon, lit lanterns and sent each other tangerines, the nighttime curfew was lifted for three days during the Tang dynasty. There is also an old saying that sacrifices were made to the silkworm deity.[244] The first and second day of the second lunar month is called Chunghwajŏl (中和節). There was a custom of playing a game with all kinds of grains in pouches made of colored silk.[245] The third day of the third lunar month was when Zeng Dian (曾點) bathed at the River Yi (沂水) and wanted to feel the breeze from the 'rain altars'.[246] Since

---

month is a 'human day', so on this day people pick seven types of wild greens, boil them in a soup and eat them." (正月七日爲人日, 以七種菜爲羹.) The seven types of wild greens are water parsley (*minari*), shepherd's purse (*naengi*), mugwort (*ssuk*), chickweed (*pyŏlkkot*), turnip sprouts, and radish sprouts.

243 Sangwŏn (C. Shangyuan 上元): The fifteenth day of the first lunar month.

244 'First Lunar Month', *Record of the Seasons of Jingchu*. "Upon examination, in *Records of Qixie* (*Qixie ji* 齊諧記) it states, 'On the fifteenth day of the first lunar month, a deity (*shen* 神) descended to the house of Chen-*shi* (陳氏) and said, if you conduct a sacrifice in the silkworm-raising room, I will ensure that your production of mulberry leaves and silkworms increases a hundredfold.'" (按齊諧記曰, '正月半有神降陳氏之宅云, 是蠶室, 若能見祭, 當令蠶桑百倍.')

245 'Zhonghejie', *Records from Mt. Tianzhong*. "Zhonghejie is the first day of the second month, and is a holiday created by Dezong (德宗) of the Tang dynasty. ...... (It was a custom) among the people to fill up blue pouches with grains and the seeds of fruits and to request and give them, and this was called 'offering for the birth of children' (K. *hŏnsaengja*; C. *xianshengzi* 獻生子)." (中和節, 二月一日爲中和. 德宗方置此節 ... 民間以青囊盛百穀瓜果種, 相問遺, 號爲獻生子.) This content is not in *Record of the Seasons of Jingchu*.

246 'Xianjin' (先進), *Analects*. When Confucius asked his disciples what each of them desired, Zeng Dian said, "In this the last month of spring, with the dress of the season all complete, along with five or six men who have assumed the cap, and six or seven boys, I would wash in the River Yi, enjoy the breeze among the rain altars (*wuyu* 舞雩), and return home singing." (莫春者, 春服既成, 冠者五六人, 童子六七人, 浴乎沂, 風乎舞雩, 詠而歸.)

the weather was cool and all things were flourishing, it was a time when the people of old enjoyed *tapchŏng* (C. *taqing* 踏青),[247] but could that be compared to the words of Zeng Dian? According to the words of Confucian scholars in the past (*sŏnyu* 先儒), 'In these words of Zeng Dian there is the spirit of Yao and Shun', so we should pay even more attention to this. Even if you wished to recount everything about the holidays of the twelve months, you would never become bored."

"Among the words that Confucius spoke to Master Zeng, there were words that Master Yan was never able to hear, and these are words that were spoken to Zilu, so isn't it good that we can all gather together to hear such words? Please, tell us more about the holidays."

"Hansik (C. Hanshi 寒食: 'cold food') occurs 105 or 106 days after the Winter Solstice."[248]

Yesŏng asked, "Is it true that the day is called Hansik because it was the day during the Jin (晉) dynasty in the Spring and Autumn Period that Jie

---

247 *Tapchŏng* (C. *taqing* 踏青): This was a custom of going for walks outside the city on the third day of the third lunar month.

248 'First Lunar Month', *Record of the Seasons of Jingchu*. In the original text of Zong Lin (宗懍) it states, "105 days after the Winter Solstice the wind blows strongly and much rain falls. This day is called Hanshi, and it is forbidden to use fires for three days, and people make taffy (*yŏt*) and barley porridge." (去冬節一百五日, 即有疾風甚雨. 謂之寒食, 禁火三日, 造餳大麥粥.) And in an annotation by Tu Gongzhan (杜公瞻), it states, "Consulting the almanac, it is 2 days before Qingming and also 106 days after the Winter Solstice." (按曆合在清明前二日, 亦有去冬至一百六日者.)

Zitui (介子推) was burned to death in a fire, so the use of fire was forbidden and people ate leftover rice?"

"People say that, but if it is the memorial ritual day of Jie Zitui's death, how could the date change every year between the second and third lunar months? In the past when the Ch'ŏngmyŏng holiday (C. Qingmingjie 淸明節) was approaching, many fierce winds blew, and as people were afraid of conflagrations, fire was forbidden, and because people ate leftover rice they called the day Hansik,[249] or it was also called Naengjŏl (C. Lengjie 冷節: 'cold holiday')."[250]

"At the time of the Tang dynasty when Liu Zongyuan (柳宗元) was exiled to Liuzhou, he said, 'I will not be able to go to my parents' graves at Hanshi',[251] so it would appear that holding a memorial service on Hansik started from the time of the Tang dynasty. How is the memorial service

---

249 'Second Lunar Month' (Eryue 二月), *Record of the Seasons of Jingchu*. "There is no record of Jie Zitui burning to death in *The Commentary of Zuo* (*Zuozhuan*) and *The Records of the Grand Historian*. In 'Sixuan-*shi*' (司烜氏), *Rites of Zhou* (*Zhouli* 周禮), it is stated, 'In the second lunar month a wooden gong was beaten to announce that it was forbidden to light fires in the country', and in an annotation it is stated, 'this is because in the third lunar month it is easy for conflagrations to occur.'" (左傳及史記, 並無介推被焚之事. 周禮司烜氏, 仲春以木鐸修火禁於國中, 注云, 爲季春將出火也.)

250 *Monthly Decrees to the Four (Groups of) People* (*Simin yueling* 四民月令). "People call 'Hanshi' ('cold food') 'Lengjie' ('cold holiday')." (齊人呼寒食爲冷節.)

251 'Biography of Liu Zongyuan' (Liu Zongyuan zhuan 柳宗元傳), *History of the Later Tang* (*Xin tangshu* 新唐書). When Liu Zongyuan was going into exile in Liuzhou (柳州), he sent letters to the metropolitan governor of the capital prefecture (*jingzhao yin* 京兆尹) Xu Mengrong (許孟容), and among them are the following words, "Nowadays the ritual of visiting one's ancestors' graves is important, but I have not been able to visit my ancestors' graves for four years. Every time Hanshi comes around, I turn northwards weeping on the road and bow my head to the ground." (近世禮重拜掃, 今闕者四年矣. 每遇寒食, 則北向長號, 以首頓地.)

performed?"

"At the time of Emperor Guangwu (光武帝) of the Han dynasty, whenever various generals would return to their hometowns, Emperor Guangwu would give them sacrificial items (*xiaolao* 小牢), so that they could conduct memorial services at the graves of their ancestors, and this was considered a great honor in their hometowns. From that time forward because of this their descendants adopted the custom of performing ancestral rites whenever Hansik came around."[252]

"What kind of game is a swing (K. *ch'uch'ŏn*; C. *qiuqian* 鞦韆)?"

"That is also a Han dynasty time game. It is also called *pansŏn* (C. *banxian* 半仙: 'half immortal'), so in general it seems to be a northern barbarian custom (Hop'ung 胡風)."[253]

---

252 'Origin of Sacrificing at the Tomb' (Muji zhi shi 墓祭之始), *Classified Collection Based on Historical Facts and on Literature from the Past and Present* (*Gujin shiwen leiju* 古今事文類聚). "Emperor Guangwu of the Han dynasty first established this great undertaking, when the various generals went to the front line, if any of them were going past their hometown, he issued an imperial edict and bestowed sacrificial items (*shaolao* 少牢) so that they could perform ancestral rites at the gravesites, and this was considered a great honor." (漢光武初纂大業, 諸將出征, 有經鄉里者, 詔有司給少牢, 令拜掃, 以爲榮.)

253 'Hanshi', *Records from Mt. Tianzhong*. "*Banxian xi* (K. *pansŏn hŭi* 半仙戱: 'half immortal game'): When the Hanshi day came around in the Tianbao (天寶) Year, in the palace, people competed with each other to make swings, and the palace imperial concubines (K. *bin*; C. *pin* 嬪) enjoyed themselves riding on them. As the emperor called this '*banxian zhi xi*' (半仙之戱), it came to be called this by the people of the country. In *Gujin yishu tu* (古今藝術圖) it states, *qiuqian* (K. *ch'uch'ŏn* 鞦韆) is a game from Shanrong (山戎) in the north." (半仙戱, 天寶宮中, 至寒食節, 競築鞦韆, 令宮嬪輩戱笑, 以爲宴樂. 帝呼爲半仙之戱, 都中士民因而呼之. 古今藝術圖云, 鞦韆, 北方山戎之戱.)

Chasŏng asked, "Is it true that Lord Mengchang (孟嘗君) Tian Wen (田文) was born on Tano Day (C. Duanwu 端午: fifth day of the fifth lunar month)?"[254]

"Lord Mengchang was born on Tano Day, and there was a folk saying that when a child born on Tano grows up and reaches the height of a door, it would be harmful to its parents and so it should be abandoned. When Lord Mengchang asked, his parents told him this reason, so Lord Mengchang said, 'raise the height of the door' and he became known as Lord Mengchang. Subsequently, Wang Zhen'e (王鎭惡) was born on Tano Day,[255] and Wang Feng (王鳳) was also born on Tano Day.[256] Hu Guang (胡廣) was born on Tano, and Hu

---

254 'Duanwu danzi' (端午誕子), *Classified Collection Based on Historical Facts and on Literature from the Past and Present.* "The mother of Tian Wen (田文) gave birth to Tian Wen on the fifth day of the fifth lunar month. His father told her not to raise him, but the mother raised Tian Wen secretly, and only when he was grown up did she reveal this fact. Finally, Tian Wen said to his father, 'Why should a child born in the fifth lunar month not be raised?' His father said, 'Because when his height reaches the height of the door, he will harm his father.' Tian Wen said, 'As fate (K. *myŏng*, C. *ming* 命) is something received from Heaven, how could it be received from a door? If fate comes from a door, why don't you raise the height of the door? If you do that, who could reach the height of the door?' His father realized his wisdom, and later he conferred the title Lord Mengchang upon him. Ordinary people shun the fifth lunar month as an unlucky month." (田文母, 五月五日生文. 父令勿擧, 母私擧文, 長以實告之. 遂啓父曰, '不擧五月子, 何也?' 父曰, '生及戸, 損父.' 文曰, '受命於天, 豈受命於户? 若受命於户, 何不高其户? 誰能至其户耶?' 父知其賢, 後封孟嘗君. 俗以五月爲惡月, 故忌.) The original source is *Yiyuan* (異苑).

255 'Duanwu danzi' (端午誕子), *Classified Collection Based on Historical Facts and on Literature from the Past and Present.* "When Wang Zhen'e was born on the fifth day of the fifth lunar month, the people in the house decided to abandon him. At that moment Wang Zhen'e's grandfather said severely, 'In the past Lord Mengchang was born on this day, and he eventually became the prime minister of Qi. This child will definitely elevate our family.' So he gave him the name Zhen'e (鎭惡: 'suppress evil')." (王鎭惡以五月五日生, 家人欲棄之. 其祖猛曰, '昔孟嘗君以此日生, 卒得相齊. 此兒必興吾宗.' 以鎭惡名之.) The original source is *Outline of Song Dynasty History* (*Songlue* 宋略).

256 'Duanwu danzi' (端午誕子), *Classified Collection Based on Historical Facts and on Literature from the Past and Present.* "When Wang Feng was born on the fifth day of the fifth lunar month, his father did not want to raise him and said, 'According to an old saying, if you raise a child

Guang's parents felt it was a shame, so they put him in a gourd and floated it in the water, so another person took him and raised him. When he grew up and had made a name for himself, his biological parents wanted to take him back. Hu Guang said, 'Abandoning your biological parents is detrimental to morality, and abandoning your adoptive parents is like forgetting your grace.' And he said he was born from a gourd (C. *hulu* 葫蘆), and so he gave himself the surname Hu and the given name Guang and later rose to the post of Sanshi (三司).[257] These are the people who were born on Tano Day, but a person who died on Tano Day was Sanlü Dafu (三閭大夫) Qu Yuan (屈原). When Qu Yuan drowned in the River Miluo, the people of Chu felt pity for him, and raced in boats to rescue him. The 'Boat Race Song' (*Jingdu qu* 競渡曲) exists until this day.[258]

---

born on this day until he reaches around the height of a door, he will either harm himself or he will harm his parents.' At this his uncle said, 'In the past Tian Wen was born on this day, but it was not misfortunate.' In the end Wang Feng was raised." (王鳳以五月五日生, 其父欲不舉曰, '俗諺舉此日生子, 長及户則自害, 否則害其父母.' 其叔父曰, '昔田文亦以此日生, 非不祥也.' 遂舉之.) The original source is *Miscellaneous Records of the Western Capital* (*Xijing zaji* 西京雜記).

257 'Duanwu danzi' (端午誕子), *Classified Collection Based on Historical Facts and on Literature from the Past and Present.* "Hu Guang's original surname was Wu (吳), and he was born on the fifth day of the fifth lunar month. His parents disliked him and so they placed him in a gourd and set him afloat on a river, then a person living by the river rescued him and raised him. After he had grown up and made a name for himself, his biological parents wanted to take him back as their son. Hu Guang thought, 'To abandon one's biological parents offends righteousness and to abandon one's adoptive parents is to forget their grace, so he did not go back to either side and it is said that because he had been 'born' from a gourd (*hulu* 葫蘆), he adopted Hu (胡) as his surname and Guang (廣) as his given name. Subsequently he rose to the official position of Sanshi (三司) and made a name for himself for keeping to the mean." (胡廣本姓吳, 以五月五日生. 父母惡之, 藏之葫蘆, 棄之河流, 岸側居人收養. 及長有盛名, 父母欲取之, 廣以爲背其所生則害義, 背其所養則忘恩, 兩無所歸, 託葫蘆而生也, 乃姓胡名廣. 後登三司, 有中庸之號.)

258 'Fifth Lunar Month' (Wuyue 五月), *Record of the Seasons of Jingchu.* "Upon examination, the folk custom of boat racing (*jingdu* 競渡) on the fifth day of the fifth lunar month is because

During the Song dynasty, the making of dumplings called *kujajong* (C. *jiuzizong* 九子粽)[259] was a custom; wine brewed from irises (K. *ch'angp'o*; C. *changpu* 菖蒲)[260] was drunk; people bathed in orchid water,[261] made human figures out of mugwort, called them 'mugwort people' (K. *aein*; C. *airen* 艾人)[262] and attached them above their doors. As they said this custom warded off evil spirits (K. *pyŏksa*; C. *bixie* 辟邪), it was handed down to later generations. Because Tano came to be designated as a holiday in this way, at the time of the Tang dynasty, clothes were made and given to the court councilors (K. *chosin*; C. *chaochen* 朝臣), so Du Fu (杜甫) received palace clothing (K. *kungŭi*; C. *gongyi* 宮衣) and composed 'Presentation of Clothes on Duanwu (Tano)' (K. Tano sa ŭi; C. Duanwu ci yi 端吾賜衣).[263]

---

it was the day Qu Yuan (屈原) threw himself into the River Miluo and died and because the people were so anguished they raced in boats to try to rescue him." (按五月五日競渡, 俗爲屈原投汨羅日, 傷其死所, 故並命舟檝以拯之.)

259 'Jiuzizong', *Classified Collection Based on Historical Facts and on Literature from the Past and Present*. "The appearance of the *zongzi* (K. *chongja* 粽子: glutinous rice and other ingredients wrapped in leaves) eaten on Duanwu are not all the same. There are *juezong* (K. *kakchong* 角粽), *zhuizong* (K. *ch'ujong* 錐粽), *lingzong* (K. *nŭngjong* 菱粽), *tongzong* (K. *t'ongjong* 筒粽), *chenchuizong* (K. *ch'ingch'ujong* 稱鎚粽) and also *jiuzizong* (K. *kujajong* 九子粽)." (端午粽子名品甚多, 形製不一, 有角粽·錐粽·菱粽·筒粽·秤鎚粽, 又有九子粽.) The original source is *Random Notes to the Events of the Annual Seasons* (*Suishi zaji* 歲時雜記).

260 'Changpujiu' (菖蒲酒), *Classified Collection Based on Historical Facts and on Literature from the Past and Present*. "On Duanwu irises are shredded or powdered and then made into wine." (端午以菖蒲, 或縷或屑, 汎酒.) The original source is *Random Notes to the Events of the Annual Seasons*.

261 'The Small Calendar of the Xia' (Xia xiaozheng 夏小正), *Records of Ritual Matters by Dai the Elder* (*Dadai Liji* 大戴禮記). "Gathering orchids is for bathing." (蓄蘭, 爲沐浴也.)

262 'Attaching Mugwort People' (Jie airen 結艾人), *Classified Collection Based on Historical Facts and on Literature from the Past and Present*. "The people of the Jingchu region dig up mugwort on Duanwu, shape it into human forms, and hang them on their doors to ward off poisonous vapors." (荊楚人端午採艾結爲人, 懸門户上, 以禳毒氣.)

263 'Presentation of Clothes on Duanwu' (Duanwu ci yi), *Classified Collection Based on Historical Facts and on Literature from the Past and Present*. This poem is included in such works as

I am on the list of those to receive clothes in the palace; (宮衣亦有名)

On Duanwu Day I encountered grace and honor. (端午被恩榮)

The delicate hemp cloth is as soft as the wind; (細葛含風軟)

The folds of fragrant gauze are light as snow. (香羅疊雪輕)

The words the Emperor wrote are still moist; (自天題處濕)

These clothes suit the heat and wearing them is refreshing. (當暑着來輕)

In my mind considering the long and the short; (意內稱長短)

All my life I will carry this sacred emotion. (終身荷聖情)

Even if we just look at this composition, we can see Du Fu's passionate loyalty (K. *ch'ungjŏng*, C. *zhongqing* 忠情). Also, in the Song dynasty there were people who, just like at the 'Beginning of Spring' (Ipch'un), would write 'Tano Day Notices' (K. Tano ch'ŏp; C. Duanwu tie 端午帖)[264] and paste them on the palace gates, so there are two poems by Ouyang Xiu (歐陽修) that are this kind of 'Tano Day announcement'.[265]

Supplementary Commentary of Du Fu's Poems (*Buzhu Dushi* 補注杜詩) under the title 'Presentation of Clothes on Duanwu Day' (*Duanwuri ci yi* 端午日賜衣).

264 'Tano Day Notices' (端午帖): A poem celebrating Tano that was presented as a 'notice' (K. *ch'ŏpcha*; C. *tiezi* 帖子) in the palace.

265 Ouyang Xiu (歐陽修), 'Notice of Remonstration' (Tiezi guijian 帖子規諫), *Classified Collection Based on Historical Facts and on Literature from the Past and Present.*

It is enjoyable to bathe together in orchid water on a good holiday; (佳辰共喜沐蘭湯)
Is there any need to dig up mugwort to counter the severe cold? (毒冷何須採艾禳)
Get a subject like Gao Yu to govern state affairs; (但得皐陶調鼎鼐)
Naturally disaster will be transformed and become auspicious. (自然灾沴變休祥)

Chu banished Qu Yuan because of an accusation; (楚國因讒逐屈原)
He never ever returned to the palace again. (終身無復入君門)
Ask about the surviving custom of the glutinous rice wrapped in leaves; (願因角黍詢遺俗)
I want people to reflect on the delusions of former kings. (可鑒前王惑巧言)

Because Ouyang Xiu was loyal, even in this ordinary composition, he remonstrated with the king, so future generations said, 'When taking up the pen, do not forget to remonstrate.'[266] When you also encounter a holiday like this, always think of the good deeds of the people of the past. Because Ch'ilsŏk (the seventh day of the seventh lunar month) is the beginning of a new autumn season, it is said, 'Among the countless trees one paulownia leaf falls.'"[267]

Maengsŏng asked, "Is it true that on the seventh day of the seventh lunar month (Ch'ilsŏk) Herd Boy (Kyŏnu 牽牛) and Weaver Girl (Chingnyŏ 織女) crossed the Milky Way (Ŭnhasu 銀河水) via the Magpie Bridge (Ojakkyo 烏鵲橋) to meet each other?"

"That story is in the book *Records of Qixie* (*Qixie ji* 齊諧記), but it is an extremely absurd tale.[268] In the past, it was said that if you put books and

---

266 'True Retainers and Officials' (Zhen shicong chen 眞侍從臣), *Classified Collection Based on Historical Facts and on Literature from the Past and Present.* "When Ouyang Xiu was a Hanlin Academician, Emperor Renzong of the Song dynasty saw a spring notice (*chun tiezi* 春帖子) pasted on the imperial pavilion. Reading it, he loved it, and he asked about it to those on his left and right, and they told him it was a composition by Ouyang Xiu. Then he collected all the notices in the palace, and upon reading them, found that each one of them had a remonstrative meaning. Emperor Renzong sighed with admiration saying, 'Lifting their writing brushes, they have not forgotten to remonstrate, so truly these are officials attending their sovereign!'" (歐陽修在翰林, 仁宗見御閣春帖子, 讀而愛之, 問左右, 曰, 學士歐某之文也. 乃悉取宮中帖子閱之, 見其篇篇有意. 歎曰, '擧筆不忘規諫, 眞侍從之臣也!')

267 Zhang Lei (張耒), 'Song of the Seventh Day of the Seventh Lunar Month' (Qixi ge 七夕歌), *Veritable Treasures of Ancient Writing* (*Guwen zhenbao* 古文眞寶). "In the world of human beings a single paulownia leaf falls, and Rushou (蓐收: the deity of autumn) presides over the progress of autumn stirring the handle of the Big Dipper." (人間一葉梧桐飄, 蓐收行秋回斗杓.)

268 'Weaver Girl Marries Herd Boy' (Zhinu jia Qianniu 織女嫁牽牛), *Classified Collection Based on Historical Facts and on Literature from the Past and Present.* "Cheng Wuding (成武丁) of Guiyang (桂陽), who had the Dao of a Daoist Immortal, said to his younger brother. 'On the seventh day of the seventh month Zhinu naturally crosses the Milky Way; the numerous Daoist

clothing out in the sunshine on Ch'ilsŏk Day, they would not get moldy, so all the households competed with each other and took pride in how many books and clothes they could put out. The house of a person called Hao Long (郝隆) was poor, but even though he did not have books or clothes, he wrote well. He went out into his courtyard and lay down looking up at the sun and sunned his belly in the sunlight, and when the people asked what he was doing, he replied, 'I do not have any clothes, but because I have many books inside my stomach, I am sunning it in the sun', so it is said that the people at that time all laughed.[269] How many books are inside the stomachs of all of you?

The fifteenth day of the eighth lunar month is called Ch'usŏk, and in the region of Guangling (廣陵),[270] the waves of the incoming tide and outgoing tide were very strong, and because people competed with each other to view it, it was called 'Viewing big waves at Guangling' (K. *Kwangnŭng*

---

immortals return to their palace.' His younger brother asked, 'For what reason did Zhinu cross the Milky Way?' So his brother replied, 'In order to meet Qianniu for a short time.' Until now people say, 'Zhinu is going to get married to Qianniu'. This is in *Continued Records of Qixie* (*Xu qixie ji* 續齊諧記). (桂陽成武丁, 有仙道, 謂其弟曰, '七月七日, 織女當渡河, 諸仙悉還宮.' 弟問曰, '織女何事渡河?' 答曰, '織女暫詣牽牛.' 世人至今云, '織女嫁牽牛也.' 續齊諧記.)

269 'Sunning Books in the Belly' (曬腹中書), *Classified Collection Based on Historical Facts and on Literature from the Past and Present*. "On the seventh day of the seventh lunar month Hao Long saw all his neighbors airing their clothes in the sunshine. Whereupon Hao Long lay down in his courtyard and sunning his belly in the sunshine said, 'I am sunning the books in my belly in the sunshine.'" (郝隆, 七月七日, 見隣人皆曝曬衣物. 隆乃仰卧曝腹於庭曰, '我曝腹中書.')

270 Guangling (廣陵) is present-day Yangzhou-shi (揚州市) in China.

kwando; C. *Guangling guantao* 廣陵觀濤).[271] At the time of the Tang dynasty, wine and candles were bestowed on the Jade Hall Scholars (Oktang haksa), so they could go out to view the moon, and in the whole sky there was not a single cloud, and the moonlight was like daylight, so it is said that the scholar Su Ting (蘇頲) said, 'the clear light is so loveable, so how could we use candlelight?'[272]

Since long ago the ninth day of the ninth lunar month has been called Chungyang kajŏl (C. Chongyang jiajie 重陽佳節). At the time of the Tang dynasty wine was bestowed upon all the office holders, and they enjoyed themselves in Shanglin Garden (上林苑), so the Jade Hall scholars composed many poems.

A person called Huan Jing (桓景) in the Runan (汝南) region got along well with the Daoist master Fei Changfang (費長房). One day the Daoist master said to Huan Jing, 'On the ninth day there will be calamity in your

---

271 'Viewing big waves at Guangling' (Guangling guantao 廣陵觀濤), *Classified Collection Based on Historical Facts and on Literature from the Past and Present.* "In 'Seven Discoveries' (Qifa 七發) by Mei Cheng (枚乘) the guest said, 'On the full moon day in the eighth lunar month, I will go to River Qu in Guangling to watch the waves with the feudal princes."' (枚乘七發, 客曰, '將以八月之望, 與諸侯並往觀濤於廣陵之曲江.')

272 'Enjoying the Moon at Jade Hall' (Yutang wanyue 玉堂玩月), *Classified Collection Based on Historical Facts and on Literature from the Past and Present.* "Su Ting (蘇頲) and Li Yi (李乂) were in charge of the emperor's memorials, and on the fifteenth day of the eighth lunar month, they were on night duty in the palace. Several scholars had prepared a drinking party to admire the moon. Finally, there was not a single cloud in the sky, and the moonlight was like broad daylight. Su Ting said, 'The clear light is so lovable, so how can we use candles?' And in the end the candles were all removed." (蘇頲與李乂, 對掌綸誥. 八月十五夜, 於禁中直宿, 諸學士翫月, 備卮酒之宴. 時長天無雲, 月色如晝. 蘇曰, '清光可愛, 何用燈燭?' 遂令徹去.) The original source is *Anecdotes from the Kaiyuan and Tianbao Periods* (*Kaiyuan Tianbao yishi* 開元天寶遺事).

house, so go down quickly and have the members of your household make a lot of red pouches, put the fruit of *Cornus officianalis* (K. *suyunang*, C. *zhuyunang* 茱萸囊) in them and tie them up with string; then go up the mountain to drink chrysanthemum wine. If you do that you will be able to avoid this catastrophe.' Huan Jing did as he had said and went up the mountain with all the members of his household, and when they returned that evening all his oxen, sheep, chickens and dogs had died suddenly. The Daoist master told him that all his domestic animals had died in his stead, so in subsequent generations every ninth day (of the ninth lunar month), the people would go up the mountain to drink chrysanthemum wine, while the women would fill purses with *Cornus officianalis* and go about with them.[273]

On the ninth day Tao Yuanming sat down without any wine, so the provincial governor of Jiangzhou sent an envoy wearing white clothes to

---

273 'Ninth Lunar Month' (Jiuyue 九月), *Record of the Seasons of Jingchu*. "In *Continued Records of Qixie* (*Xu qixie ji* 續齊諧記) it states, 'A person called Huan Jing in the Runan region went around with Fei Changfang and learned from him, and Fei Changfang said, "As there will be a calamity in your house on the ninth day of the ninth lunar month, if you quickly have the people of your household make pouches, fill them with *Cornus officianalis* and tie them to the upper part of their arms, and then go up the mountain and drink chrysanthemum wine, you will be able to avert this calamity." In accordance with his words Huan Jing took all the members of his household up the mountain, and when he returned in the evening, he found that his chickens and dogs, oxen and sheep had all died suddenly at the same time. Upon hearing this Fei Changfang said, "They were able to take your place." Nowadays on the ninth day of the ninth lunar month, people go up to a high place and drink wine, and in general women wearing pouches of *Cornus officianalis* started from here."' (續齊諧記云, 汝南桓景, 隨費長房遊學, 長房謂之曰, '九月九日, 汝家中當有災厄, 急令家人縫囊盛茱萸繫臂上, 登山飮菊花酒, 此禍可消.' 景如言, 擧家登山, 夕還, 見雞犬牛羊, 一時暴死. 長房聞之曰, '此可代也.' 今世人九日登高飮酒, 婦人帶茱萸囊, 蓋始於此.)

him bearing wine. Consequently, there is also a composition Tao Yuanming wrote when he received it and drank it."[274]

Chinsŏng asked, "Did Wang Bo write 'Preface to Prince Teng's Tower' (Tengwangge xu 滕王閣序)[275] on the ninth day?"

"In the annotations to 'Preface to Prince Teng's Tower', it states that it was written on the ninth day.[276] It said, 'The time was the Ninth Lunar Month (*shi wei jiuyue* 時維九月), and the season was in the Third Lunar Month of Autumn' (*xu shu sanqiu* 序屬三秋). You didn't understand this because you just read it in a cursory way."

---

274 'Picking Handfuls of Chrysanthemums' (Zhai ju yingba 摘菊盈把), *Classified Collection Based on Historical Facts and on Literature from the Past and Present.* "Tao Yuanming had no wine on the festival of the ninth day of the ninth lunar month, so he gathered handfuls of chrysanthemums from around his house, put them down and absent-mindedly sat next to them for a long time. Finally, a white clad person came who was someone the provincial governor of Jiangzhou (Jiangzhou cishi 江州刺史) Wang Hong (王弘) had sent to bring him wine." (陶潛嘗九月九日無酒, 宅邊菊叢摘盈把, 坐其側, 悵望久之. 見白衣至, 乃江州王弘送酒也.) The original source is *Continuation of the Annals of Jin* (*Xu jin yangqiu* 續晉陽秋).

275 'Preface to Prince Teng's Tower' (Tengwangge xu 滕王閣序): The son of Emperor Gaozu (高祖) of Tang Li Yuanying (李元嬰) built a splendid pavilion, which he called Prince Teng's Tower (滕王閣). Subsequently, the governor of Hongzhou (Hongzou mushi 洪州牧使) Yan Baiyu (閻伯嶼) held a great banquet on the Chongyang Festival, and among all the guests on that day, the youngest Wang Bo (王勃) wrote 'Preface to Prince Teng's Tower' and gained a reputation for himself.

276 In an annotation at the beginning of 'Preface to Prince Teng's Tower', *Veritable Treasures of Ancient Writing*, it states, "Wang Bo's courtesy name was Zian (子安), and he was outstandingly talented from his childhood. ...... On his way to attend his father at his official post in the provinces, he passed by Zhongli (鍾離), and at this pavilion on the ninth day of the ninth lunar month, he composed this preface." (勃字子安, 少有逸才. ... 後到父任所, 省侍, 道過鍾離, 九月九日, 會此而作此序.)

Fascicle 3

The Origins of Holidays and Seasonal Customs II

"Indeed that is so."

"Because the *yang* energy (K. *ki*; C. *qi* 氣) first appears at the Winter Solstice, and the days start to get longer little by little, the palace women of the Jin (晉) dynasty measured the shadow cast by the sun with red threads, and because after the Winter Solstice they increased every day by one strand, it was called 'increasing palace thread' (K. *ch'ŏm kung sŏn*; C. *tian gong xian* 添宮線)."[277]

277 'Eleventh Lunar Month' (十一月), *Record of the Seasons of Jingchu.* "Also, during the Wei-Jin period the shadow cast by the sun was measured with red threads, and after the Winter Solstice every day the shadow grew longer by the length of one thread." (又晉魏間, 宮中以紅線量日影, 冬至後日影添長一線.)

Yesŏng asked, "What is the reason for cooking red bean porridge on the Winter Solstice?"

"Long ago the son of Gonggong-*shi* (共工氏) died on the Winter Solstice and became an epidemic demon. Because he was afraid of red beans, people warded him off by cooking and eating red bean porridge."[278]

"From when did bean curd begin to be made with soya beans?"

"It is said that Liu An (劉安) the King of Huainan (淮南王) under the (Western) Han (漢) was reluctant to let his people have any power, so he made bean curd and fed it to them to make them fat and dull.[279] From ancient times Laping (臘平) is a well-known day; at the time of the Xia dynasty, it was known as Jiaping (嘉平); at the time of the Yin dynasty, it was called Qingsi (清祀); and at the time of the Zhou dynasty, it was called Dala (大蜡). At the time of the Han dynasty, it was called La (臘), and the appearance of the character for the word '*la*' is similar to the character '*lie*' (獵) in '*tanlie*' (田獵).[280] In the Tang dynasty the assistant minister of the Ministry of Revenue

---

278 'Eleventh Lunar Month' (十一月), *Record of the Seasons of Jingchu*. "Gonggong-*shi* had a son who was lacking in talent, and he died on the Winter Solstice and became an epidemic demon. Because he was afraid of red beans, people made red bean porridge on the Winter Solstice to drive away the epidemic demon." (共工氏有不才之子, 以冬至死爲疫鬼. 畏赤小豆, 故冬至日作赤豆粥以禳之.)

279 'Bean Curd' (豆腐), *Compendium of Medicinal Herbs* (*Bencao gangmu* 本草綱目). "The way of making bean curd began with King Liu An of Huainan under the Han." (豆腐之法, 始於漢淮南王劉安.)

280 'La' (臘), *Classified Collection Based on Historical Facts and on Literature from the Past and Present.*

(Hubu shilang 戶部侍郎) Xiao Jiong (蕭炅), when talking together with Yan Jun (嚴俊), misnamed the days known as *fula* (伏臘) with the word *fulie* (伏獵), so the people of that time mocked him by calling him the 'Fulie shilang' (伏獵侍郎).'[281]

When Helping Others, Continue Until the End

Ten *li* to the west of Wanshu Garden was the house of an impoverished scholar with no official position (K. *p'oŭi hansa*; C. *buyi hanshi* 布衣寒士). He intended to give his daughter's hand in marriage, and he had only just been able to buy the clothing and marriage articles (K. *chajang*; C. *zizang* 資裝),[282] when a thief

---

"In the Han dynasty it was called 'Jiaping' (嘉平); in the Yin dynasty it was called 'Qingsi' (清祀); in the Zhou dynasty it was called 'Dala' (大蜡); and in the Han dynasty it was revised and called 'La' (臘), and 'La' comes from 'Lie' (獵) meaning 'to hunt'. People hunted and caught animals, which they offered as sacrifices to their ancestors." (夏日嘉平, 殷日清祀, 周日大蜡, 漢改日臘, 臘者獵也. 因獵取獸以祭先祖.)

281 'Not Knowing the Character *La* (臘)' (Bu shi la zi 不識臘字), *Classified Collection Based on Historical Facts and on Literature from the Past and Present*. "In the 'Biography of Yan Jun' (Yan Jun *zhuan* 嚴浚傳) in the Tang dynasty, the assistant minister of the Ministry of Revenue (Hubu shilang 戶部侍郎) Xiao Jiong (蕭炅), when discussing with Yan Jun, mistakenly said '*fulie*' (伏獵) instead of '*zheng chang fula*' (蒸嘗伏臘). Yan Jun asked, 'Is there a Fulie shilang (伏獵侍郎) in the court?' And Xiao Jiong was sent away to be the provincial governor of Qizhou (Qizhou cishi 岐州刺史)." (唐嚴浚傳, 户部侍郎蕭炅, 嘗與浚言蒸·嘗·伏·臘, 乃爲'伏獵.' 浚曰, '省中而有伏獵侍郎乎?' 乃出炅爲岐州刺史.)

282 *Chajang* (C. *zizang* 資裝): Marriage articles (K. *honsu* 婚需).

came during the night and stole both the clothes and the marriage articles. The wedding date was coming up in a few days, and the poor scholar's wife was at her wit's end. Day and night she was consumed with worry and sighed helplessly. She wanted to borrow clothes from Yuhandang, but she did not dare trouble an elderly person in this way. A neighbor came and told Yuhandang about what had happened. When Yuhandang heard this, she felt pity and decided to send some clothes.

Her granddaughter said, "Grandmother how will you send the clothing? We have to send young people's clothes."

"The fact they want to borrow clothes from me in that household is because they know I am old and have many children and grandchildren. Since it is right to do it freely according to the will of that person, I would like to lend them my clothes."

Finally, she told the female servant to go to the pavilion and bring out a box with clothes in it. She prepared various items of clothing by hand and sent them even before the poor scholar's wife asked for them. The poor scholar's wife was deeply moved. When she opened everything, she found various items of clothing with nothing lacking and felt even more gratitude. After using them for the wedding day and the day of greeting the in-laws

(K. *hyŏn kugo*; C. *xian jiugu* 見舅姑),[283] she intended to send the clothing back. But the next night, it suddenly rained heavily. The house leaked, and the clothes in the boxes all became spoiled, so they could not be worn again. Not only was the poor scholar's wife worried about the clothes that her daughter needed to wear for the day of greeting the in-laws that was approaching, but also because all the clothes she had just borrowed from Yuhandang had become spoiled. She felt so dreadful about it day and night that she became ill and had to take to her bed.

Upon hearing this rumor, Yuhandang felt pity and said to her granddaughter, "That household is deserving of our pity. In the past every morning Han Xin (韓信) would get food to eat from the house of the magistrate (*tingzhang* 亭長) of Nanchang (南昌). The magistrate (*tingzhang*) fed him every day, but later he got tired of doing this, so he cooked and ate his breakfast at dawn, so when Han Xin came in the morning he said, 'I can't make breakfast' and Han Xin went away without eating. Afterwards Han Xin became the king of Qi (齊), and when he was passing Nanchang, he called the magistrate and rebuked him saying, '*wi tŏk pu chol*' (C. *wei de bu zu* 爲德不卒),[284] which means 'When bestowing a favor, you stopped half way.'

---

283 *Hyŏn kugo* (C. *xian jiugu* 見舅姑): See footnote 50.

284 'Biography of the Marquis of Huaiyin' (Huaiyin Hou liezhuan 淮陰侯列傳), *Records of the*

Now I hear that my first loan of clothing to the poor scholar's household has ended in failure, if I do not loan again, it will be like the saying, 'When bestowing a favor, you stopped half way.'"

"You took pity on them for a small thing, but this situation is truly deserving of pity, so you guessed that you would have to send them something again."

Yuhandang sent a female servant to bring the clothing box, and opening it, she prepared various items of clothing and marriage articles and sent them off with a letter saying, "I heard that the clothes I sent first got dirty and cannot be used, so I feel pity and am sending clothing once more, so you can carry out the great rite (*taerye* 大禮) of greeting the in-laws with peace of mind." The wife of the poor scholar expressed her gratitude one hundred times over. After receiving the clothes and carrying out the ceremony for greeting the in-laws, she put them all in the box and sent them back, but Yuhandang would not receive them. Instead, she returned them with a letter that said, "Even if you have completed the *hyŏn kugo*

Grand Historian. After defeating Xiang Yu (項羽), Liu Bang (劉邦) transferred Han Xin from being King of Qi (齊王) to being King of Chu (楚王). When he returned to his home country of Chu, he gave a thousand gold pieces to an old washerwoman who had given him food when he had been starving, but to the magistrate (*tingzhang*) of Nanchang, he only gave 100 *qian* (錢), and spoke these words, "You are an inferior person. When bestowing a favor, you stopped half way." (公, 小人也. 爲德不卒.)

ceremony, I know that you do not have any clothes to wear in the future, so please keep them and wear them."

Because she sent them back, the wife of the poor scholar turned towards the east every day and prayed that Yuhandang would have a long life.

A Poetry Meeting at Wanshu Garden

On Hansik Day, Tu Ch'ŏnbok and Yuhandang went sightseeing together to Wanshu Garden and climbed up to Yangguan Terrace (仰觀臺); after looking around thoroughly Tu Ch'ŏnbok said to Yuhandang, "My wife you have been skilled in writing all your life, but you have never written a single poem, because you think it is inauspicious to compose poetry. For nearly seventy years, I also have nothing to pass down. Not only is the scenery of birds and flowers beautiful today, but my wife you are already old, so it is permissible for you to write poetry. I think it would be good if you just wrote one today."

"Long ago the wife of Yang Pu (楊璞) and Liu-*shi* (劉氏) the wife of Du Gao (杜羔) wrote compositions for their husbands, but I do not know if those ladies had engaged in academic studies. I too have refrained from writing poems until now for fear that it would be greatly detrimental to morality, so it would not be easy for me to write as I would wish after sixty or seventy years of refraining from literary composition."

Her niece who was attending her then said, "I once heard that the wife of Yang Pu (楊璞) wrote a poem called 'Poem of Farewell' (Songxing shi 送行詩),[285] but I never heard about the wife of Du Gao writing anything. As grandmother has memorized the poem, please recite it for me."[286]

"After failing the civil service entrance examination several times Du Gao was returning home, so Yu-*shi* wrote for the first time sending him back with these words:

---

285 'A Wife's Poem of Farewell' (Qi shi jianxing 妻詩餞行), *Classified Collection Based on Historical Facts and on Literature from the Past and Present.* "Emperor Zhenzong of the Song dynasty was offering a sacrificial rite at Mt. Tai and was looking for hermits throughout the nation and a person from Qi (杞) brought Yang Pu. He wrote poetry well but said that he couldn't write poetry for the emperor. When the emperor asked 'When you left home was there no one who wrote a poem (of farewell) for you?' Yang Pu said, 'My wife wrote one and gave it to me. 'Do not lose your mind and indulge in alcohol; do not recite poems just as you please. Today if you are arrested and taken to the government office, your old head will be cut off at once, and you will return.' The emperor laughed out loud, released him, and sent him back to the mountain." (眞宗東封, 訪天下隱者, 得杞人楊璞, 能爲詩, 召對自言不能. 上問, '臨行有人作詩送卿否?' 璞曰, '獨臣妻有詩一首云. 更休落魄貪盃酒, 亦莫猖狂愛詠詩, 今日捉將官裏去, 這回斷送老頭皮.' 上大笑, 放還山.)

286 'A Wife's Poem Encouraging Her Husband' (Qi shi mian fu 妻詩勉夫), *Classified Collection Based on Historical Facts and on Literature from the Past and Present.* At the time of the Tang dynasty the literatus Du Gao was on his way back home after repeatedly failing the civil examination when his wife sent him her first poem. Reading the poem Du Gao immediately turned around and finally passed the civil examination. The content of the poem is the same as that presented in the main text.

My husband clearly has outstanding talent; (良人的的有奇才)
Why is it that he returns year after year having failed the exam? (何事年年被放回)
I am now ashamed to see my husband's face; (如今妾面羞君面)
So if you come back please return in the night time. (君到來時近夜來)

When Du Gao read this poem, he immediately returned and took the civil exam. As he came high up on the list of successful candidates (K. *ch'ambang*, C. *canbang* 參榜), Yu-*shi* wrote another poem and sent it to him. The poem was as follows:

Chang'an is not far from here; (長安此去無多地)
A vigorous and auspicious aura arises. (鬱鬱蔥蔥佳氣浮)
My husband who has passed the exam is still young; (良人得意正年少)
So when he gets drunk on wine tonight, where will he sleep? (今夜醉眠何處樓)

"Since she wrote in this way, people of later generations have honored her saying, 'She was capable of encouraging (*kwŏnmyŏn* 勸勉) her husband along the right path.'"[287]

"I wondered if there were women who wrote poetry in the past."

"She was not the only woman who wrote poetry. There have been many."

Tu Ch'ŏnbok said, "I know that women in the old days also wrote compositions, so do not refuse now, and if you write one, I will reply to your poem using the same rhyme (K. *ch'aun*; C. *ciyun* 次韻)."

"As you are pleading in this way, how could I refuse? If you write one couplet first, I will write one couplet and keep going until we complete an eight-line poem (K. *yulsi*; C. *lüshi* 律詩)."

Tu Ch'ŏnbok finally picked up his writing brush and wrote one couplet, so Yuhandang wrote one couplet, then Tu Ch'ŏnbok wrote another couplet, and Yuhandang wrote another couplet and in this way an eight-line poem was created.

---

287 'A Wife's Poem Encouraging Her Husband', *Classified Collection Based on Historical Facts and on Literature from the Past and Present.* "It deserves to be said that she counseled her husband in the right way." (可謂能勉其君子以正矣.)

Tu Ch'ŏnbok recited the poem and said, "My wife, the verses you wrote, even though you have never practiced, are better than my poetic verses."

Laughing Yuhandang said, "Do not even discuss the merits and demerits of the poem; rather, it is laughable that that through your urging today, you made me go against my lifetime resolve not to write poetry."

As she said these words, Lady Wŏn came up with her grandchildren and great-grandchildren, so Tu Ch'ŏnbok and Yuhandang came down from the pavilion to greet her. One young lady spread out the paper on which the poem was written in front of Lady Wŏn, and explained about how it came to be written.

Lady Wŏn laughed out loud and said, "This is a wonderful way to welcome Hansik."

As she was saying this, a man came riding a horse along the road through the rice fields.

The young lady pointed and said, "The person is too far away so I can't see who it is, but this is what is called 'welcoming Hansik on horseback'."[288]

Lady Wŏn said, "Your words are very quick witted."

---

288 'En Route to Hanshi' (Tuzhong Hanshi 途中寒食), *Tangyin* (唐音). "As I welcomed Hanshi (K. Hansik) on horseback, on the way late spring arrived." (馬上逢寒食, 道中屬暮春.) This poem is by Song Zhiwen (宋之問).

As he got closer, they saw that he was the grandson of Yuhandang's daughter. He tied his horse to the root of an old pine tree outside the door and rushed up to the raised platform, greeted them in turn, and sat down. Then Lady Wŏn said, "This is a poem written by your maternal grandparents so take a look."

Then she gave him what had been written, and after the maternal grandchild had finished reading it, he asked Lady Wŏn, "How could great-grandmother not write a composition, too?"

"I came after the poem was written."

"If great-grandmother also wrote a poem, I could have poems written by my great-grandmother and grandmother that I could show my mother when I go back home, and she will be so happy. Please write one."

"As you are pleading so much, it would be good if you write the first line of the poem. I will write the next line and that will form the first couplet. If I then write one more line, and Yuhandang writes the next line, those lines will form the second couplet. If Yuhandang then writes one more line, and our granddaughter-in-law writes one line, together they will form the third couplet. And if our granddaughter-in-law writes one more line, and I write one more line, then that will complete an eight-line poem."

Yuhandang said, "It would be good if each of us uses a memorized phrase from ancient poems (*kosi* 古詩) and in this way form four phrases, then there will be no suspicion of us composing a new poem."

The maternal grandson wrote down the first memorized line, and Lady Wŏn said, "I will write a rhyme (K. *ch'aun*; C. *ciyun* 次韻) that matches the poem that my son and daughter-in-law wrote before, then I will read it out, and you can all respond to it."

Then they slowly recalled lines of ancient poems from memory and in turn tried to write them down. Then Lady Wŏn had her granddaughter-in-law read them out once and said, "There are few women in my family who cannot write poetry, and because the scenery of Wanshu Garden, Shuiyue Pavilion and Yangguan Terrace is renowned, there are no guests with literary ability who do not write some sentences. The women in our family say that writing poetry is not the role of women, and we have always admonished each other about this, so we never write poetry. Today is the first time we have written a poem."

The maternal grandchild said, "Would it be sinful for women to write compositions? Today this writing is indeed valuable in various ways. If we speak about heavenly times, the third lunar month of spring (*ch'unsamwol* 春三月) is when all forms of life are born. If we speak about geography, the scenery in front of Qiantang Lake (錢塘湖) is outstanding. If we speak about literary compositions, the most outstanding are poems written in response by using the same rhyme. Responding by using the same rhyme is one class of poetry, and if they are linked together (*yŏn'gu* 連句) that is another class. And since three generations of parents (*kobu* 姑婦) are gathered together to make a poem one after the other, it is a happy event and a rare occurrence in a long time. My mother was absent, but I came and participated in the first and last verses, so I am going to copy this poem and show it to my mother."

Then he copied it, put it in his sleeve, went back home, and showing it to his mother, told her the story. When she saw it, she said, "I left my parents like thoughts of the spring water flowing to the River Qi.[289] It is a daily occurrence for the elders to enjoy themselves at Wanshu Garden, but this is the first time they have gathered together to write. It is a pity that I could not participate in the event, but I will also write a verse in response using the same rhyme."

She picked up a writing brush and wrote a composition. Yuhandang's maternal grandson read it once and said, "As mother has also written in

---

289 See footnote 82.

this way, a scroll of verses (K. *sich'uk*; C. *shizhou* 詩軸) has now been created. This single scroll of verses is a rare thing in this world. Because our maternal grandparents' happiness and wealth in their old age is boundless, even though they engage in everyday enjoyments on the mountain behind their house, their male and female descendants all flourish. It is a rare thing in this world to be prosperous and wealthy, as a scholar writing compositions is something that comes from the efforts made in the family. But it is valuable to see the writing talents of men and women spanning three or four generations of a family all revealed in one scroll of poems. All the writings of the elders reveal a spirit of filial piety, fraternal duty and kindness (K. *hyo che in hu*; C. *xiao ti ren hou* 孝悌仁厚) and gentle virtue and rectitude (K. *yu hwa chŏng chŏng*, C. *rou he zhen zheng* 柔和貞正), so this cannot be viewed as just an ordinary scroll of poetry."

Do Not Pick Blossoms in the Spring

Yuhandang, together with her daughters-in-law and granddaughters, was sitting under a pine tree when Ch'ilbong came with blossoms he had picked.

"In spring the sunshine becomes warm, and all things have encountered this good time, but by just breaking off one of those branches, you are harming the life force (K. *saenggi*; C. *shengqi* 生氣) between heaven and earth (K. *ch'ŏnji*; C. *tiandi* 天地). From now on, do not pick them."

"I picked them because they looked so beautiful, but listening to your words, that is indeed true. For that reason, in the past when Emperor Renzong (仁宗)[290] of the Song dynasty broke off a willow branch, Master Cheng (程子) told him not to do that.[291] Mother's words are the same as those of Master Cheng."

"Not only the words of Master Cheng, but also in the *Book of Rites* it states, 'To fell a single tree, or kill a single animal, not at the proper season, is contrary to filial piety.'[292] So there is a proper time for cutting down a plant or killing an animal. For this reason, the sage kings (K. *sŏngwang*; C.

---

290 Renzong was the fourth emperor of Northern Song (1010–1063, r. 1022–1063).

291 'Remonstration Against Breaking Off a Willow Branch' (Jian zhe liuzhi 諫折柳枝), *Classified Collection Based on Historical Facts and on Literature from the Past and Present*. "One day when Cheng Yi (程頤) was the crown prince tutor (C. *shuoshu* 說書) in the Palace of the Supreme Government (Chongzhengdian 崇政殿), after having finished his lecture (C. *jinjiang* 進講), but when he still had not taken his leave, the emperor suddenly arose and leaning over the railings, lightheartedly broke off a willow branch. The master stepped forward and said, 'Now is the beginning of spring and the moment when the life force is growing; it is not right to break it off without reason.'" (程頤召充崇政殿說書, 一日講罷未退, 上忽起憑檻, 戲折柳枝. 先生進曰, '方春發生, 不可無故摧折.') This account also appears in *Collected Comments on Reflections on Things at Hand* (*Jinsi lu jizhu* 近思錄集註) and *Records of the Origins of the Yi Luo School of the Cheng Brothers* (*Yiluo yuanyuan lu* 伊洛淵源錄).

292 'The Meaning of Sacrifices' (Jiyi 祭儀), *Book of Rites*. "To fell a single tree, or kill a single animal, not at the proper season, is contrary to filial piety." (斷一樹, 殺一獸, 不以其時, 非孝也.)

shengwang 聖王) of old in the first lunar month forbade the breaking of the eggs of birds and the hunting of animals in the fields or fish because they valued life that was just coming into being.'"[293]

Hearing this one of the granddaughters said, "As the benevolent mind of the sage kings is clearly expressed in the laws they enacted, how could the way they governed their country not be admirable? If the ruler's governance is like this, how could ordinary people have the mental attitude to recklessly harm a single plant or tree or even a tiny insect."

And pointing to the bamboo thicket she said, "If you cut down those bamboo shoots to make wild vegetable side dishes, it is alright as long as you do it at the right time."

"Just as with bamboo shoots, it is the same for the shoots of trees."

Ch'ilbong asked, "There are two gingko trees in the garden. One produces fruit each year, and one does not produce fruit, so someone said, 'Trees are also male and female.'"

"That is true. Not only the gingko tree, but it is said that there are male and female hemp plants in the field and male and female bamboo trees in the garden.'"[294]

---

293 First Lunar Month, 'Yueling', *Book of Rites*. "Nor fawns (young animals); nor eggs (should be destroyed)." (毋麛, 毋卵.)

294 'Small Commentaries' (Xiaozhu 小註), *Added Comments to the Combined Cheng Yi's and Zhu Xi's Commentaries to the Book of Changes* (*Zhouyi zhuanyi fulu* 周易傳義附錄). "Also, as things such

"That is the first time I have heard these words. In which text are they to be found?"

"They are in the 'Small Commentaries' (Xiaozhu 小註) of the *Book of Changes* (*Yijing*)."

Questions and Answers with Her Son upon His Return from Qiantang Lake

One day Ilbong got together with several brothers and friends and went boating on Qiantang Lake, so Yuhandang had her eldest daughter-in-law prepare food and then had a servant take it to them in a small boat. Ilbong, his brothers and friends enjoyed themselves all day long, and when they returned after the moon had risen, Yuhandang asked Ilbong, "Who were your friends who you met up with today, and what are their writing skills like?"

---

as plants and trees are male and female, the same is true for gingko, paulownia, mulberry, hemp and bamboo." (又如草木之有雌雄, 銀杏桐楮, 牝牡麻竹之類, 皆然.)

"There were twenty friends who met together, and among them there were two who are engaged in scholarship and fifteen who write compositions. Two are master calligraphers (*myŏngp'il* 名筆) and one is good at painting pictures, so he painted the scenery, and then we came back."

Yuhandang looked at the painting and pointed out scenic spots with her hand, saying, "The bridge to the west of Yulian Hall (玉蓮堂)[295] is Liushui Bridge (溜水橋), to the east of Mt. Baoshi (寶石山)[296] is Zhiguo Temple (智果寺), and I think that spring's name is Canliao Spring (參寥泉). Zhiguo Temple was built during the Shaoxing reign (紹興, 1131–1162) in the Song dynasty,[297] Canliao Spring is the name of a spring that was given to it by Su Dongpo when he came to enjoy sightseeing with Canliaozi (參寥子)[298] from Hangzhou."[299]

---

295 Yulian Hall (Yuliantang 玉蓮堂) is a lodge (K. *pin'gwan*; C. *binguan* 賓館) on the lakeside when you come out of Qiantang Gate (錢塘門) at West Lake (Xihu 西湖).

296 Mt. Baoshi (Baoshishan 寶石山) is a small mountain located on the northern shore of West Lake.

297 *West Lake Sightseeing Gazetteer* (*Xihou youlan zhi* 西湖遊覽志) by Tian Rucheng (田汝成) of the Ming dynasty. "In the past Zhiguo Temple was located on Mt. Gu (孤山) and was built by the kings of Wu and Yue. It was moved to this place during the Shaoxing reign in the Song dynasty." (智果寺舊在孤山, 吳越王所建. 宋紹興間, 徙築於此.)

298 Canliaozi (參寥子) is the brush name of the Buddhist monk Dao Qian (道潛), a close friend of Su Dongpo.

299 *West Lake Sightseeing Gazetteer.* "Long ago when Su Dongpo was in Hangzhou, he became friends with the Buddhist monk Canliaozi from Zhiguo Temple, and he gave the name 'Canliao Spring' to the spring where he lived." (先是蘇子瞻守杭州, 與智果院禪師參寥子善, 名其所居泉曰, '參寥泉'.)

"These words are unknown to myself and my friends. Where are they from?"

"They are in *Record of Famous Mountains* (*Mingshan ji* 名山記)."[300]

"We tied up the boat at the edge of the spring. We drank the spring water, and as the water was very cold, we all debated about it saying, 'There are cold springs and hot springs, but it is strange that there are no 'cold fires (*naenghwa* 冷火) among fires.' But there was one person who said there is a 'cold fire', and also one person who said there is not, so we could not come to a conclusion."

"Saying there is such a thing is right, and saying there is not is also right."

Ilbong laughed out loud and said, "Both statements are right. How can that be?"

"According to the words of Shao Kangjie (邵康節), 'water has hot springs' (K. *su yu onch'ŏn*; C. *shui you wenquan* 水有溫泉) but 'fire does not have a cold flame' (K. *hwa mu hanyŏm*; C. *huo wu hanyan* 火無寒炎),[301] and these words are not

---

300 *Record of Famous Mountains* (*Mingshan ji* 名山記) appears to be a reference to *General Record of the Scenery of Famous Mountains* (*Mingshan shenggai ji* 名山勝槩記).

301 'Hot Springs, Cold Fires' (溫泉寒火), *Rustic Talks from the East of Qi* (*Qi dongye yu* 齊東野語). "Shao Kangjie says, 'In the world there are hot springs, but there are not cold fires.'" (邵康節曰, '世有溫泉而無寒火.') The same content can also be found in *Comprehensive Correct* [*Dictionary*] (*Tongya* 通雅) and *The Insignificant Collection* (*Baibian* 稗編).

wrong. Nevertheless, according to Lord Liu (劉公), 'there is a cold fire in the Xiaoqiu (蕭丘) region',[302] and these words are also not wrong."

"Everyone says that it is good to make many friends, but there are also those who say it is good to only make a few friends, so which is right?"

Yuhandang laughed and said, "Both opinions are correct."

Ilbong laughed and said, "What are you saying?"

"In the *Analects* it says, 'He should overflow in love to all (K. *pŏm ae chung*; C. *fan ai zhong* 汎愛衆) and cultivate the friendship of the good' (K. *yi ch'in in*; C. *er qin ren* 而親仁).[303] Overflowing in love to all means making many friends, but if you discriminate by cultivating the friendship of the good that is just making a few friends."

"I think it would be good to put both these sayings into practice together."

---

302 'Hot Spring, Cold Fire', *Rustic Talks from the East of Qi*. "In the chapter 'Conghua' (從化) in *Liuzi* (劉子) it says, 'The nature of spring water is to be cold, but in Huayang (華陽) there are hot springs. Nevertheless, we say that spring water is cold because there are many springs that are cold. The nature of fire is to be hot, but in Xiaoqiu (蕭丘) there is a cold fire. Nevertheless, we say that fire is hot because there are many fires that are hot." (劉子從化篇曰, '水性宜冷而有華陽温泉. 猶曰泉冷, 冷者多也. 火性宜熱而有蕭丘寒燄. 猶曰火熱, 熱者多也.')

303 'Xue'er', *Analects*. "Confucius said, 'A youth when at home should be filial, and, abroad, respectful to his elders. He should be earnest and truthful. He should overflow in love to all, and cultivate the friendship of the good. When he has time and opportunity, and after the employment of these things, he should employ them in polite studies.'" (子曰, '弟子, 入則孝, 出則悌, 謹而信, 汎愛衆而親仁. 行有餘力, 則以學文.')

"That is right. Because generally we discriminate when making friends, in the past Liu Anshi (劉安世) said, 'Better not to read literary works for one year than to be close to an inferior person even for a day.' Master Zhu praised these words, so succeeding generations have taken them as a model."[304]

Ch'ilbong said, "Mother keeps on saying that both sayings are correct. Today there was something that the majority of people weren't able to come to a conclusion about, so it could not be decided."

"If one is right, and one is wrong, why are you unable to distinguish between right and wrong?"

"The people who met today spoke about Tao Hongjing (陶弘景)[305] who resigned from his official post when he was young. One person said that the character for 'Hong' in his name was '*hong*' (弘) meaning 'broad', and another person said that it was the character '*hong*' (洪) meaning 'big'."

"Those two sayings are also both correct."

---

304 'Yu Chen Chengxiang Shu' (與陳丞相書), *Collected Works of Huian* (*Huian ji*). "Liu Anshi, whose brush name was Yuancheng and whose posthumous epithet was Zhongding, said to his children, 'I would rather not read for a whole year than get close to an inferior person even for a day.' These words are truly meaningful." (元城劉忠定公有言子弟, '寧可終歲不讀書, 而不可一日近小人.' 此言極有味.)

305 Tao Hongjing (陶弘景, 456–536) was a Chinese scholar from the Northern and Southern dynasties period. He resigned from his official post early and lived in seclusion on Mt. Juqu (句曲山).

Ch'ilbong laughed out loud and said, "I asked mother in order to come to a decision. If *hong* meaning 'big' is wrong then *hong* meaning 'broad' must be right, but if *hong* meaning 'broad' is wrong then *hong* meaning 'big' must be right—so how can both be correct?"

Yuhandang laughed and said, "It is not right to pretend one clearly knows the right and wrong of everything. There are grounds for both these opinions. We cannot just forcefully say that one is wrong. The character *hong* in Tao Hongjing's name is *hong* meaning 'big', but because in the Song dynasty, the character *hong* meaning 'big' was forbidden (*hwi* 諱),[306] from that time onwards the character was written in books as *hong* meaning 'broad'. Therefore, *hong* meaning 'big' was the original character in the name of the person, but the other one is how his name was written after it was revised, so neither of these opinions is wrong."

---

306 Emperor Taizu of Song Zhao Kuangyin's father was Zhao Hongyin (趙弘殷). Because of this, the use of the character *hong* meaning 'big' was forbidden (*hwi*) in people's given names.

The Reign Periods of Past Sovereigns

At the age of eight Yuhandang's second grandson Ch'ŏnsŏng read *Outlines and Details of the Comprehensive Mirror to Aid in Government* (*Zizhi tongjian gangmu* 資治通鑑綱目)[307] and asked, "All in all how many years has it been since Emperor Yao Taotang-*shi* (帝堯陶唐氏)[308] ascended the throne in the Kapchin Year (甲辰年, BC 2357) until this year the Sinyu Year (辛酉年, 1621)?"

"You are reading about it, so why don't you try and find out."

"*Outlines and Details* (*Gangmu* 綱目) has many volumes, and not only is it difficult to find, but because Yao, Shun, Xia, Shang and Zhou are not mentioned in *Outlines and Details*, grandmother please tell me."

"As this is different from passages in the usual classics, please find out about this from your grandfather."

---

307 *Outlines and Details of the Comprehensive Mirror to Aid in Government* (*Zizhi tongjian gangmu* 資治通鑑綱目): Zhu Xi compiled this history book based on the *Comprehensive Mirror for Aid in Government* (*Zizhi Tongjian* 資治通鑑) by Sima Guang of the Song dynasty, and following the model of the *Spring and Autumn Annals* (*Chunqiu* 春秋), he divided it into 'outlines' (*gang* 綱) and 'details' (*mu* 目).

308 Emperor Yao Taotang-*shi* (帝堯陶唐氏): Emperor Yao. Yao's family name was Yiqi (伊祁), his given name was Fangxun (放勛), and his brush name was Taotang-*shi* (陶唐氏).

Ch'ŏnsŏng went out straight away and asked his grandfather, and his grandfather replied, "Your grandmother knows, but without telling you, she is always telling me to tell you, so please go back inside and study."

Ch'ŏnsŏng went back inside and told his grandmother what had happened and asked her to teach him, so Yuhandang laughed and said, "Very well then I will tell you. The length of Emperor Yao's reign was 100 years, and as the length of Emperor Shun's reign was 50 years that is a total of 150 years. The seventeen generations of the rulers of the Xia dynasty lasted for 441 years, and the twenty-eight generations of the rulers of the Shang dynasty lasted for 644 years. Concerning Zhou, the twenty generations of the rulers of Western Zhou (Xizhou 西周) lasted for 350 years, and the twenty-six generations of the rulers of Eastern Zhou (Dongzhou 東周) lasted for 520 years, and as the thirty-eight generations of the rulers of Western and Eastern Zhou together lasted for 870 years, are not the accumulated meritorious deeds and benevolence (K. *chŏkdŏk nuin*, C. *jide leiren* 積德累仁) of King Wen, Tairen and Taisi sacred?

The two generations of rulers of Qin (秦) lasted for 30 years,[309] so it was because of the First Emperor of Qin's violence and cruelty that it

309 In the original Han'gŭl text and in the Nason version, 'thirty' is written as "스십" (forty), which appears to be a scribal error for "슴십" (thirty). In fact, the reign of the First Emperor of Qin (秦始皇) lasted twenty-six years, and his successor's reign lasted only three years.

collapsed that quickly. Concerning the Han dynasty, Western Han (Xihan 西漢) lasted for twelve generations, so altogether the reign period lasted for 240 years, Eastern Han (Donghan 東漢) lasted for ten generations so altogether the reign period lasted for 196 years, Shuhan (蜀漢) lasted for two generations and altogether the reign period lasted for 43 years. Between the two periods of Western Han and Eastern Han, Wang Mang (王莽) usurped the throne, so altogether, Western Han, Eastern Han and Shu Han lasted twenty-six generations, and in total the reign period lasted 469 years.[310]

The Jin (晉) dynasty founded by Shima-*shi* (司馬氏) lasted four generations and altogether the reign period lasted 52 years, as Eastern Jin (Dongjin 東晉) lasted eleven generations and altogether the reign period lasted 104 years, so the two Jin dynasties together lasted fifteen generations and altogether the reign period lasted 156 years. The eight generations of Liusong (劉宋)[311] altogether lasted 60 years, and the reign period of the seven kings of Qi (齊) altogether lasted 24 years. The reign period of the four kings of Liang (梁) lasted 56 years, and the five kings of Chen (陳) altogether lasted 30 years.

---

310 If the numbers of years in the main text are added together, they actually come to 479 years, but the number is 469 because the 10-year reign of the usurper Wang Mang has been excluded from the calculation.

311 The Liusong (劉宋) dynasty was founded by the Eastern Jin (東晉) general Liu Yu (劉裕, 363–422) and is referred to as Liusong in order to distinguish it from the later Song dynasty.

The reign period of the three kings of Sui (隋) lasted 38 years, and altogether the reign period of the 20 generations of Tang (唐) lasted 290 years. The reigns of the two kings of Later Liang (Houliang 後梁) together lasted 17 years, and the four kings of Later Tang (Houtang 後唐) together lasted 14 years. The reigns of the two kings of Later Jin (Houjin 後晉) together lasted 11 years; the reigns of the two kings of Later Han (Houhan 後漢) lasted 4 years, and the three generations of Later Zhou (Houzhou 後周) altogether lasted 10 years.

The reign period of the nine generations of Song (宋) altogether lasted 168 years, and the reign period of the nine emperors of Southern Song (Nansong 南宋) altogether lasted 153 years, so together the reign period of the eighteen generations of the rulers of the two Song dynasties lasted 320 years. The reign period of the ten emperors beginning with Shizu (元世祖) Hubilie (忽必烈) of the Yuan dynasty altogether lasted 90 years.

Emperor Taizu of the Ming dynasty rectified all under heaven in the Musin Year (C. Wushen nian 戊申年, 1368). Taizu reigned for 31 years; Huizong (惠宗) reigned for 4 years; Chengzu (成祖) reigned for 22 years; and Renzong (仁宗) reigned for 1 year. Xuanzong (宣宗) reigned for 10 years; Yingzong (英宗) reigned for 22 years; Daizong (代宗) reigned for 7 years; Xianzong (憲宗) reigned for 18 years; Wuzong (武宗) reigned 16 years; Shizong (世宗) reigned for 45 years; Muzong (穆宗) reigned for 6 years; and so the 230 generations from when Emperor Yao ascended the throne in the Kapchin Year (C. Jiachen nian 甲辰年) until our current emperor ascended the throne in the Kyeyu Year (C. Guiyou nian 癸酉年, 1573) have lasted 3,930 years. This is the number you get if you add up all the numbers of years of the past generations of rulers' reign periods."

Just as Ch'ŏnsŏng picked up his writing brush to write this down in a book, Tu Ch'ŏnbok came in, and seeing this, asked Yuhandang, "As you already worked this out, why didn't you tell the child from the start but instead sent him to me?"

"I did not tell him because a woman affecting to know the history of the past generations of rulers cannot speak about them concisely. Now the children have grown up, I am reluctant to answer their questions. After telling them the words recorded in the classics, my explanations naturally get longer, and the studies that all my life I have intended to keep simple, instead become very longwinded. As I was worried about this, I sent him to you."

"Even though one's words are appropriate, can they not be harmful to studying if there are too many of them?"

"As the saying goes, 'Even if 10,000 words are correct 10,000 times' (K. *man ŏn man tang* 萬言萬當) 'they are not equal to keeping silent once' (K. *pul yŏ il muk* 不如一默), so what is better than to be sparing with words?"

"When Mencius' mother moved three times for the sake of her son's education (K. *sam ch'ŏn chi kyo* 三遷之敎), how could she have taught him if she had only moved once?" Tu Ch'ŏnbok asked and laughed out loud.

Ch'ŏnsŏng recorded everything and showed it to his father and his various uncles, so they examined everything and said not only must it have been difficult for their mother to have read so many books, but from what she had read when she was young, there was not a single mistaken Chinese character in all that she had said and that it was truly fortunate that her intelligence had not diminished.

How to Engage in Astronomy

When Yuhandang's third grandson Unsŏng was eleven years old, he asked Yuhandang, "Last night, around sunset, my sixth uncle and youngest uncle climbed up to Yangguan Terrace, looked at the stars, discussed their positions, and said to each other, 'Looking at the stars, 'Hibernators stir' (K. Kyŏngch'ip; C.

Jingzhe 驚蟄)[312] will be the day after tomorrow.' I asked if I could learn, too, but my youngest uncle told me to learn by looking at a specialist book (K. *pangsŏ*; C. *fangshu* 方書), and he did not teach me. Grandmother as you know, please teach me."

"It is difficult to predict the auspiciousness or inauspiciousness of the future by using astronomy and looking at the energy or the light of the stars, but the regular passage of the sun according to the 'junctures' (*chŏlgi*) is precise, so it is not difficult to understand. As now is the day called 'Hibernators stir', in the second lunar month at the earliest, the sun is in the 10th degree of the Wi (Rooftop) Constellation (K. Wisu; C. Weixiu 危宿) among the Twenty-Eight Constellations (K. *su*; C. *xiu* 宿); on the day 'Clear and bright' (K. Ch'ŏngmyŏng; C. Qingming 淸明), the sun is in the 8th degree of the Pyŏk (Wall) Constellation (K. Pyŏksu; C. Bixiu 壁宿). The 'Beginning of Summer' (K. Ipha; C. Lixia 立夏) is the first day of the fourth lunar month and is at the beginning of the Wi (Stomach) Constellation (K. Wisu; C. Weixiu 胃宿); 'Grain in ear' (K. Mangjong; C. Mangzhong 芒種) is in the fifth lunar month and is in the 8th degree

312 'Hibernators stir' (K. Kyŏngch'ip; C. Jingzhe 驚蟄) is the third of the twenty-four 'junctures'. According to the solar calendar, this day occurs around the beginning of March, when the angle (*hwanggyŏng* 黃經) of the sun is 345°. In the Shixian calendar (時憲曆), the day the *hwanggyŏng* is 0° is the Spring Equinox (Ch'unbun), and each time it moves 15°, the 'junctures' change one by one, until the day when the *hwanggyŏng* is 270°, which is the Winter Solstice.

of the P'il (Net) Constellation (K. P'ilsu; C. Bixiu 畢宿); 'Little heat' (K. Sosŏ; C. Xiaoshu 小暑) is on the first day of the sixth lunar month and is in the 10th degree of the Chŏng (Well) Constellation (K. Chŏngsu; C. Jingxiu 井宿).''[313]

Unsŏng said, "If you do not tell me what comes after the seventh lunar month, I will work it out."

And so counting on his fingers, he worked everything out saying, "'Beginning of Autumn' (K. Ipch'u; C. Liqiu 立秋) is in the 7th degree of the Yu (Willow) Constellation (K. Yusu; C. Liuxiu 柳宿); 'White dew' (K. Paengno; C. Bailu 白露) is the first day of the eighth lunar month and is in the 11th degree of the Chang (Extended Net) Constellation (K. Changsu; C. Zhangxiu 張宿); 'Cold dew' (K. Hallo; C. Hanlu 寒露) is the first day of the ninth lunar month and is in the 6th degree of the Chin (Square) Constellation (K. Chinsu; C. Zhenxiu 軫宿); 'Beginning of Winter' (K. Iptong; C. Lidong 立冬) is the first day of the tenth lunar month

---

313 The Twenty-Eight Constellations (K. *su*; C. *xiu* 宿) are the division of the stars in the sky into twenty-eight sectors: the seven northern constellations are Dipper (K. Tu; C. Dou 斗), Ox (K. U; C. Niu 牛), Girl (K. Yŏ; C. Nü 女), Emptiness (K. Hŏ; C. Xu 虛), Rooftop (K. Wi; C. Wei 危), Encampment (K. Sil; C. Shi 室) and Wall (K. Pyŏk; C. Bi 壁). The seven western constellations are Legs (K. Kyu; C. Kui 奎), Bond (K. Nu; C. Lou 婁), Stomach (K. Wi; C. Wei 胃), Hairy Head (K. Myo; C. Mao 昴), Net (K. P'il; C. Bi 畢), Turtle Beak (K. Cha; C. Zi 觜), Three Stars (K. Sam; C. Shen 參). The seven southern constellations are Well (K. Chŏng; C. Jing 井), Ghost (K. Kwi; C. Gui 鬼), Willow (K. Yu; C. Liu 柳), Star (K. Sŏng; C. Xing 星), Extended Net (K. Chang; C. Zhang 張), Wings (K. Ik; C. Yi 翼) and Chariot (K. Chin; C. Zhen 軫). The seven eastern constellations are Horn (K. Kak; C. Jiao 角), Neck (K. Hang; C. Kang 亢), Root (K. Chŏ; C. Di 氐), Room (K. Pang; C. Fang 房), Heart (K. Sim; C. Xin 心), Tail (K. Mi; C. Wei 尾), and Winnowing Basket (K. Ki; C. Ji 箕). The size of each sector occupied by each constellation is different. In the text the twenty-four junctures and the positions of the sun are mentioned in order.

and is in the 2nd degree of the Chŏ (Root) Constellation (K. Chŏsu; C. Dixiu 氐宿); 'Great snow' (K. Taesŏl; C. Daxue 大雪) is the first day of the eleventh lunar month and is in the 2nd degree of the Mi (Tail) Constellation (K. Misu; C. Weixiu 尾宿); 'Little cold' (K. Sohan; C. Xiaohan 小寒) is in the twelfth lunar month, and it is in the 5th degree of the Yŏ (Girl) Constellation (K. Yŏsu; C. Nüxiu 女宿), isn't that so?"

"You also know how to work out the 'degree numbers' well. That is indeed correct."

Unsŏng was extremely happy and went outside to his various uncles to proudly let them know saying, "After working it out with my hands, I realized all the degree numbers of the movement of the sun."

"In that case tell us in detail."

Unsŏng worked out the twelve months and told them, so his uncle said, "Among the stars there is a star called Kusŏng (C. Jiuxing 臼星)[314] that is shaped like a mortar, which is why it is called *ku* (mortar) *sŏng* (star). Also,

---

314 Kusŏng (C. Jiuxing 臼星) is a star in the seventh northern constellation, the Wi Constellation (C. Weixiu 危宿). *Astronomical Categories* (*Tianwen leichao* 天文類抄). "The Jiuxing star is the star that rules over pounding (grain) in a mortar. If it is upside down, there will be a great famine; if it is the right way up there will be a bountiful harvest. If the star is not bright the people will starve; if the stars gather together it will be a carefree year; if they are scattered or agitated there will be a famine. If there is a supernova (K. *kaeksŏng*; C. *kexing* 客星), or if a comet enters, there will be armed uprisings, and the whole nation will be swept by war." (主舂. 覆則大饑, 仰則大豐. 不明民飢, 星衆歲樂, 疎或動饑. 客彗入杵臼, 兵起, 天下聚米.)

there is a star called P'aegusŏng (C. Baijiuxing 敗臼星: 'failed mortar star')[315] that is also shaped like a mortar, so why don't you go and ask (Yuhandang) why it is called P'aegusŏng?"

Unsŏng went back and asked, so Yuhandang laughed and said, "Kusŏng is in the shape of an upright mortar and above it there is a star like a pestle Chŏsŏng (C. Chuxing 杵星),[316] so it is naturally called Kusŏng ('mortar star'). As the star called P'aegusŏng does not have a Chŏsŏng ('pestle star'), it is a mortar that cannot be used, so naturally is called P'aegusŏng ('failed mortar star'), so how could there be any question about that?"

Unsŏng went out and told his uncle, so Ch'ilbong laughed out loud and said, "Last night we saw the two stars and wondered about their different

---

315 P'aegusŏng (C. Baijiuxing 敗臼星: 'failed mortar star') is a star in the seventh northern constellation, the Hŏ Constellation (K. Hŏsu; C. Xuxiu 虛宿). *Astronomical Categories*. "The Baijiuxing star governs destruction and disaster. If a single star is not visible the people will be made to sell their earthenware steamers and iron pots; if no stars are visible, the people will have to leave their hometowns. If Mercury (Susŏng), Jupiter (Moksŏng), Venus (Kŭmsŏng) or Mars (Hwasŏng) enter, old things will be discarded and new things will spread. If there is a supernova or if a comet enters, the people will starve and become vagabonds, and there will be armed uprisings." (主敗亡災害. 一星不具, 民賣甑釜, 不見, 民去其鄉. 五星入, 除舊布新, 客彗犯之, 民飢流亡, 兵起.)

316 Chŏsŏng (C. Chuxing 杵星: 'pestle star') is a star in the seventh northern constellation, the Wi Constellation (K. Wisu; C. Weixiu 危宿) and forms a constellation together with the Kusŏng (C. Jiuxing 臼星: 'mortar star'). It is located above the 'mortar star' like a pestle. *Astronomical Categories* (*Tianwen leichao* 天文類抄). "The Jiuxing star governs the pounding of (grain) in mortars and military supplies. If Chuxing is pointing directly at Jiuxing below it, this is auspicious, but if it is not pointing directly at it, grain will be in short supply. If Chuxing is not upright the people will starve; if the constellation is not properly formed, the people will have to sell their earthenware steamers and iron pots." (主舂軍糧. 正直下臼吉, 不相當糧絶. 不直民飢, 不具民賣甑釜.)

names, which is why I said that to you. Hearing mother's words, not only do you know, but now I know, too!"

A Family Gathering at Shuiyue Pavilion

One day, Minister Tu took all his sons and grandsons up to Shuiyue Pavilion where they viewed the flowers, and he had them write poems. And after enjoying themselves, he sent his grandson Ch'ilbong to tell his wife to come together with their daughters-in-law, daughters their grandsons' wives and granddaughters. Lady Wŏn went together with her three daughters-in-law, thirteen daughters, her grandsons' wives, various granddaughters and young great-grandchildren. The flowers were blooming in the garden; the cranes were gamboling in pairs; beyond the balustrade Qiantang Lake spread around about; and the sounds of boating songs could be heard from here and there.

Minister Tu emptied his wine cup and said to his wife, "In the old days countless poets and men of letters (K. *mukkaek*; C. *moke* 墨客) would go with their friends up to raised pavilions by rivers and lakes (K. *kangho*; C. *jianghu* 江湖),

but I have only seldom heard of the men and women, old and young of three or four generations of one family all enjoying themselves together. The kind of enjoyment our household is having today is not an easy attainment for human beings."

"Our eldest daughter-in-law Yuhandang has read many ancient books, so what family in the past accomplished this kind of thing?"

Yuhandang said, "In 'Preface to a Spring Night Banquet in the Peach and Plum Garden'[317] by Li Bai (李白), he mentions the pleasure (K. *naksa*; C. *leshi* 樂事) of family bonds (K. *chŏllyun*; C. *tianlun* 天倫), but he only met up with his brothers. Master Zhu wrote in a letter he sent to a friend, 'the entire family touring the mountains; what a marvelous thing that is!'[318] That friend had gone on a pleasure trip with all his family to the mountains. How could he have known about the hardships of traveling over mountains and rivers with little children, too? Our family's enjoyment today does not have any of the tiring effects of travelling. The outstanding scenery of Qiantang Lake is

---

317 'Preface to a Spring Night Banquet in the Peach and Plum Garden' (Chunye yan taoli yuan xu 春夜宴桃李園序). "Gathering in a garden where peach and plum blossoms are blooming, brothers enjoy relaxing within the family circle. The younger brothers are all as wonderful as Xie Huilian (謝惠連). We compose poems and recite them. I alone am ashamed to fall short of Xie Lingyun (謝靈運)." (會桃李之芳園, 序天倫之樂事. 羣季俊秀, 皆爲惠連, 吾人詠歌, 獨慚康樂.) A work by the Tang dynasty poet Li Bai (李白, 701–762), it is also included in *Treasury of Ancient Writings* (*Guwen zhenbao* 古文眞寶).

318 'Letter Answering Liu Dexiu' (答劉德修), *Collected Works of Huian Zhu Xi* (*Huian ji*). "A whole family touring the mountains is truly an extraordinary thing." (盡室遊山, 大是一段奇事.)

stretched out below the balustrade. Regardless of the seasons, the men and women, old and young of one household have never departed from this place. Indeed, it is the most enjoyable thing between heaven and earth, and it cannot be compared to cases in the past."

Minister Tu said, "Our family's previous generations (*sŏndae* 先代) have accumulated a lot of virtue, so the glory and splendor of our family is very great, and their descendants are prospering in this way. Indeed, when the superiors and subordinates of the same family, adults and children alike, go in and out with a fearful heart, are very cautious in their conduct, and are especially frugal in their clothing and food, it is only right for us to pour cups of wine and pledge to each other never to discard the dying injunctions (*yuhun* 遺訓) of our ancestors."

Yuhandang said, "Indeed, today's words of caution are better than 'the warning against satiety' (*sŏng man chi kye* 盛滿之戒),[319] so who among their descendants will not obey this command?"

The eldest grandson Ilbong came before Minister Tu with a wine cup, while his wife (*chongsonbu* 宗孫婦) came before Lady Wŏn with a wine cup.

---

319 In 'Excellent conduct' (Shanzai xing 善哉行) by Cao Cao (曹操) in the Three Kingdoms era it states, "If one can maintain things at fullness without superfluity, a person with virtue can bring things to a good result." (持滿如不盈, 有德者能卒.)

They poured cups of wine in turn, and after even the children had drunk, Minister Tu said, "How many cups of wine have we drunk?"

His grandson's wife replied, "Today, we have drunk about fifty cups."

Minister Tu told them to bring *Reflections on Things at Hand* (*Jinsi lu* 近思錄)[320] and *Biographies of Women.*[321] He had his grandsons each read a passage from *Reflection on Things at Hand*, and then had his daughters-in-law and granddaughters-in-law each read a passage from *Biographies of Women* in front of Lady Wŏn.

Yuhandang said, "We intend to study by looking at these texts, but if we put our minds to learning, it will be beneficial to our conduct if we understand even the insects and plants in front of us, even though they are not texts."

Lady Wŏn said, "Indeed that is so. Zhou Lianxi (周濂溪) said about those lotuses in that pond, 'The lotus is a superior person among flowers',[322] so

---

320 *Reflections on Things at Hand* (*Jinsi lu* 近思錄) is a book compiled and edited by the Song dynasty scholars Zhu Xi and Lü Zuqian from material selected from the most important parts of the writings of Zhou Dunyi, Cheng Hao, Cheng Yi and Zhang Zai and is a core text of Neo-Confucianism (Sŏngnihak).

321 *Biographies of Women* is a collection of anecdotes about women compiled by Liu Xiang (劉向), a scholar of the Western Han dynasty, that were intended to be an example and an admonition for women.

322 'On Love of the Lotus' (Ailian shuo 愛蓮說). "I think that the chrysanthemum is the hermit among flowers, the peony is the wealthy and honored one among flowers, and the lotus is the superior person among flowers." (予謂, 菊, 花之隱逸者也; 牡丹, 花之富貴者也; 蓮, 花之君子者也.) 'On Love of the Lotus' (Ailian shuo 愛蓮說) is found in such works as Zhou Lianxi's

indeed we think of the 'studies of a superior person' (*kunja chi hak* 君子之學); the crows in that wood supporting their parents in their old age (*panp'o* 反哺) were called 'Zeng Shen among birds'[323] in a poem by Bai Letian, so we think of the 'way of filial children' (*hyoja chi to* 孝子之道); if we look at the mother ox licking her calf in the field, we will be able to think about 'feelings of love for children' (*chaae chi chŏng* 慈愛之情); if we look at Echinacea flowers (*chahyŏnghwa* 紫荊花)[324] and tree branches that grow together as one (*yŏlliji* 連理枝),[325] we will be able to think about the relationship between brothers (*hyŏngje chi ryun* 兄弟之倫). If we look at the ants under the rocks, we will think of the righteousness between a ruler and his ministers, so what cannot become a subject of academic study?"

Yuhandang said, "Shao Kangjie said, 'You can make a chapter of the *Book of Changes* with everything in front of you.'[326] Even the grass, trees,

---

collected works, *Zhou Yuangong ji* (周元公集) and *Treasury of Ancient Writings*.

323 'Compassionate Crows Crowing at Night' (*Ciwu ye ti* 慈烏夜啼), "O filially pious crows, O filially pious crows, you are the Zeng Shen among birds." (慈烏復慈烏, 鳥中之曾參.) Baby crows later bring food in their beaks for their elderly mother crow. It became known as a filially pious bird and became a byword for the filial piety of supporting parents in their old age (*panp'o chi hyo*; C. *fanbu zhi xiao* 反哺之孝). This poem is included in such works as *Baixiangshan shiji* (白香山詩集), the collected poems of the Tang dynasty literatus Bai Juyi (白居易), and *Treasury of Ancient Writings*. Letian (樂天) is Bai Juyi's brush name.

324 The flowers of the Echinacea (*Cercis chinensis*) bloom profusely on one branch, so it is considered to be a symbol for harmonious brothers.

325 *Yŏlliji* (連理枝)' refers to tree trunks with separate roots that merge together and grow as a single tree.

326 Source unknown.

birds of the air and beasts of the field in front of this pavilion right now are sufficient to be understood as the 'teaching of the five relationships' (*oryun chi kyo* 五倫之敎)."

A Family Tradition of Frugality

One day Wŏnsŏng's sixth younger brother's wife Lady Chu came on the day for greeting the parents-in-law of one's offspring (K. *ch'inyŏng il*; C. *qingying ri* 親迎日). After the banquet was over Lady Chu said to Yuhandang, "More than 100 women relatives, who came as guests today, gathered in lavish and luxurious clothes with beads, jade, and silk. However, close to a hundred women from Lord Minister Tu's family wore upper and lower garments made from cotton fabrics; not one among them wore clothes made from patterned silk, so I admire the frugal and unsophisticated family tradition of Lord Minister Tu. Furthermore, even though the young women who were wearing cotton garments were sitting among others who were wearing clothes of silk adorned with beads and jade, they did not show the slightest sense of embarrassment, so I can see that they have been extremely well educated."

Yuhandang laughed and said, "When the young women first entered my household, although there were some occasions when they felt that kind of embarrassment, over the years they have become much better."

"According to the words of a person of old, Even among the disciples of Confucius, it is said that only Zilu (子路) was not ashamed to be dressed in ragged clothes while standing next to someone in a coat of white fox fur (*hobaekku* 狐白裘), so it is not to be wondered at that young women might feel that way.[327] On the contrary, isn't the fact that they soon improved after a few years of living in one household a reformation? In an ancient text it states, 'If one family is benevolent, one nation's benevolence will flourish',[328] so I would like to make the family tradition of Lord Minister Tu's family the custom of the whole world."

---

327 'Zihan' (子罕), *Analects*. "Confucius said, 'Dressed himself in a tattered robe quilted with hemp, yet standing by the side of men dressed in furs, and not ashamed—ah! It is You (Zilu) who is equal to this!'" (子曰, '衣敝縕袍, 與衣狐貉者立, 而不恥者, 其由也與.')

328 *Great Learning*. "If one family is benevolent, benevolent customs will arise in that country; if one family puts others first, the custom of putting others first will arise in that country; if one person is covetous and vicious, the country will be in turmoil, and its foundations will be like this." (一家仁, 一國興仁, 一家讓, 一國興讓, 一人貪戾, 一國作亂, 其機如此.)

Sage Rulers and Sages

Yuhandang's eldest granddaughter asked, "The great men of letters call Yao, Shun, Yu, Tang, King Wen and King Wu sage rulers, and Confucius, Yanzi, Zengzi, Zisi, Mencius and the various wise men of the *Lianluo* (濂洛) are all called sages. But I do not know their full names and the years of their birth and death. Even though it might be said that as a woman I do not need to know such things, I feel ashamed to know so little and would like to study from grandmother today."

"As a woman, why should you know such things? Nevertheless, to know so little is to be extremely behind the times, so I will give you my rough outline.

The family name of Emperor Yao Taotang-*shi* (帝堯陶唐氏) is Qi (祁); his given name is Fangxun (放勛), and he is the son of Emperor Ku Gaoxin-*shi* (帝嚳高辛氏). His mother is the daughter of Chenfeng-*shi* (陳鋒氏), who gave birth to him fourteen months after conception, which was the Chŏnghae Year (C. Dinghai nian 丁亥年) in the 63rd year of Gaoxin-*shi's* reign. Emperor Yao reigned for 100 years, and died at the age of 117.[329]

---

329 Emperor Yao's family name was Yiqi (伊祁). His given name was Fangxun (放勛), and his brush name was Taotang-*shi* (陶唐氏). 'Annals of the Five Emperors' (Wudi benji 五帝本

The family name of Emperor Shun Youyu-*shi* is Yao (姚); his given name is Zhonghua (重華); his father is Gusou (瞽瞍) and his mother is Wodeng (握登). She saw a rainbow and moved by this gave birth to Shun. This occurred in the 41st year of the reign of Emperor Yao, a Kapsin Year. Succeeding to the throne after Emperor Yao, the first year of his reign was the Kapsin Year (C. Jiashen nian 甲申年). He reigned for fifty years and died at the age of 110.[330]

The family name of Xia Yu-*shi* (夏禹氏)[331] is Si (姒), and his given name is Wenming (文明). He is the son of Gun (鯀) and his mother is Xiuji (修己). She saw a star and was moved, and she gave birth to Yu on the 6th day of the sixth lunar month of the 55th year of Emperor Yao's reign, a Musul Year (C. Wuxu nian 戊戌年). He succeeded to the throne after Shun in the Kapsul Year (C. Jiaxu nian 甲戌年), reigned for ten years and died at the age of 106.

紀), *Records of the Grand Historian*. "Emperor Yao Taotang-*shi's* family name is Qi (祁). His mother Qingdu (慶都) was pregnant for fourteen months and then gave birth to Yao." (帝堯陶唐氏祁姓也. 母慶都十四月生堯.) *Imperially Approved Annual Tables of Historical Events* (*Yuding lidai jishi nianbiao* 御定歷代紀事年表). "She married Gaoxin-*shi*, and fourteen months after she conceived, she gave birth to Yao in Danling in the Dinghai Year." (孕十四月於高辛氏, 丁亥歲生堯於丹陵.)

330 Emperor Shun's family name is Yao (姚) and his given name is Zhonghua (重華). 'Gan shuxing sheng' (感樞星生), *Collection of Matters from the Past and Present*. "Wodeng, seeing a rainbow, responded in her heart and gave birth to Shun." (握登見虹意感而生舜.)

331 Xia Yu-*shi* (夏禹氏) is the name of Emperor Yu of Xia. 'Swallowing a Pearl and Becoming Pregnant with Yu' (Tun zhu yun Yu 呑珠孕禹), *Extended Investigations of the Mountain Hall* (*Shantang sikao* 山堂肆考). "Xiuji went to the mountain and observing a meteor piercing the Pleiades, she also swallowed a divine pearl and responded by giving birth to Yu at Mt. Shiniu." (修己山行, 見流星貫昴, 又呑神珠, 意感而生禹于石紐.)

The family name of King Tang of Yin (殷王成湯)[332] is Zi (子), and his given name is Lü (履). His mother is Fudu (扶都), who saw a white aura around the moon and was moved and gave birth to Tang. This occurred in the Musin Year (C. Wuchen nian 戊辰年), the 27th year of the reign of Kongjia (孔甲)[333] of Xia. Jie (桀) was cruel, so the princes elevated Tang (湯) and made him ascend the throne. The founding year of his reign (*wŏnnyŏn* 元年) was the Ŭlmi Year. He reigned for three years and died at the age of 100.

The family name of King Wen (文王) of Zhou is Ji (姬). His given name is Chang (昌), and he was the sixteenth generation descendant of Houji (后稷).[334] His mother was Tairen, and he was born in the Imin Year (C. Renyin nian 壬寅年) in the first year of the reign of Gengding (庚丁),[335] the King of Yin (殷). He was invested with the rank of Count of the West (Xibo 西伯) and died in the Muin Year at the age of ninety-seven.

King Wu (武王) was the son of King Wen, and his given name was Fa (發). King Wen took Taisi to wife and gave birth to King Wu. She gave birth

---

332 King Tang of Yin (殷王成湯): 'A White Energy Pierces the Moon' (Baiqi guan yue 白氣貫月), *Collection of Matters from the Past and Present*. "Tang's mother Fudu saw a white energy piercing the moon, and responding to this, she gave birth to Tang." (湯母扶都, 見白氣貫月, 意感而生湯.)

333 Kong Jia (孔甲) was the fourteenth ruler of Xia.

334 Houji (后稷) was the founder of the Zhou dynasty, and because he was skilled in farming, he was given the posthumous title, 'Lord of Millet' (Houji 后稷).

335 Gengding (庚丁) was the 27th ruler of Yin.

to King Wu in the Kyech'uk Year in the twelfth year of the reign of King Gengding of Yin. When King Wen died (K. *hung*, C. *hong* 薨), he succeeded him as Count of the West. As King Zhou (紂) of Yin was tyrannical (*mudo* 無道), King Wu gathered all the dukes and defeated him, so all the dukes elevated King Wu and revered him as the 'Son of Heaven'. The first year of his reign was the Kimyo Year. He reigned for seven years and died at the age of ninety-three. These six kings were the sage kings of antiquity. Their royal virtues and historical deeds (*sajŏk* 史蹟) are recorded in the Classics and history books.

Confucius' family name is Qiu (丘), and his courtesy name is Zhongni (仲尼). His father is Shuliang He[336] from Lu, and his mother is Zhengzai (徵在). As Shuliang He was very old, she prayed at Mt. Niqiu and gave birth to a son Boni (伯尼). Then she prayed again and gave birth to Zhongni. Confucius was born in the Kyŏngsul Year (C. Gengxu nian 庚戌年, BC 551), the 21st year of the reign of King Ling of Zhou (周靈王) and died in the Imsul Year (C. Renxu nian 壬戌年, BC 479), the 41st year of the reign of King Jing (敬王) of Zhou at the age of seventy-three.

---

336 Shuliang He, the father of Confucius, was from the state of Lu (魯) and lived during the Spring and Autumn period.

The given name of Yanzi (顏子) is Hui (回), and his courtesy name is Ziyuan (子淵). His father is Yan Wuyou (顏無繇) from Lu and his mother is Jiang-*shi* (姜氏). He was born in the Muja Year (C. Wuzi nian 戊子年, BC 513), the seventh year of the reign of King Jing of Zhou, and he died in the Kimi Year (C. Jiwei nian 己未年, BC 482), the 38th year of King Jing's reign, at the age of thirty-two.

The given name of Zengzi (曾子) is Shen (參), and his father was Zeng Dian (曾點) of Lu. His mother's name has not been handed down to posterity. Zengzi was born in the Pyŏngsin Year (C. Bingshen nian 丙申年, BC 505) in the 15th year of the reign of King Jing of Zhou, and he died in the Ŭlsa Year (C. Yisi nian 乙巳年, BC 436) in the fifth year of King Kao (考王) of Zhou at the age of seventy.

The given name of Zisi (子思)[337] is Ji (伋); he was the grandson of Confucius and the son of Boyu (伯魚). The year of his birth has not been handed down to posterity, He died in the Chŏngch'uk Year (C. Dingchou nian 丁丑年), the 22nd year of King Weilie (威烈王) of Zhou. Some people say he was 110 years old when he died.

---

337 Zisi (子思) was the grandson of Confucius who studied under Zengzi and was the teacher of Mencius. He wrote the *Doctrine of the Mean*.

Mencius' given name is Ke (軻); his courtesy name is Ziyu (子輿); his father is Ji (激) from Zou (鄒); and his mother is Zhang-*shi* (仉氏). He was born in the Kiyu Year (C. Jiyou nian 己酉年), the 4th year of King Lie (烈王) of Zhou, and he died in the Imsin Year (C. Renshen nian 壬申年), the 26th year of King Nan (赧王) of Zhou at the age of eighty-four.

These five sages are the five great sages of antiquity, so the virtue and words of Confucius' *Analects*, Mencius' *Mencius*, Zengzi's *Great Learning* and Zisi's *Doctrine of the Mean* are all worth reading. Only Yanzi did not leave behind any writings because he left this world early.

If we discuss all the sages of *Lianluo*, in the Chŏngmyo Year (C. Dingmao nian 丁卯年, 967), the 5th year of the reign of Taizu (Qiande 乾德) of Song, it mentions that because the five planets, Venus, Jupiter, Mercury, Mars and Saturn were all in the Legs Constellation (K. Kyusŏng; C. Kuixing 奎星)[338] various sages were born.

---

338 'The Five Planets Congregate in the Legs Constellation' (Wuxing ju Kui 五星聚奎), *Collection of Matters from the Past and Present*. "In the 3rd lunar month of the fifth year of the Qiande (乾德) reign era of Emperor Taizu of Song, five planets like a string of beads descended after the Bond Constellation (Lou 婁). In the first place, Dou Yi (竇儀) was in the court of Zhou Xiande (周顯德) of Later Zhou (Houzhou 後周) and soon said to his fellow minister Yang Huizhi (楊徽之) and others, 'As the five planets have congregated in the Legs Constellation (Kui 奎) in the Dingmao Year, all under heaven will be at peace from now on.'" (宋太祖乾德五年三月, 五星如連珠, 在降婁之次. 初, 儀周顯德中嘗謂楊徽之等曰, '丁卯歲, 五星聚奎, 自此天下太平.')

Master Shao Kangjie's[339] given name is Yong (雍). His courtesy name is Yaofu (堯夫), and his brush name is Kangjie. As a person from Luoyang (洛陽), he was born in the Sinhae Year (C. Xinhai nian 辛亥年, 1011), the 4th year of the Dazhong xiangfu (大中祥符) reign era of Emperor Zhenzong (眞宗) of Song, and he died in the Chŏngsa Year (C. Dingsi nian 丁巳年, 1077), the 10th year of the Xining (熙寧) reign era of Emperor Shenzong of Song at the age of sixty-seven.

Master Zhou Lianxi's[340] given name is Dunyi (敦頤) and his courtesy name is Maoshu (茂叔), so Lianxi is his brush name. His father was Sub-Governor of Guiyang (桂陽令) Fucheng (輔成), who was from Daozhou (道州), and his mother was Zheng-*shi* (鄭氏). He was born in the Chŏngsa Year (C. Dingsi nian 丁巳年, 1017), the 1st year of the Tianxi (天禧) reign era of Emperor Zhenzong, and he died in the Kyech'uk Year (C. Guichou nian 癸丑年, 1073), the 6th year of the Xining (熙寧) reign era of Emperor Shenzong (神宗) of Song at the age of fifty-seven.

The given name of Master Zhang Hengqu (張橫渠)[341] is Zai (載), and his courtesy name is Zihou (子厚), so Hengqu is his brush name. His father was Auxiliary Secretary in the Imperial Household (Dianzhong cheng 殿中丞) Di (迪),

---

339 Shao Kangjie was the Northern Song Confucian scholar Shao Yong (邵雍, 1011–1077). He was skilled in divination using the *Book of Changes*.

340 Zhou Lianxi: See footnote 29.

341 Zhang Hengqu: See footnote 110.

who was from Kaifeng (開封). He was born in the Kyŏngsin Year (C. Gengshen nian 庚申年, 1020) in the 4th year of the Tianxi reign era of Emperor Zhenzong of Song and died in the Chŏngsa Year (C. Dingsi nian 丁巳年, 1077) in the Xining reign era at the age of fifty-eight.

Master Cheng Mingdao's[342] given name is Hao (顥) and his courtesy name is Bochun (伯淳). His father was Superior Grand Master of the Palace (Taizhong dafu 太中大夫) and was from Henan (河南). His mother was Hou-*shi* (侯氏). The master was born in the Imsin Year (1032) in the 1st year of the reign of Emperor Renzong of Song and died in the Ŭlch'uk Year (C. Yichou nian 乙丑年, 1085) in the 8th year of the Yuanfeng (元豊) reign era of Emperor Shenzong of Song at the age of fifty-four.

The given name of Master Cheng Yichuan (程伊川)[343] is Yi (頤) and his courtesy name is Zhengshu (正叔), so Yichuan (伊川) is his brush name. He is the younger brother of Cheng Mingdao and was born one year after Mingdao in the Kyeyu Year (1033) and died in the Chŏnghae Year (1107) in the 1st year of the Daguan (大觀) reign era of Emperor Huizong (徽宗) of Song at the age of seventy-five.

---

342 Cheng Mingdao: See footnote 30.

343 Cheng Yichuan (程伊川) was Cheng Yi (程頤, 1033–1107), a Song dynasty Neo-Confucian scholar.

The given name of Zhuzi is Xi (熹). His courtesy name is Yuanhui (元晦), and his brush name was Master Huian (晦庵先生). His father was Auxiliary Secretary for the Ministry of Personnel (Libu yuanwailang 吏部員外郎), and his mother was Zhu-*shi* (祝氏). He was born in the Kyŏngsul Year (1130) in the 4th year of the Jianyan (建炎) reign era of Emperor Gaozong (高宗) of Song. Confucius was born in the Kyŏngsul Year and so was Master Zhu, so there are some people who have written about him who call him the sage of the Kyŏngsul Year.[344] He died in the 6th year of the Qingyuan (慶元) reign era (1200) of Emperor Ningzong (寧宗) of Song at the age of seventy-one. Master Zhu transmitted the way of Yao, Shun, Confucius and Mencius (*Yao Shun Kong Meng zhi dao* 堯舜孔孟之道), so his successors have referred to him as the 'reincarnated Confucius'."

Yuhandang's eldest granddaughter listened and said, "I will write this down and reflect upon it."

344 'Letter to Sub-Governor Liu Requesting the Repair of Ziyang Confucian Academy' (Shang Liu Zhixian chongxiu Ziyang shuyuan shu 上劉知縣重修紫陽書院書), *Chinese Parasol Tree Ridge Collection* (*Wugang ji* 梧岡集) by Tang Wenfeng (唐文鳳) of the Ming dynasty. "Earlier in the Gengxu Year, the Zhou dynasty moved its capital to the east, and Confucius was born; later, in the Gengxu Year, the Song dynasty moved its capital to the south, and Zhuzi was born. Ah, could this be connected with the births of these sages?" (前庚戌而孔子生于東遷, 後庚戌而朱子生於南渡, 嗚呼, 聖賢之生關乎.)

The Secret of Enjoying Blessings

One day Minister Tu's female maternal younger cousin (*oejongmae* 外從妹) Lady Sŏp came and asked Yuhandang, "Your father-in-law is over ninety years of age. I know that he has a strong physical constitution, but in general what is his daily routine?"

"Ever since he was a child, he has memorized texts at dawn, and until today he has never stopped doing this. He gets washed and visits the ancestral shrine to greet the ancestors (*sinallye* 晨謁禮),[345] and he never fails to do this regardless of whether the weather is extremely cold or hot (*kihan sŏngsŏ* 祁寒盛暑). In the evening he always goes to Wanshu Garden and Shuiyue Pavilion without fail and sits there before coming back down; and when he is going up the stone steps or up to the raised pavilion (*nugak* 樓閣), he always tells his children not to support him and just goes up; and this generally shows how his physical strength is."

"I knew that he is always engaged in academic studies, but what kind of dietary regime (*yangsaeng* 養生) has he studied and what kind of food does he eat?"

---

345 *Sinallye* (C. *Chenye li* 晨謁禮) is the ritual of greeting one's ancestors in the family shrine in the early morning.

"Food is no different from the body, so he cannot eat much by nature, and he has been that way ever since he was a child until now. Even on a very hot day, he doesn't drink water and does not fan himself. Even though he drinks wine, he never drinks so much that he becomes drunk. He does not spit profusely, and he does not speak loudly. He does these things because he has engaged in academic studies, and naturally these things do not go against the way of maintaining good health (*yangsaeng pang* 養生方)."

Lady Sŏp also asked, "If he does not speak loudly, are the people who attend him also able to refrain from speaking loudly?"

"My father-in-law really dislikes noisiness, so how could his three sons dare to speak loudly, and as women, how much more could we dare to speak loudly? We are extremely careful."

"As you yourself are over seventy years old, isn't it tiring to manage all your tasks?"

"In the *Book of Rites* it states, 'When one's parents are alive one should never refer to oneself as being old through words or actions.'[346] As I am attending my father-in-law, even though I am seventy years old, how could I say 'I have grown old'? Since I am taking care of my two elderly

346 'Record of the Dykes' (Fangji 坊記), *Book of Rites*. "The Master (Confucius) said, 'Before his parents (a son) should not speak of himself as old.'" (子云, '父母在, 不稱老.')

parents-in-law, it is not only a child's duty to personally attend to their meal requirements, but also it is a pleasure for human beings to take care of our white-haired elders, so how could I say that it is tiring? Just as Emperor Gwangwu of Later Han said, 'It is my pleasure to do this' so 'I do not suffer.'[347] I think of it as my joy to do what I do, so I never think of it as being hard work. My daughters-in-law are very wise, so they are fully capable of doing everything in my stead, but because I want to show my respect in person, I never ask them to do anything on my behalf."

Lady Sŏp also asked, "You have an extremely burgeoning family of five generations of men and women in one household, so how do you manage to prepare food every day?"

"The men and women require one *toe* (1.8 liters) of rice per person, so I prepare cooked rice using two straw sacks (*sŏm*: 180 liters) of rice at one time, and in one day I use four straw sacks of rice.[348] The servants cook and eat

---

347 'Annals of Emperor Guangwu' (Guangwudiji 光武帝紀), *History of Later Han*. Every day Emperor Guangwu of Later Han participated in the morning palace assembly and did not leave until after sunset. He often called his ministers to discuss the principles of the Classics and did not sleep until it was late at night. When the crown prince, who was worried about his father, remonstrated with him, Emperor Guangwu responded, "I am enjoying myself, so I do not get tired." (我自樂此, 不爲疲也.)

348 'Four straw sacks (*sŏm*) of rice': In the original text, there is a footnote stating, "*tyung wŏn il yŏ syŏk mal*" (In China 10 *tu* [C. *dou* 斗] equal 1 *sŏk* [C. *dan* 石]). This footnote was added in the original text because in Chosŏn 1 *sŏm* of lesser grains (*sogok* 小斛) equaled 15 *mal* and 1 *sŏm* of major grains (*taegok* 大斛) equaled 20 *mal*. 1 *toe* (572 ml approx.) of rice was prepared per person, and two *sŏm* of rice were prepared at one time. As in China 1 *sŏm* equaled 10

eight straw sacks of rice in a day."

"As you have so much food to prepare, how do you supervise all the food preparation?"

"Nowadays, my daughters-in-law supervise it. In the past I used to do everything myself, so my two sisters-in-law (*tongsŏ*: husband's brother's wives) sincerely asked me if they could personally serve food to our parents-in-law. As our parents-in-law granted their permission, I decided that we would share the task between the three of us by each of us serving for ten days per month. This is following the example of Lu Jia (陸賈) in the Han dynasty, who used stay with each of his five sons for ten days at a time.[349] Apart from the morning and evening meals, I cannot delegate to anyone else the serving of special meals either early in the morning or late at night or making sure that they are neither too cold nor too hot. As I know their daily eating habits very well, that's why I take care of them myself."

---

mal, the number of men and women in Yuhandang's family would have been around 200 persons.

349 'Historical Biography of Li Yeqi and Lu Jia' (酈生陸賈列傳), *Records of the Grand Historian.* Lu Jia gave his five sons 200 pieces of gold each and said, "I am contracting a promise with you. When I come to your house, you must provide wine and food for me and my attendants and horses. After receiving everything I want for ten days, I will change homes, and if I die, my jeweled sword and chariot, horses and servants will all go to that (son's) household." (與汝約. 過汝, 汝給吾人馬酒食, 極欲, 十日而更, 所死家, 得寶劍車騎侍從者.)

Lady Sŏp also asked, "What kind of work do the men and women have to do every day?"

"They attend the two elders, and all their male and female descendants greet them in the morning (*munch'im* 問寢) and supervise their meals (*sisŏn* 視饍),[350] and in the remaining time, the sounds of classic texts being read out loud and weaving never stop."

"Who attends your parents-in-law during the night time?"

"Where my father-in-law stays, there is an adjacent room where his three sons stay day and night, and the grandsons take it in turns to attend him in pairs for three days at a time. Where my mother-in-law stays, the three daughters-in-law and the granddaughters-in-law also do the same thing."

"How many brothers and children are there overall?"

"Five or six years ago when my parents-in-law were sitting in Wanshu Garden and enjoying themselves with their sons and grandchildren, from among their sons and grandsons who had gone through the capping ceremony (*kwallye* 冠禮), each one of them read out the text for one hexagram

350 Paying respects and supervising meals (*munan sisŏn* 問安視膳): Children serving their parents in accordance with Confucian etiquette involves them greeting their parents every morning and being at their side to serve them at meal times.

(*kwae* 卦) from the *Book of Changes*, and even though the texts for the sixty-four hexagrams were all read out, there were still over ten people remaining. Since that occasion tens or more persons have also gone through the capping ceremony."

Lady Sŏp also asked, "As there are so many persons in one household, you must have followed the way of Zhang Gongyi (張公藝) who wrote down the Chinese character for 'self-restraint', '*in*' (C. *ren* 忍), one hundred times[351]—and as your family is always harmonious what did you study to achieve that?"

"As every person's innate character seems to have a different intellectual level, their sturdiness, gentleness and alacrity (*kang yu wan kŭp* 剛柔緩急) are also different. How could one person's character be the same as everyone else's? However, every person in the same family, regardless of their age or sex, should simply be studying day and night how to keep the heart of the

---

351 'Good Conduct' (Shanxing 善行), *Elementary Learning*. "Zhang Gongyi lived together with nine generations, and was well known for his virtuous conduct in Northern Qi (Beiqi 北齊), Sui (隋) and Tang (唐). During the Linde (麟德) reign era Emperor Gaozong (高宗) of Tang, after offering sacrifices to Heaven (*fengshan* 封禪) at Mt. Tai, went to Zhang Gongyi's house and calling Zhang Gongyi into his presence asked him the reason why he was able to live in harmony with his family, so Zhang Gongyi took up a writing brush and some paper and wrote down the Chinese character '*ren*' (忍), meaning 'self-restraint', one hundred times." (張公藝九世同居, 北齊隋唐, 皆旌表其門. 麟德中, 高宗封泰山, 幸其宅, 召見公藝, 問其所以能睦族之道, 公藝請紙筆以對, 乃書忍字百餘以進.) The original sources are *History of the Early Tang* (*Jiu tangshu* 舊唐書) and *Sima Guang's Family Example* (*Wengong jiafan* 溫公家範).

parents-in-law from being disturbed in the slightest. How could there be any other way? Even though people of later generations have mentioned the words of Zhang Gongyi, people only have to have self-restraint because there is something lacking in their heart. I study so that there is nothing that I have to exercise self-restraint about in my home. As all the people in one household cannot discard their relationships as brothers and sisters, uncles, aunts, nieces and nephews, if thoughtless words are spoken among brothers and sisters, that is close to being a violation of morality. If such a thing should happen, how could we be called a household of superior persons who study the classics?"

"Even though both old and young in one family all practice harmony among people, filial piety and fraternal duty (*inhwa hyoje* 人和孝悌) to the utmost, as there are also hundreds of male and female servants in one household, how do you manage?"

"Each one of them has a different character, but as they are carefully watched, they feel extremely ashamed if they engage in wrongdoing or violent behavior, and for this reason they do not commit evil deeds and live out their whole lives into old age as filially pious husbands and wives."

"Before now, I thought Tu Ch'ŏnbok's dream omen was extraordinary, but this kind of good fortune (*pongnok* 福祿) is due to your merit Yuhandang."

"As the nature of my parents-in-law is benevolent and virtuous, they will enjoy good fortune for ten thousand years, and this is something all the world knows. How could it be because of the merit of a single daughter-in-law?"

Approving and praising these words Lady Sŏp said, "Long life, wealth, honor and many sons are all extolled as good fortune by human beings, and your elderly father-in-law is not far from becoming 100 years old. In terms of honor he has a first rank government position. In terms of wealth he has ten thousand pieces of gold. Both he and his wife are growing old together, and they are caring for hundreds of their descendants under one roof. There seems to be no one who can compare with them since the times of Yao, Shun, Xia, Yin and Zhou."

"In the past and present there have been noble people; those who have a long life; those who have wealth; and those who have many sons. However, there is one thing that my parents-in-law have achieved that no one else could achieve."

"What is that?"

"None of the offspring of my parents-in-law have been lost due to a miscarriage or abortion after conception, and none of their offspring have died early after being born. I have attended my parents-in-law for over sixty years, but I have never had to call a doctor even for a mild cold, and this is not a common thing in other people's homes."

"Hearing these words, such a thing will never happen again between heaven and earth. For this reason even if relatives and friends just come to see the faces of your parents-in-law, there will be none among them who will not feel as proud as if they had seen the Three Mountains (K. Samsan; C. Sanshan 三山)[352] and the Ten Islands (K. Sipchu; C. Shizhou 十洲)[353] where the Daoist immortals (Sinsŏn) live."

Lady Sŏp also asked, "Teaching boys to write is something that happens naturally as the older ones study together with the younger ones, but the women who come into the family (i.e. daughters-in-law) are different from children, as they were born and raised in a different household. So how do you teach them?"

"Teaching children to write is a common thing in people's households. It may be rare for others to teach women, but in my house, I teach them reading first as soon as the women arrive."

---

352 The 'Three Mountains' (K. Samsan; C. Sanshan 三山) is a reference to the three mountains where the Daoist immortals are said to live, namely, Mt. Pangjang (C. Fangzhangshan 方丈山), Mt. Pongnae (C. Penglaishan 蓬萊山) and Mt. Yŏngju (C. Yingzhoushan 瀛洲山).

353 The 'Ten Islands' (K. Sipchu; C. Shizhou 十洲) is a reference to the ten islands where the Daoist immortals are said to live, namely, Choju (C. Zuzhou 祖洲), Yŏngju (C. Yingzhou 瀛洲), Hyŏnju (C. Xuanzhou 玄洲), Yŏmju (C. Yanzhou 炎洲), Changju (C. Changzhou 長洲), Wŏnju (C. Yuanzhou 元洲), Yuju (C. Liuzhou 流洲), Saengju (C. Shengzhou 生洲), Pongninju (C. Fenglinzhou 鳳麟洲) and Ch'wigulchu (C. Jukuzhou 聚窟洲).

"What kind of texts do you teach them?"

"I teach them the 'Pattern of the Family' (Neize 內則) chapter in the *Book of Rites* as well as *Biographies of Women* and *Elementary Learning*."

"Are the young women able to study well right from the start?"

"As they are all women from the family of literati, they are not completely ignorant, and as studying is something they do habitually after coming into my home, they try to learn using their intelligence. If they are intelligent and gifted, they learn immediately, but even if they are a little slow, they still learn quite quickly."

"What kind of study did you undertake so that even though you have many offspring, they do not get ill, and they rarely have to see a doctor?"

"Sickness first comes about due to wind, cold, heat and dampness. There are naturally few cases of illness because I never let the people in my household get very cold. They are never exhausted or distressed by going on long journeys, and they hardly have any arduous tasks."

"It's not unusual that the people in your family have been raised that way since childhood, but how is it that the women who each came from different homes (i.e. daughters-in-law) are also just the same?"

"How could it be possible that a person never contracts a minor illness? But after they enter my house, the family rules (*kapŏp* 家法) are strict, so how could anyone dare to transgress even a single word of the admonitions of my parents-in-law. Therefore, as everyone is careful about their behavior, they do not stay in cold places; they do not drink cold water; they do not expose themselves to the wind; and they do not climb up to dangerous places. If they are told not to drink wine, even the men do not dare to get drunk, so by personally putting these principles into practice, they not only become the principles of all the offspring, but they are also the way of protecting the health (*sŏpsaeng* 攝生) of the children."

"Even though each of the women from different homes learn this way after coming here, how can they all be of one heart in behaving so kindly and sensibly?"

"First of all when seeking a spouse for one's son, one should neither be greedy to find a wealthy family nor avoid a poor and humble family, but rather one should find a family that is scholarly and renowned for its benevolence and high moral character and then marry one's son to a daughter from that family. Some of the people coming into our family are mature and some are immature, so each of them is different, but because they have a kind and virtuous character, and they have learned everything from their family tradition, they are better than someone who grew up in a wealthy but ignorant family."

Lady Sŏp also asked, "As my maternal grandfather enjoys wealth and prosperity in this kind of pavilion in nature, when the scenery is good in spring or autumn, do you enjoy singing and dancing?"

"Not only do my parents-in-law dislike singing and dancing, but they admonish us with the words of Wang Yucheng (王禹偁) in 'Record of a Bamboo Tower in Huangzhou' (Huangzhou zhulou ji 黄州竹樓記), "They are only places where female entertainers (C. *jinü*; K. *kinyŏ* 妓女) sing and dance; they are not something a poet should have anything to do with.'[354] As he said, hearing the clear sound of your children and grandchildren reading is like hearing a good song, and seeing your children and grandchildren walking in accordance with the Way is like watching a good dance, so do not envy the songs of Yan and the dances of Zhou (Yange Zhaowu 燕歌趙舞).'[355]

"Isn't it troublesome when your children and grandchildren come to greet you?"

"How could it be troublesome and boisterous when our many descendants come to greet us? Three of our sons first ask after our well-

354 'Bamboo Tower Record' (Zhulou ji 竹樓記), *Collection of Matters from the Past and Present.* "Qiyun Tower and Luoxing Tower are very high, and Jinggan Tower and Liqiao Tower are very splendid. But they are only for gathering female entertainers to sing and dance in and that is all, so they have nothing to do with poets, and I do not choose such places." (彼齊雲落星, 髙則髙矣, 井幹麗譙, 華則華矣. 止于貯妓女, 藏歌舞, 非騷人之事, 吾所不取.)

355 In ancient times the people of Yan and Zhao were said to be skilled in singing and dancing.

being, then after watching six or seven of our grandsons take it in turns to bow four times each, we watch five or six of our great-grandchildren each take it in turns to bow several times, and then we watch our great-great-grandchildren follow their example. After receiving the morning greeting in the family shrine (*sadang*), we then go into the inner quarters (*naedang*), and our daughters-in-law, granddaughters-in-law, great-granddaughters-in-law and great-great-granddaughters-in-law all greet us in the same way, and our daughters, granddaughters, great-granddaughters, and great-great-granddaughters all do the same. As we watch the young boys and girls all standing in line to perform their bows to carry out this ritual, their sincerity and solemnity make us feel like field marshals (*taejanggun*) sitting on a dais in front of our generals at the head of their troops in a military parade, so how could such an occasion possibly be noisy and boisterous?"

"You have often been asked the exact number of your grandchildren, but you only reply in rough terms and never answer precisely, so why is that?"

"By all means one should avoid shining too much light on other people's business, and this is to avoid the spreading of rumors."

"If you hardly ever argue over what is right or wrong, that seems to be close to the Way of the Daoists (道家)?"

Yuhandang laughed and said, "Indeed, that is correct. In our family everyone laughs among themselves, saying that my reluctance to be exacting in everything seems to be close to the way of Laozi, and my reluctance to kill even the smallest of insects is close to the doctrine of Buddhism."

"As you are well known for your talents and extensive knowledge, I would like to ask you this question. Is there a principle determining whether someone has a long or short life and whether they have many or few descendants?"

"Because even among physiognomists and fortunetellers there are only a few who can predict the future accurately, as a woman, my innate disposition is inadequate, so how could I know? But having many or few descendants depends on the harshness and gentleness of one's character. As there are a great many people in my household, I have naturally heard many things about what happens in other people's homes. Very gentle and kind people have many children; after such people, those who are kind and gentle have a lot of children; while those who have a harsh character only have a few; and those who have an extremely harsh character are harmed greatly by that fact.

Even looking at my own family, there are those who have seven or eight children, and those who have five or six. Because there are no harsh persons in our household, however, there is no one who has not given birth to three sons, so we can easily see the innate character of the women."

"That is indeed usually the case, nevertheless there are those who are extremely benevolent and kind, and yet they have no children, and there are also those who have many children even though they are evil. Isn't that strange?"

"There are less wicked people with many children than kind people with many children, and there are less benevolent and good people who are childless than wicked people who are childless. For the sake of comparison, even though it is the natural way of things for fire to be hot, there are sparks that are cold, and even though it is the natural way of things for water to be cold, there are exceptions to this principle in the case of such things as hot springs. How can we discard a basic principle and accept another principle based on just a few exceptions? As Master Zhu said, 'even in the midst of the great cold of severe frost, how can there not be a few warm and mild days?'[356] These words are based on the natural principle of referring to winter as being cold regardless of whether there are some

---

356 'Letter answering Pan Shudu' (Da Pan Shudu shu 答潘叔度書), *Collected works of Huian* (*Huian ji*). "But even when the bitter frost blows, and it is very cold, how could there be no sign of gentle winds and warm sunlight? So whatever occurs the most wins." (然嚴霜大凍之中, 豈無些小風和日暖意思? 要是多者勝耳.)

warm and mild days in the extreme cold of winter. The early death of Yan Hui (顏回) and the fact that Bodao (伯道) was childless[357] are exceptions to the rule."

"Because the fortune or misfortune of a home naturally depends on women, we can indeed see that the rulers of the past gained and lost their kingdoms due to the goodness or evilness of their consorts. For example, even if we just look at the *Records of the Grand Historian*, when King Yu of Xia arose, Tushan-*shi* (塗山氏)[358] was there, when Jie (桀) lost the throne Moxi (妺喜) was there. When Tang (湯) was king of Yin (Shang), Youshen-*shi* (有莘氏)[359] was there; when Zhou (紂) fell Daji (妲己) was there. Concerning the queen consorts of the Zhou dynasty, Taisi was the queen consort of King Wen,

---

357 'Good Conduct', *Elementary Learning*. "Deng You (鄧攸), the vice director of the right (You puye 右僕射) of Jin (晉), in the final years of the Yongjia (永嘉) reign era was defeated by Shi Le (石勒) and crossed over the River Si (泗水). Deng You ran away with his wife and children on horses and oxen. Also, they encountered robbers who took their oxen and horses, so he continued on foot with his son and his younger brother's son on his back. Deng You thought that he would not be able to save the lives of both these children and said to his wife, 'My younger brother died young, and this is his only child, in principle I cannot cut off his line of descendants. It is only right that we should abandon our own child. If we are fortunate enough to survive, we will naturally have more children later.' In tears his wife complied. After that they abandoned their child and left, and in the end they had no descendants." (晉右僕射鄧攸, 永嘉末, 沒于石勒, 過泗水. 攸以牛馬負妻子而逃, 又遇賊, 掠其牛馬, 步走, 擔其兒及其弟子綏, 度不能兩全, 乃謂其妻曰, '吾弟早亡, 唯有一息, 理不可絶. 止應自棄我兒耳. 幸而得存, 我後當有子.' 妻泣而從之, 乃棄其子而去之, 卒以無嗣.) The original source is 'Historical Biographies of Virtuous Officials' (Liangli liezhuan 良吏列傳), *History of the Jin* (*Jinshu* 晉書). Bodao (伯道) is Deng You's courtesy name.

358 Tushan-*shi* (塗山氏) was the queen consort of King Yu of Xia.

359 Youshen-*shi* (有莘氏) was the queen consort of King Tang of Yin (Shang).

and Jiang-*shi* (姜氏) was the queen consort of King Wu, but when King You (幽王) went into decline, Baosi (褒姒) was there. Can the fortune and misfortune of a family not be dependent upon the women? Yuhandang's words today have naturally made me realize this principle."

"Concerning the men in a home, how can the gains and losses and the fortune and misfortune depend solely upon the women in a family? Diligently being benevolent and engaging in virtuous conduct is said to be the entire role of men, while for those who are women, it is said that fortune and misfortune depend upon them assisting their spouses. So it is rare for a household not to prosper if the women are diligent in being benevolent and carrying out good deeds."

Lady Sŏp responded by saying that what she had said was good.

"Your family is famous for being benevolent and good and harmonious, and there is no one in this world who does not envy you, so I am always hearing people asking what kind of study brought this about. Listening to Yuhandang's words, I can naturally grasp the basics."

Lady Sŏp's third daughter, who was eight years old, followed after her mother and said, "In *Unity of the Three in the Book of Changes* (*Zhouyi cantongqi* 周易參同契) it states, 'Swallows and sparrows cannot give birth to phoenixes, and foxes and rabbits cannot suckle a horse',[360] so without virtuous mothers, how could sages such as Confucius, Mencius, Chengzi and Zhuzi have appeared?"

Yuhandang said, "Worldly women are unable to do this and instead respect shamans and fortunetellers (*mubok* 巫卜). Are they not truly deplorable? Your words are intelligent, and it is admirable that you have understood the meaning of my words."

Soon afterwards Yuhandang's eldest son Ilbong came in. As Yuhandang told him what Lady Sŏp's daughter had been saying about Confucius, Mencius, Chengzi and Zhuzi, Ilbong said, "Confucius' father Shuliang He was a person who had accumulated merit (*chŏk tŏk chi in* 積德之人), and Mencius' mother is renowned for her example of moving house three times (for the sake of her son's education), so how could there not have been any teaching of his father Jigongyi (激公宜). Not only were Lady Hao and Lady Zhu virtuous, but the two elder men Cheng Taizhong (程太中)[361] and Zhu Weizhai (朱韋齋)[362] were also both virtuous, so generally for benevolent children to be born, there must be a benevolent father."

---

360 *Investigation of Discrepancies in Unity of the Three in the Book of Changes* (*Zhouyi cantongqi kaoyi* 周易參同契考異). "Swallows and sparrows cannot give birth to phoenixes, and foxes and rabbits cannot suckle a horse." (燕雀不生鳳, 狐兎不乳馬.)

361 Cheng Taizhong (程太中) was the father of Cheng Mingdao.

362 Zhu Weizhai (朱韋齋) was the father of Zhu Xi.

Lady Sŏp said, "These words are the same as what was just said. Because these words are fitting, it is said that children resemble their fathers."

Lady Sŏp's daughter laughed and said, "According to an old saying 'a father like a tiger cannot sire an offspring that is like a dog' (*hobu pul saeng kyŏnja* 虎父不生犬子), so these words have just such a meaning."

Famous Sights of Qiantang Lake

Lady Sŏp asked Yuhandang, "Qiantang is renowned throughout the world as a famous scenic spot. As you spend your daily life in the midst of this scenery, people of this world all envy you—so have you seen all the scenic spots of Qiantang Lake?"

"As a woman I have lived next to Qiantang Lake for sixty years, and it is extremely regrettable that I have not been able to see all the sights."

"Even though you could not see all the mountains and streams around Qiantang Lake, you will have heard all their names, so please tell me all that you have heard about?"

"I cannot tell you everything in order, but I will tell you what I have heard about from time to time. There is a gate at the water's edge of Qiantang, the name of which is Yulian Hall, and on its northern side there is a house called Laique Pavilion (來鵲樓). On its western side there is a bridge called Liushi Bridge, and below the bridge there are many lakes, so the sound of waterfalls is like shattering jade. Over the bridge there is a Buddhist temple called Zhaoqing Temple (昭慶寺), and on its western side there is a bridge called Shihan Bridge (石函橋).

There is a mountain called Mt. Baoshi to the west, so in the past the four Chinese characters *ho san sung kae* (C. *hu shan sheng gai* 湖山勝槩: 'Beautiful view of a mountain and lake') were inscribed there in the calligraphy of Zhang Jizhi (張卽之),[363] and the mountain peak is called Shizi Peak (獅子峰: 'Lion peak'). Because there is a rock shaped like a fallen star beneath a pine tree, its name is Luoxing Rock (落星石: 'Fallen star rock'), and next to it there is a raised terrace called Kansong Terrace (看松臺: 'Guardian pine terrace'). Below the terrace there is a spring, and because it tastes sweet like mother's milk, it is called Ruquan Well (乳泉井: 'Breast milk well'); next to it there is a rocky cliff that is like a natural painting, and people say that the First Emperor of Qin tied up his

---

363 Zhang Jizhi (張卽之, 1186–1263) was a Southern Song calligrapher. His courtesy name is Wenfu (溫夫), and his brush name is Yunliao (樗寮).

boat to this rock when he was searching for Daoist immortals, so it is called Lanchuan Rock (纜船石: 'Mooring boat rock'). They say the hills and fields are ruddy; the fields are green and the dwellings are scattered about like *paduk* (*go*) pieces; the sound of roosters crowing and dogs barking seems to come from the clouds.

In the valley there is the Ziyang Confucian Academy (紫陽書院), which is the Confucian academy where Master Zhu Huian held ancestral rites. Also, there is a place called Geweng Well (葛翁井). This is a well that is said to have been where Zhichuan (稚川)[364] made cinnabar (K. *tansa*; C. *dansha* 丹砂). Because the mountain peak called Hutou Rock (虎頭巖: 'Tiger head rock') was shaped like a tiger's head, it was given this name, but because in the past someone who interpreted auras (K. *manggi*; C. *wangqi* 望氣) said that there was a royal energy (K. *wanggi*; C. *wangqi* 王氣: i.e. energy that could result in the birth of a king) in Hangzhou (杭州), it was destroyed.[365]

---

364 Zhichuan (稚川) is the Eastern Jin Daoist adept Ge Hong (葛洪, 283–343). Zhichuan is his courtesy name, and his brush name is Baopuzi (抱朴子).

365 *West Lake Gazetteer* (*Xihu youlan zhi* 西湖遊覽志). "The appearance of Hutouyan protruding from the mountain is just like the head of a tiger. At the time when the states of Wu and Yue were flourishing someone who could interpret auras said, 'there is a royal energy in Hangzhou.' The emperor ordered it to be destroyed, so now it has been cut off and has fallen down." (虎頭巖, 山形突出, 若虎頭然. 吳越王盛時, 望氣者云, '杭州有王氣.' 藝祖命鑿之, 今斷落矣.)

To the north of Jianmen Pass (劍門關: 'Sabre gate pass'), there is Jingu Cave (金鼓洞: 'Gold drum cave'), where it is said that if you strike the rocks, they make a sound like golden drums. Below there is the tomb of the Song dynasty general Yue Fei (岳飛).[366] Mt. Qinghua (慶化山) is where the scholar without an official government position in the Jin dynasty Chen Chongzhen (陳崇眞)[367] lived, so every year on the 24th day of the sixth lunar month until now the local people have gathered there without fail to conduct a memorial rite.

On a cliff in the place called Tongtian Cave (通天洞: 'Communication with Heaven cave') the name Jiang Zhiqi (蔣之奇)[368] has been written using seal script. Also, to the north of Yanzhi Ridge (臙脂嶺: 'Red cosmetics ridge') there is a stone peak, so if you go up there and take in the view, you can see all the mountains surrounding Qiantang Lake like a folding screen. The lake itself is as clear as a mirror, and the clouds are reflected in it upside down.

---

366 Yue Fei (岳飛, 1103–1142) was a Southern Song general who contributed greatly in the defense against Jin (金) but was unfairly put to death as a result of a plot by the prime minister Qin Hui (秦檜).

367 Chen Chongzhen (陳崇眞): *West Lake Gazetteer*. "Concerning Shenxiao leiyuan (神霄雷院), in the Xianchun (咸淳) reign era (1265–1274) of the Song dynasty, a Daoist adept called Chen Chonzhen came from the country of the Min (Fujian) region and settled down here. Because he was good at controlling thunderbolts, by imperial order he built a 'thunder institution' (K. *noewŏn*; C. *leiyuan* 雷院) and lived there, and the brush name Chongsu zhenren (冲素眞人) was bestowed upon him. Until now, every year without fail, on the 24th day of the sixth lunar month, the people gather there and at their own expense hold a memorial rite." (神霄雷院, 宋咸淳間, 羽士陳崇眞者, 自閩來卜居於此. 善雷法, 因勑建雷院以居之, 賜號冲素眞人. 六月二十四日, 郡人雲集, 設醮捨貲, 至今不廢.)

368 Jiang Zhiqi (蔣之奇, 1031–1104) was a Northern Song literatus whose courtesy name was Yingshu (穎叔).

Fishing boats and pleasure boats (K. *ch'aebang*, C. *caifang* 彩舫) float on the water, appearing and disappearing like seagulls on the mist-covered water (K. *yŏnp'a*; C. *yanbo* 煙波). Between them, the river is spread out like freshly washed white silk, and there is a broad and endless vista towards distant Canghai (滄海).

There is a place called Juesheng Gate (絶勝門), and it is said that its name is written in the calligraphy of Ge Hong (葛洪) or the calligraphy of Song Zhiwen (宋之問).[369] If you come out of Qiantang Gate (錢塘門), the colors of the mountains are different in layers as though a thousand hibiscus flowers were blooming, and there is a place called Jindai Bridge (錦帶橋: 'Brocade girdle bridge'), where peach, willow, and flowering plants flourish all around.

Next to this is a place called Sixian Hall (四賢堂: 'Hall of the four worthies'), which is where memorial rites are held for the Marquis of Ye (鄴侯), Li Mi (李泌),[370] the drafting advisor of the imperial secretariat (Zhongshu sheren 中書舍人) Bai Juyi (白居易)[371] of the Tang era, the Song dynasty academician Su Shi (蘇

---

369 *West Lake Gazetteer*. "Lingyinchan Temple (靈隱禪寺) was built by a Buddhist monk called Huili (慧理) in the first year of the Xianhe (咸和) reign era (326–334) of the Jin (晉) dynasty. 'Juesheng jue chang' (絶勝覺場) is written on the name plaque, and it is said that either Ge Hong (葛洪) or Song Zhiwen (宋之問) wrote it." (靈隱禪寺, 晉咸和元年, 僧慧理建山門. 扁曰, '絶勝覺場', 相傳葛洪所書, 或云宋之問書.) Ge Hong was a Daoist adept of Eastern Jin (Dongjin 東晉) whose courtesy name is Zhichuan (稚川) and Song Zhiwen was a Tang poet whose courtesy name is Yanqing (延清). The characters on the name plaque mentioned above are now 'Zui sheng jue chang' (最勝覺場: a place where countless people become enlightened).

370 Li Mi (李泌, 722–789) was a Tang dynasty politician who left behind many wonderful achievements and exercised good governance while he was the governor of Hangzhou.

371 Bai Juyi (白居易, 772–846) was a Tang dynasty poet who exercised good governance when

軾)[372] and the scholar without an official position in the government Lin Bu (林逋).[373] Three of these persons spent time in the Hangzhou administration, and as this was the place where regional inspector Lin Bu had originally lived, his grave is also there. In front of it there are a pair of plum trees, and it is called the 'place where Lin Bu's cranes played'.

Next to it is Wanghu Pavilion (望湖亭: 'Viewing lake pavilion') and the verdant layers of lofty mountains surround the lake. Huxin Pavilion (湖心亭: 'Lake heart pavilion) stands in the midst of the water like a crane; the wind rings the bells hanging from the eaves, and the moonlight moves like a flower's shadow, so if you ascend to the raised pavilion, there is no one who does not feel as though they were 'ascending to heaven and becoming a Daoist immortal' (K. *uhwa tŭngsŏn*; C. *yuhuan dengxian* 羽化登仙).

To the north of Qiantang there is Qingbo Gate (清波門: 'Clear wave gate'). Inscribed on its stone walls are the text of the 'Family' (Jiaren 家人) hexagram from the *Book of Changes* and the 'Record of Music' (Yueji 樂記) chapter from

---

he was the governor of Hangzhou and left behind many outstanding administrative achievements such as the construction of the embankment called Baidi (白堤).

372 Su Shi (蘇軾, 1037–1101) was a Northern Song dynasty poet who also exercised good governance when he was the governor of Hangzhou and left behind many outstanding administrative achievements such as the construction of the embankment called Sudi (蘇堤) at West Lake.

373 Lin Bu (林逋, 967–1028) was a Northern Song dynasty hermit poet who lived in seclusion on Mt. Gu (Gushan 孤山) near West Lake in Hangzhou.

the *Doctrine of the Mean*, which are said to be in the calligraphy of Sima Wengong (司馬溫公).[374]

Even if I could not see the magnificent view of these splendid mountains of Qiantang myself, whenever my sons and grandsons come back from sightseeing, they explain the sights to me more or less like this, but how can you describe such extraordinary scenery in words?"

"Even if I cannot visit all the mountains and rivers of Qiantang, people say that seeing the landscape of your family's landscaped garden (K. *wŏllim*; C. *yuanlin* 園林) is just as good as touring around the rivers and mountains."

"In the garden, when spring is at its height many flowers bloom on all sides. Rare birds chirrup in pairs and fly from tree to tree, so it is well worth seeing in the third lunar month when the spring breezes blow. When the autumn weather is clear and cool, every tree passes through the frost season, and there is an abundance of ripe fruits, so it is exactly the same as the words in Du Fu's poem, 'Either red as cinnabar or black as lacquer'.[375] When the autumn leaves have changed their colors, it is like

---

374 Sima Wengong (司馬溫公) was the Northern Song literatus Sima Guang (司馬光, 1019–1086). He compiled *Comprehensive Mirror to Aid in Government* (*Zizhi tongjian* 資治通鑑).

375 'Punitive Expedition to the North' (Beizheng 北征), *Supplementary Commentary on Du Fu's Poems* (*Buzhu Dushi* 補注杜詩). "Numerous small mountain fruits, acorns and chestnuts are intermingled. Either things as red as cinnabar, or things as black as lacquer." (山果多瑣細, 羅生雜橡栗, 或紅如丹砂, 或黑如點漆.)

being surrounded on all sides by a curtain of embroidered silk. It is just like the phrase in the Tang poem 'Frosty red leaves like blossoms in the second lunar month',[376] so this scenery is well worth seeing in the cool autumn of the eighth and ninth lunar months.

Concerning Shuiyue Pavilion, beyond the balustrade there is not a single speck of dust. Fishing boats are scattered here and there, and the call and response of the boating songs are well worth listening to during the day. The moon rising by the lake illuminates the balustrades as brightly as in the daytime. The light of the peaks on all sides is splendid, and heaven and earth seem to be empty, so such moonlit nights are also worth seeing. Which scenery do you intend to see first?"

"As I came in spring, I want to see the spring scenery of Wanshu Garden, and today I want to see the daytime scenery of Shuiyue Pavilion. As the moon will be full in a few days' time, on that day I want to see the night view of Shuiyue Pavilion. This year I will come again in the autumn and see the fall scenery of Wanshu Garden, and I hope not to miss a single night view."

---

376 'Mountain Hike' (Shanxing 山行), *Sounds of Tang* (*Tangyin* 唐音). "The cart stopped because I love the forest colored by the leaves of late autumn; the red of the maple leaves is more intense than the flowers of the second lunar month." (停車坐愛楓林晩, 霜葉紅於二月花.) This poem was written by the Tang poet Du Mu (杜牧).

Sightseeing around Wanshu Garden

Yuhandang ordered the gate into Wanshu Garden to be opened and went in together with over ten of her daughters and nieces, her younger sister-in-law, Lady Sŏp, and Miss Wang followed. As they went out of the northern gate, the bamboo groves to the left and right were green, and walking about twenty meters,[377] the garden was flat and spacious and could seat over a thousand people. On all sides of the open space, beautiful flowers and plants bloomed resplendently, and beyond the flowers, the (pine) trees were luxurious and almost reached up to the sky. The green (willow) trees hung down beautifully to touch the ground. As they slowly walked over a hundred paces between the pine trees and willow trees up to Yangguan Terrace, Qiantang Lake was spread out below their knees, and the sky gradually expanded, so it seemed that they had ascended to a special realm that was not of this world. Lady Sŏp said, "Such scenery as this does not seem to be of this world, so it is not for the eyes of women. Even among men, only those with the constitution of Daoist immortals would be worthy to see it."

---

377 In the original text it says 'over 10 *kan*', and 1 *kan* is approximately 1.8 meters.

Miss Wang said, "Ascending to the terrace and looking down on the lake, the words in the writings of a Confucian scholar of the Song dynasty (K. *Songyu*; C. *Songru* 宋儒) 'The clouds and rays of light from heaven linger together'[378] are appropriate."

Yuhandang said, "Listening to the words that Miss Wang just mentioned from Lian and Luo's writings, they are indeed just right for this moment."

Lady Sŏp said, "What kind of terrace is this?"

"This is the terrace that the men use to view the constellations."

"If you climb up to this terrace, it seems that there would be no stars that you could not see. What kind of place is the clearing in the forest of bamboo and pine that we saw before?"

"Because there are so many people, if men and women, old and young all wish to sit down side by side, even though the raised pavilion is spacious, it is always insufficient, so my parents-in-law come here, so that all their offspring can sit down together at the same time."

---

378 'Feelings while Reading Two Poems' (Guanshu you gan er shou 觀書有感二首), *Collected Writings of Huian* (*Huian ji*). "The small, square lotus pond is spread out like a mirror, and the light from the sky and shadows of the clouds linger together." (半畝方塘一鑑開, 天光雲影共徘徊.)

"Do you often attend them here in this open space?"

"When the men and women come out here occasionally, if they are only a small group, they gather in one of the raised pavilions, but when everyone gathers together, we come here."

"How many times have you gathered here together until now?"

"In spring and autumn when the weather is clear, there are only a few days when my parents-in-law do not walk around here. We meet here three or four times a year for banquets, and in the last fifty years or so we have gathered here over thirty times to hold a congratulatory banquet (*munhŭi yŏn* 聞喜宴)[379] after the civil examination."

Lady Sŏp led the way and walked about one hundred paces to the north where there was a grove of peach trees and plum trees. To the left was a grove of apricot trees, and to the right there was a grove of Japanese apricot trees. This was the moment when the peach blossoms were in full bloom, and the late blooming flowers were also just about to bloom. Patterns of flowers filled the valley; between the rocks came the sounds of chickens, birds and dogs, and the reds and greens that covered the mountains (*mansan hongnok* 滿山紅綠) were so resplendent and magnificent that they were beyond description.

---

379 Congratulatory banquet (*munhŭi yŏn* 聞喜宴): A congratulatory banquet held for those who gained the highest mark in the civil examination.

Lady Sŏp said, "As there are so many trees here, it is natural that it is called Wanshu Garden (萬樹園: 'Ten thousand trees garden'), but from today's discussion, I barely know more than the names of pine and bamboo, plum and willow, peach and apricot, but not those of all the unusual plants."

"There are many plants that even men do not know the names of."

Yuhandang's grandchild spoke, "The words 'the colors of the leaves by the mountain stream can barely be distinguished' and 'I do not know the names of the flowers blooming in the mountains'[380] are indeed fitting."

Lady Sŏp said, "Grandmother's literary skill has been handed down to her grandchild!"

After walking about a hundred steps through the woodland to the west, the trees dwindled away, and there was a small raised pavilion on the hill.

Lady Sŏp said, "What is this raised pavilion?"

"We had it made because the open space in front of it is extensive, and because in the spring and in the autumn the men come here to enjoy the view, its name is Guanjia Pavilion."

---

380 'Evening walk through a plain of hemp' (Ma ping wan hang 麻平晚行), *Collected Works of Wang Zi'an* (*Wang Zi'an ji* 王子安集). "The colors of the leaves by the mountain stream can barely be distinguished, and I do not know the names of the flowers blooming in the mountains." (澗葉纔分色, 山花不辨名.)

"As this open space is more than ten *li*, does all the land belong to this house?"

"Yes, it does."

"When you do the harvest, where do you store it, and how do you use it?"

"As there is a separate storehouse (*pyŏlgo* 別庫) next to the 'righteous storehouse', we store it there and use it for food. The men come to this raised pavilion and personally oversee things and place the harvested grain in the 'sacrificial offerings warehouse' (*chemulgo* 祭物庫) so that 'sacrificial grain' (*chasŏng* 粢盛)[381] can be offered for one year."

Finally, several tens of servants carrying tables came through the flowering trees to the pavilion and offered tables laden with food in turn, so Lady Sŏp said, "You prepared this food in a hurry, so how could it be this magnificent?"

"Ours is a house where elderly parents are cared for, so there is always some food prepared. This food was not prepared separately."

Miss Wang said, "According to the words 'constant supply of delicacies' (K. *sangjin*; C. *changzhen* 常珍) in the *Book of Rites*, it is a matter of etiquette to serve delicacies."[382]

---

381 'Sacrificial grain' (*chasŏng* 粢盛): Clean grain used for ancestral rites.
382 'Royal Regulations' (Wangzhi 王制), *Book of Rites*. "For those of fifty the grain was (fine and)

Yuhandang said, "Food is always on hand, but delicacies are not so easy (to provide)."

When the tables were taken away, as Lady Sŏp returned, Yuhandang said, "If you intend to go back by the way we came, not only is it further, but in order to see more trees and flowering plants, let's go back along a new pathway."

Lady Sŏp agreed that this would be good, and they went down the stairs and walked about ten steps through the grove of trees to where there were six little pavilions. Lady Sŏp asked, "What kind of pavilions are these?"

"These pavilions are called the Liuyi Pavilions (六藝樓: Six Confucian Arts Pavilions). In the first pavilion ritual books (*yesŏ* 禮書) are stored; in the second pavilion music books (*aksŏ* 樂書) are stored; in the other four pavilions writings on archery (*sa* 射), charioteering (*ŏ* 御), calligraphy (*sŏ* 書) and mathematics (*su* 數) are stored. If the men intend to discuss etiquette, they come to the first pavilion to consult the ritual books and discuss them. If they intend to discuss music, they come to the second pavilion to consult

---

different (from that used by younger men). For those of sixty, flesh was kept in store. For those of seventy, there was a second service of savory meat, and for those of eighty, there was a constant supply of delicacies." (五十異粻, 六十宿肉, 七十貳膳, 八十常珍.)

the music books and discuss them, and if they intend to discuss archery, charioteering, calligraphy or mathematics, they just go to the appropriate pavilion."

"Lord Minister Tu's way of studying in the family (*kahak* 家學) is like this. When people in this world discuss the Six Confucian Arts, there is no one who does not mention Minister Tu and his children. How could things be this way without this kind of studying?"

Lady Sŏp ascended to the first pavilion and after looking at the ritual books collected there, she came down and said, "In an ancient classic it states, 'Ceremonies (禮) and music (樂) should not for a moment be neglected by anyone,'[383] so ceremonies and music are the best things for scholars to study. Collecting books like this and making an effort to study them is not just the duty of men. How can women not also see and hear a lot?"

"My father-in-law built this house and said that he had a plan for his sons and grandsons, so the men always come here to pursue their studies, but as we women do not know how to study even a little, we feel embarrassed."

---

383 'Record of Music' (Yueji 樂記), *Book of Rites*. "Ceremonies (禮) and music (樂) should not for a moment be neglected by anyone." (禮樂不可斯須去身.)

Lady Sŏp went up to look at the three pavilions for archery, charioteering and calligraphy in turn and afterwards sat down in the sixth pavilion and said to Miss Wang, "You always liked mathematics, so as we have come to this pavilion, let us study by asking Yuhandang."

Yuhandang said, "As you are young and intelligent, you must know a lot about mathematics."

And then Yuhandang asked Miss Wang, "What should women know about mathematics, and what should they use mathematics for? But I am going to ask you about something that pertains to women, so please give me your reply. In "A Peacock Flying to the Southeast" (Kongque dongnan fei 孔雀東南飛), it states 'I weave five bolts of cloth in three days',[384] so if the length of one bolt is forty *ch'ŏk* (尺, 30.72 cm) in one day how much was woven in terms of *ch'ŏk* (尺, 30.72 cm), *ch'i* (*ch'on* 寸, 3.072 cm) and *pun* (分, 0.3072 cm)?"

Miss Wang answered immediately, "This cannot be expressed as a number after two *ch'i* are left, so I would say that dividing one *ch'i* by three, would result in two."

---

384 'The Wife of Jiao Zhongqing' (Jiao Zhongqing qi 焦仲卿妻), *Collected Songs of the Music Bureau Style* (*Yuefu shiji* 樂府詩集). "Even though I weave five bolts of cloth in three days, my mother-in-law dislikes me for being slow." (三日斷五匹, 大人故嫌遲.)

Laughing Yuhandang said, "I just asked you out of the blue, but you answered promptly, so I can see that you are interested in mathematics."

Lady Sŏp descended from the sixth pavilion and went up to Shuiyue Pavilion. The water of the lake was blue; the sunset had disappeared, and shadows were reflected upside down in the blue waters of Qiantang Lake. The scenery beyond the lake was boundless, and the water and the sky were so distant that it was impossible to distinguish which was which. Lady Sŏp said, "This scenery with the call and response of the boating songs is like the words of Yuhandang."

Miss Wang pointed to the boundlessly expansive sky and said, "In a work by Su Dongpo there is the phrase, 'I could not tell if it was a mountain or a cloud because it was so far away.'[385] Concerning the water, in Du Fu's poem it says 'A boat on the water in the spring seems to be sitting up in the sky',[386] and this is just like what we have seen from Shuiyue Pavilion today."

---

385 'Written on a Painting of a Misty River and Serried Hills, Owned by Wang Dingguo' (書王定國所藏煙江疊嶂圖), *Complete Works of Su Dongpo* (*Dongpo quanji* 東坡全集). "I couldn't tell if it was a mountain or a cloud because it was so far away, but when the fog and the cloud lifted, it was definitely a mountain." (山耶雲耶遠莫知, 煙空雲散山依然.)

386 'Riding in a Boat on the Day Before the Spring Festival' (Xiao Hanshi zhouzhong zuo 小寒食舟中作), *Supplementary Commentary on Du Fu's Poems* (*Buzhu Dushi* 補注杜詩). "A boat floating on the spring river water, seems to be sitting up in the sky, and in my aging years viewing flowers is like looking into the mist." (春水船如天上坐, 老年花似霧中看.)

Lady Sŏp said, "Your words are indeed true, but in the following line of that couplet are the words 'in my ageing years viewing flowers is like looking into the mist', and this exactly describes my flower viewing today."

Yuhandang said, "Even if the words of a grownup and a child refer to two different passages by Du Fu, they are both perfectly fitting, so I can see that the women of a family that engages in literary studies are indeed different. As every word that Miss Wang speaks quoting literary passages are all fitting, are all her siblings like this, too?"

"Even if this child had been born as a man, her elder brothers would not have been able to outdo her ability. It saddens me that she was born a woman."

Lady Sŏp Offers Wishes for Longevity

Lady Sŏp and Yuhandang walked back slowly with each other, and Lord Minister Tu came in and said to Lady Sŏp, "Did you see all of Wanshu Garden and Shuiyue Pavilion? How were they?"

"Concerning Shuiyue Pavilion, the vastness and immensity of the color of sea water is like the bosom of grandfather; the numerous mountains of Qiantang Lake are luxuriant, and standing massively, they are like grandfather's majestic spirit; and among the imposing trees of Wanshu Garden, the greenery of the pine trees and bamboo is like grandfather's lofty integrity, and if one ascends Yangguan Terrace to view the sun, moon and stars, their brilliance is like grandfather's literary compositions."

Laughing Minister Tu said, "Even though my younger sister's hair has become white, her wittiness has not declined. Please do not exaggerate so much and just speak about what you saw as it actually was."

"The lake water was clear and without a blemish. The deportment of the reflections of the sky and clouds is like grandfather's elegant deportment. The appearance of the mountains standing loftily with countless peaks spread out before and behind and to the left and right is like the endless burgeoning of grandfather's sons and grandsons. The sprouting leaves and blooming blossoms of the trees and flowering plants are like grandfather flourishing for a hundred years. The rare and precious animals and exotic birds calling to one another is like the harmoniousness of grandfather's family, and the rising of the sun and moon at Yangguan Terrace is as though it is matched to grandfather's daily life and meal times."

"The more my younger sister speaks, the more mysterious her words are."

"Upon seeing Qiantang Lake and Wanshu Garden, I spoke about the scenery of Shuiyue Pavilion, so quoting the *Book of Odes*, I will speak about three scenes together. In the *Book of Odes* it states, 'As the stream ever coming in, like the moon advancing to the full, like the sun ascending to the heavens, like the age of the southern hills, never waning, never falling',[387] so grandfather's blessings are like flowing water, and like the rising of the sun and like the movement of the moon, like the flourishing of the pine, like the vigorous sprouting of the bamboo, and like the southern mountains whose numbers never diminish. With these words I offer you my felicitations."

And she came forward to pour wine for Minister Tu and his wife. Minister Tu received it and drank. Greatly pleased, he turned to his wife and said, "Not only does my younger sister have talent and eloquence because from the outset she has been greatly blessed, as there is so much precious energy in her words of felicitation, ordinary women in general ought to learn to speak as abundantly as this."

---

387 The phrases 'As the stream ever coming in' (如川之方至), 'Like the moon advancing to the full' (如月之恒), 'Like the sun ascending to the heavens' (如日之升), 'Like the age of the southern hills, never waning, never falling' (如南山之壽, 不騫不崩) are all quoted from 'Heavenly Protection' (Tianbao 天保), *Book of Odes*, and 'firm as the roots of a clump of bamboo' (如竹苞矣) and 'like the luxuriant head of a pine tree' (如松茂矣) are quoted from 'These Banks' (Sigan 斯干), *Book of Odes*.

"The three speeches that Lady Sŏp just made would become good literary compositions if they were written down."

Then he poured the wine again and gave it to Lady Sŏp, saying, "I dedicate this single cup of wine to Lady Sŏp."

After Lady Sŏp received it and drank it, Yuhandang said to Lady Sŏp, "Why do you not speak about the Liuyi Pavilions?"

"The scenery of the Liuyi Pavilions is also good, but when speaking about them one should not talk about the scenery. They are an accumulation of wisdom that exists nowhere else under heaven. The men study in their midst to enter government and assist our emperor to govern with courtesy and music, and through civil administration for the sake of the nation, we will once again see the bright fortune of the 800-year civilization of the Zhou dynasty. These Liuyi Pavilions alone are the most magnificent sight."

As Minister Tu went outside, Lady Sŏp asked Yuhandang, "As grandfather wrote many compositions throughout his life, does he still write now? Surely there must be a composition that is worth listening to, so please tell me more."

"Nowadays he writes occasionally, but I don't know what precisely. Nevertheless, because one passage among his writings was so good, I memorized it."

Lady Sŏp asked if she could listen to it, so Yuhandang recited it from memory:

> Facing one thousand blossoming trees at the pavilion; (樓對千花樹)
> In the garden, a fifth-generation descendant walks with big strides. (庭趨五世孫)

Lady Sŏp read it repeatedly and said in admiration, "The composition is good, but the blessings in this piece of writing do not exist in this world."

The Eldest Son Ilbong's Sixtieth Birthday Celebration

When Minister Tu was ninety-four years of age, his eldest son Ilbong's sixtieth birthday occurred. Tu Ch'ŏnbok informed Minister Tu, "As it is not long until Ilbong's sixtieth birthday, I want to buy some wine and food and gather your descendants together."

"If I counted all the birthdays of my descendants, would there be a single day without a birthday in the year?"

"The sixtieth birthday is different from ordinary birthdays, and as it is a truly rare and grand occasion to see the sixtieth birthday of a third-generation descendant, it would be regrettable not to host a banquet."

Without granting his permission, Lord Minister Tu went into the inner quarters and informed Yuhandang saying, "Today, Ch'ŏnbok told me that Ilbong's sixtieth birthday is not far off, and he asked permission to organize a banquet, but I did not allow it."

"It is truly a rare and grand event under heaven to celebrate the sixtieth birthday of a third-generation descendant in one family. It is not a normal thing among households to respond to such a rare and grand event with silence. I will keep the wine, food and other expenses simple and ensure there are limits to prevent any excesses—also, to not have a banquet would appear strange."

"Indeed you are right. If one encounters a minor occasion one should celebrate it in a small way, but it is only right and proper when one encounters a major occasion to celebrate it in a grand way. As a descendant's sixtieth birthday is a rarity, a banquet should be held, but only summon the children and grandchildren and do not invite guests from far and wide."

Tu Ch'ŏnbok provided 5,000 pieces of gold to buy the wine and food, and thoroughly cleaned the grounds in Wanshu Garden. Of the thousands of people who gathered on that day, over a thousand were descendants of Lord Minister Tu. Lord Minister Tu's son-in-law, grand academician Wi Ch'ŏn'gyŏng, composed the following 'Preface to a Sixtieth Birthday Banquet' (*suyŏn sŏ* 壽宴序):

People of old said, 'Heaven sends down good people and without fail grants them many blessings',[388] and today these words are being proven to be true in the family of Lord Minister Tu. Because people in this world call living to a ripe old age a blessing; and call having many descendants a blessing; and call passing the civil examination and attaining a high ranking government position a blessing, even if you were only to attain one of these three blessings, there would be no one who would not envy you, so how much more must this be the case for Lord Minister Tu who has attained all three of these blessings? So how could they not have been granted by Heaven?

---

388 'In Distress' (Zai'e 在厄), *The School Sayings of Confucius* (*Kongzi jiayu* 孔子家語). "Heaven repays those who do good deeds with blessings and, Heaven repays those who do evil deeds with catastrophes." (爲善者, 天報之以福, 爲不善者, 天報之以禍.)

If we speak about living to a ripe old age in general, Lord Minister Tu is ninety-four years old. He has three sons who are almost eighty years old, and his grandson is today celebrating his sixtieth birthday, so we can say that this is a rare blessing under heaven. If we speak about having many descendants, there are 3 sons, 17 grandsons, 50 great-grandsons, 180 great-great-grandsons and over 20 great-great-great-grandsons arrayed in front of us. If we speak about the kindred of the great-grandsons, great-great-grandsons and great-great-great-grandsons, it is impossible to know how many would come out before us, so this can also be said to be a rare blessing under heaven. If we speak about passing the civil examination and entering government service, Lord Minister Tu is a minister in the Board of Rites who retired due to his age when he was seventy years old. His eldest son refrained from taking the civil examination and obtained the official rank of vice minister (*sirang* 侍郎). His second son and third son served as a minister and a grand academician respectively and relinquished their government positions at the age of seventy. Ten of his grandsons have passed the civil examination, and his eldest grandson is a minister. All the rest hold upright and prominent positions (*chŏnghyŏn chik* 淸顯職) of vice minister and below. Among the great-grandsons, thirty have passed the civil examination, and among the great-great-grandsons, over forty have passed the civil exam and are embarking on diverse government careers, becoming famous for their literary talent. It is impossible to calculate how many more will follow the same path in the future. If we speak about the daughters' children, the three generations of descendants beginning with the daughters of Lord Minister Tu amount to several hundred, of whom more than fifty have passed the civil examination. As the offspring of Lord Minister Tu and his wife have flourished in this way, it is considered a rare blessing under heaven.

How could these three kinds of blessings have happened without a basis? This has come about as a consequence of the benevolent and virtuous deeds that have been performed for hundreds of years beginning with the ancestors of Lord Minister Tu. With the utmost benevolent and generous character between heaven and earth, Lord Minister Tu has personally put into practice the teachings of his family since his childhood, and after becoming an adult and learning from the scholarship of his teachers, throughout his whole life he has not transgressed against the four characters *inhu* (仁厚: kindness and generosity) and *yusŏn* (有善: being virtuous) by a single word or a single deed. Therefore, between his eyes there is the peacefulness of the 'harmonious energy of a spring breeze' (*ch'unp'ung hwagi* 春風和氣) and not the slightest trace of any intention to 'injure people or harm things' (*sangin haemul* 傷人害物), and as those who watch the people bowing before his table feel unworthy, not knowing whether they might not be witnessing 'an auspicious unicorn and a propitious phoenix' (*sangnin sŏbong* 祥麟瑞鳳), this is not something that people can achieve through their own efforts. In other words, is it not right and proper to say that Heaven has bestowed these various blessings on such a superior man?

One's sixtieth wedding anniversary (*hoehollye* 回婚禮) is called one of the secular rites (*songnye* 俗禮) of the world. Lord Minister Tu has celebrated his sixtieth wedding anniversary, and his three sons have, too. This year is the sixtieth year since I first came as a young lad to get married in Lord Minister Tu's house and become his son-in-law. Also, as I will celebrate my sixtieth wedding anniversary in the spring of this year, this can also be said to be yet another propitious event to take place under the protection and care of Lord Minister Tu. Among the people gathered here today for the sixtieth birthday of Lord Minister Tu's grandson over a thousand are all his descendants. Even if we include all people who have had many descendants from antiquity until now, Lord Minister Tu is the foremost.

Lord Minister Tu commanded me to write the congratulatory address for this birthday banquet. As I have respected and admired him all my life with my utmost sincerity and heart, how could I dare to say before Lord

Minister Tu that it would be difficult for me to write because of my old age and ill health. I have forced myself to take up the writing brush and have briefly recorded these three kinds of blessings, and if people of this world read this and would like to obtain the blessings of Lord Minister Tu, they should study his lordship's uprightness of heart. I am not recording all the luxuriousness of the mountains and rivers and the magnificence of the banquet.

○Year ○Month ○Day, recorded by Grand Academician Wi Ch'ŏn'gyŏng.

Explication of *Record of the Words and Deeds of Yuhandang Sa-ssi* (*Yuhandang Sa-ssi ŏnhaengnok*)

1. Summary of *Record of the Words and Deeds of Yuhandang Sa-ssi*

Record of the Words and Deeds of Yuhandang Sa-ssi is a work depicting the ideal female figure of the Chosŏn dynasty through its protagonist, the fictional female character Yuhandang (幽閒堂) Sa-*ssi* (謝氏). According to the custom of novels at that time, the novel is set in China during the reign of the Wanli Emperor in the Ming dynasty, and it recounts anecdotes in chronological order from the birth of Yuhandang through her childhood, youth, middle age, and old age.

There are more than thirty extant copies of this work in the collections of major institutions such as the National Museum of Korea, the Kyujanggak Institute (奎章閣) for Korean Studies at Seoul National University, and the Jangseogak Archives (藏書閣) at the Academy of Korean Studies. In addition, it is listed in the Yŏngyŏng Hall (Yŏngyŏngdang 演慶堂) *List of Han'gŭl Books* (*Ŏnmunch'aek mongnok* 諺文冊目錄), a list of books kept in

Yŏngyŏng Hall, Ch'anggyŏng Palace (昌慶宮), where Han'gŭl books for royal women were mainly kept, so it seems to have been widely read primarily by women of the royal family and noble families.

By way of comparison, there are only single surviving copies of the personal writings of Kim Hoyŏnjae (金浩然齋) and Im Yunjidang (任允摯堂), two representative female intellectuals of the Chosŏn dynasty, and *New Record of Education in the Womb* (*T'aegyo sin'gi* 胎教新記) by Yi Sajudang (李師朱堂). There are twelve copies of *Encyclopedia of Women's Daily Life* (*Kyuhap ch'ongsŏ* 閨閤叢書) by Yi Pinghŏgak (李憑虛閣), which is a relatively well known work. On the other hand, in the case of *Record of the Words and Deeds of Yuhandang Sa-ssi*, there are more than thirty duplicate copies written in Korean and Chinese characters. In order to explore the general consciousness, orientation and characteristics of upper-class women in the Chosŏn dynasty, *Record of the Words and Deeds of Yuhandang Sa-ssi*, therefore, may be a more suitable material with a greater degree of universality than any other extant work.

The author and creation date of *Record of the Words and Deeds of Yuhandang Sa-ssi* have not yet been discovered. Among the other copies in Keimyung University's collection, there is one that was copied before 1833. It is also possible to speculate that the main character Yuhandang was modeled after Hong Wŏnju (洪原周 1791–?), a historical person in the late

Chosŏn dynasty who had the same title 'Yuhandang' as Yuhandang Sa-*ssi*. Both the P'ungsan Hong clan (豐山洪氏) on Hong Wŏnju's father's side, and the Talsŏng Sŏ clan (達城徐氏), on her mother's side, were considered to be noble families. In addition, her brother Hong Sŏkchu (洪奭周 1774–1842) was a representative scholar and writer in the nineteenth century, serving as an intendant of education (*taejehak* 大提學) and a second state councilor (*chwaŭijŏng* 左議政). Similarities can be found in the fact that Yuhandang Sa-*ssi* of *Record of the Words and Deeds of Yuhandang Sa-ssi* was also born into a prestigious family and learned to read from her eldest brother Sa Manch'un at an early age, and that her other elder brothers also appeared in the narrative as outstanding writers. However, based on the surviving data discovered so far, there is still insufficient evidence to suggest that the protagonist of *Record of the Words and Deeds of Yuhandang Sa-ssi* was actually modeled after the historical person Hong Wŏnju.

Keimyung University Dongsan Library has in its Old Books Collection four Korean Han'gŭl versions and one Chinese character version of the text. The *Record of the Words and Deeds of Yuhandang Sa-ssi* published in this book is not only the most complete of all the published versions discovered so far, but as it also contains several anecdotes that have been omitted in other versions, it has a very high value as a primary source text.

2. Structure and Content

Record of the Words and Deeds of Yuhandang Sa-ssi, which is held in Keimyung University Dongsan Library, comprises three fascicles and three books, which together loosely comprise the dialogues that the protagonist Yuhandang has with members of her family without following any particular order. Among the contents of *Record of the Words and Deeds of Yuhandang Sa-ssi*, the most representative passages are 1) Birth, 2) Childhood, 3) Eldest daughter-in-law Yuhandang, 4) Children's education, and 5) Eldest son's sixtieth birthday celebration.

(1) Birth

Yuhandang (幽閒堂) of the Sa descent group (Sa-*ssi* 謝氏) was the daughter of Scholar (Ch'ŏsa) Sa Kwanghan (謝光翰), while her mother was from the No descent group (No-*ssi* 盧氏) and was the daughter of the Hanlin Academy scholar No Wŏn'gyŏng (盧元景). The Sa family generally excelled in scholarship and was looked up to by people in the world, and the No family members were also outstanding in their conduct and words, and from generation to generation, it was a family that occupied high rank and was exceptional in its moral behavior.

Lady No gave birth to Yuhandang on the 19th day of the fourth lunar month of the Chŏngch'uk Year (丁丑年, 1577) in the fifth year of the reign of the Wanli Emperor (萬曆), Shenzong (神宗) of the Ming dynasty. The family was upright and prominent (*ch'ŏnghyŏn* 清顯) and strict in its morals. Yuhandang was intelligent and concentrated on studying from a young age, so all her relatives said, "The intelligence and ability of personages in this world produces seeds (*chongja* 種子)."

Yuhandang was born on the 19th day of the fourth lunar month, in the 5th year of the Wanli reign era (1577), to Sa Kwanghwan and his wife No-*ssi*. Yuhandang's family had been highly cultured for generations, and her relatives admired her because she was very intelligent and devoted to learning from an early age.

Yuhandang learns *Elementary Learning* and several other classic texts from Vice Director Sa Manch'un, who is her eldest brother. After waking up early every day and greeting her parents, she always sits in the inner quarters and immerses herself in studying all day.

(2) Childhood

When Yuhandang read the 'Subject Matter of the *Elementary Learning*' (*Xiaoxue* tici 小學題辭), she asked Vice Director Sa, "'The great and originating' (*wŏn* 元), 'the penetrating' (*hyŏng* 亨), 'the advantageous' (*li* 利), and 'the correct and firm' (*chŏng* 貞) follow the order of spring (*ch'un* 春), summer (*ha* 夏), autumn (*ch'u* 秋) and winter (*tong* 冬), but the order of benevolence (*in* 仁), righteousness (*ŭi* 義), courtesy (*ye* 禮) and wisdom (*chi* 智) is different. Benevolence belongs to spring, righteousness belongs to autumn, courtesy belongs to summer, and wisdom belongs to winter, so even though the order ought to be 'benevolence, courtesy, righteousness and wisdom', it is 'benevolence, righteousness, courtesy and wisdom'. Do you know why this is so and what it signifies?"

"There is no particularly deep significance. 'The great and originating', 'the penetrating', 'the advantageous', and 'the correct and firm' are mentioned in accordance with the order of the four seasons, and benevolence, righteousness, courtesy and wisdom are mentioned in accordance with the order of east, west, south and north because benevolence is associated with the east (*tong* 東), righteousness is associated with the west (*sŏ* 西), courtesy is associated with the south (*nam* 南) and wisdom is associated with the north (*puk* 北)."

Vice Director Sa then asked with deliberation, "Wouldn't it be possible to say 'east, south, west and north' as well as 'east, west, south and north'?"

"As 'the great and originating', 'the penetrating', 'the advantageous' and 'the correct and firm' are listed in heaven's natural order, we say them in that order, and because east, west, south and north are geographical terms, they are referred to in that way based on the directions that are facing each other. How is it that you do not know 'the principle of the orderly passage of time and the pairing of opposites' (*yuhaeng taedae chi li* 流行待對之理)?"

Vice Director Sa struck his knee in admiration and praised her, saying, "Even among men who read books, there are only a few who know about 'the principle of the orderly passage of time and the pairing of opposites'. Even though you are just a young girl, you already know such things. How extraordinary you are!"

Yuhandang surpassed all others in terms of her academic level from the age of seven or eight. She clearly explains the logic of coined words such as 'the great and originating, the penetrating, the advantageous, and the correct and firm' as well as 'benevolence, righteousness, courtesy and wisdom'. She also predicted that the Imjin War would occur ten years later by citing the classic texts mentioned when her father and brother had been talking about astronomy. Before turning ten, Yuhandang explained why the word '*sokchŏ*' (屬猪) was used as another name for the Song dynasty better than her brother, and the anecdote concerning the origin of the word '*wangyŏ*' (王餘魚) shows that her knowledge of and ability to expound on classic texts surpassed that of many advanced scholars.

(3) The Eldest Daughter-in-law Yuhandang

Yuhandang had already spent a long time at the home of her parents-in-law. She attended her parents-in-law with filial piety and was obedient towards her husband. She was extremely friendly towards her brothers-in-law and sisters-in-law, and she treated her relatives and servants with benevolence, so people in her neighborhood all sang her praises. Minister Tu and his wife considered the sagacity of their eldest daughter-in-law to be quite out of the ordinary. One day Minister Tu's wife became slightly ill, so for over a day she was unable to get up from her bed. Yuhandang exerted all her sincerity day and night, personally tasted her medicine and never left her side. The outstanding virtue of the filially pious daughter-in-law, was such that people who witnessed it were all deeply impressed.

Minister Tu also considered this to be extraordinary and said to his wife, "As the conduct of the bride is not such that can be attained by a young woman, if she had not been born as a noble lady how could this be possible?"

"As I experienced this illness, her boiling of tea and porridge with her own hands in a way suitable for my sick body, as well as the way she sat me up and laid me down was well beyond the strength of a child. In spite of my daughter-in-law's weak body, she was able to ease my difficulties, and I was able to recover from this illness easily. How could this not be considered to be extraordinary?"

As Yuhandang grew up, requests for her hand in marriage came pouring in from many wealthy families. However, Scholar Sa disregarded them all and married her to the eldest son Ch'ŏnbok (天復) of Minister Tu Wŏnyong (杜元庸). Ch'ŏnbok was a person who was called Hyoja ('filial son') by the local people because of his excellent filial piety from an early age. Even in *Record of the Words and Deeds of Yuhandang Sa-ssi*, Ch'ŏnbok is always referred to as 'Hyoja' or 'Tu Hyoja', but for the sake of clarity, he is referred to as Tu Ch'ŏnbok or just Ch'ŏnbok throughout this translation. Yuhandang, who married Tu Ch'ŏnbok, was recognized as a good daughter-in-law in her husband's family because she took good care of her mother-in-law and skillfully made her father-in-law's court robe. In addition, she suggested to her husband to establish a 'righteous storehouse' (*ŭigo* 義庫) through careful management of the household economy and earned the trust of all the family members by performing ancestral rites with sincerity and purity.

(4) Children's Education

Yuhandang said, "What arises from the 'private nature of form-and-energy' is called the 'human mind' and what arises from the 'rectification of life' is called the 'moral mind'."

Her granddaughter replied, "If it arises from the 'private nature of form-and-energy', is it human greed?"

"According to the words of Master Zhu, 'the human mind is certainly not human greed.' How can you ask if we have two minds? The human mind and the moral mind are not separate. It is called by many names such as the 'original mind' (*ponsim* 本心), the 'conscience' (*yangsim* 良心), the 'mind of a newborn baby' (*chŏkchasim* 赤子心), and it is also called the 'great human mind' (*taeinsim* 大人心), so please read the *Classic of Mind-and-Heart* (*Xinjing*) carefully."

"If the human mind arises from the private nature of 'form-and-energy' and the moral mind arises from the 'rectification of life', when Yao and Shun passed on their way of using the mind in the *Book of History* (*Shujing*), why did they not mention the moral mind that arises from the rectification of life but first mentioned the human mind that arises from the private nature of form-and-energy?"

"Generally in language, lighter matters are mentioned first and serious matters are mentioned later, but also sometimes important things are mentioned first and lighter things later. The sequential order of the human mind and the moral mind does not necessarily have any bearing on their relative importance. I think it was because there is more in the human mind to be wary of. In the deliberations of previous Confucian scholars, we cannot see any discussion about the sequential order of the human mind and the moral mind. When people read texts, they have to diligently put into practice their 'admonitions about the rectification of the heart-mind' (*chŏngsim chi hun* 正心之訓) and their 'admonitions about the existence of the mind' (*chonsim chi hun* 存心之訓), Whether it is the moral mind or the human mind, if we only memorize passages from the classics by reciting them how can they benefit our physical being?"

"Grandmother's teaching is indeed like that."

Yuhandang directly taught her seven sons various Confucian texts and classics. After the sons grew up, they also taught their grandchildren and great-grandchildren. In scenes where several children ask questions and Yuhandang answers them, Yuhandang's extensive knowledge and brilliant memory are clearly demonstrated. Yuhandang does not simply emphasize knowledge for its own sake. Rather, it is emphasized repeatedly that the purpose of studying is not simply to acquire knowledge, but to put it into practice. In other words, textual passages are not only to be memorized, but also practiced to make them beneficial.

After Yuhandang became old, she led her granddaughters and grandsons' wives on a tour of Wanshu Garden and Shuiyue Pavilion, and sometimes even entertained women of the same age and conversed with them. Through these dialogues, the wisdom and strategies of Yuhandang, who managed the household of a noble family, such as prenatal education and childcare, childbirth, hospitality, health care, disease prevention, and admonitions in words and deeds, are all explained one by one.

(5) Eldest Son's Sixtieth Birthday Party

When Minister Tu was ninety-four years of age, his eldest son Ilbong's sixtieth birthday occurred. Tu Ch'ŏnbok informed Minister Tu, "As it is not long until Ilbong's sixtieth birthday, I want to buy some wine and food and gather your descendants together."

"If I counted all the birthdays of my descendants, would there be a single day without a birthday in the year?"

"The sixtieth birthday is different from ordinary birthdays, and as it is a truly rare and grand occasion to see the sixtieth birthday of a third-generation descendant, it would be regrettable not to host a banquet."

Without granting his permission, Lord Minister Tu went into the inner quarters and informed Yuhandang, "Today, Ch'ŏnbok told me that Ilbong's sixtieth birthday is not far off, and he asked permission to organize a banquet, but I did not allow it."

"It is truly a rare and grand event under heaven to celebrate the sixtieth birthday of a third-generation descendant in one family. It is not a normal thing among households to respond to such a rare and grand event with silence. I will keep the wine, food and other expenses simple and ensure there are limits to prevent any excesses—also, to not have a banquet would appear strange."

"Indeed you are right. If one encounters a minor occasion one should celebrate it in a small way, but it is only right and proper when one encounters a major occasion to celebrate it in a grand way. As a descendant's sixtieth birthday is a rarity, a banquet should be held, but only summon the children and grandchildren and do not invite guests from far and wide."

> Tu Ch'ŏnbok provided 5,000 pieces of gold to buy the wine and food, and thoroughly cleaned the grounds in Wanshu Garden. Of the thousands of people who gathered on that day, over a thousand were descendants of Lord Minister Tu.

At the end of *Record of the Words and Deeds of Yuhandang Sa-ssi*, a sixtieth birthday celebration is held for Ilbong, the eldest son of Yuhandang. His father originally refused to allow the sixtieth birthday party, but Yuhandang convinced her father-in-law that it was a rare event for the representatives of three successive generations to celebrate their sixtieth birthdays while all were still living. Thousands of family members and relatives gathered at the sixtieth birthday party held at Wanshu Garden, and among them, about 1,000 were descendants of Minister Tu. The son-in-law of Minister Tu, Grand Academician Wi Ch'ŏn'gyŏng, composes 'Preface to a Sixtieth Birthday Banquet' (*suyŏn sŏ* 壽宴序), enumerating the blessings of his father-in-law and his family, and in this way he concludes the work.

3. Significance

Record of the Words and Deeds of Yuhandang Sa-ssi is a literary work with such a diverse character that it is difficult to define its genre in one word. In the explications of the versions held by Seoul National University's Kyujanggak Institute for Korean Studies and the National Library of Korea, this work was introduced as an 'ethics book'.[389] Yi Chiyŏng views this work as a kind of 'question-and-answer-style encyclopedia' that embodies the female intelligence of the Chosŏn dynasty,[390] and Sŏ Kyŏnghŭi, paying attention to the fictional nature of the events, regards it as belonging to the category of 'didactic novels for women' (*kyuhun sosŏl*).[391] Yuhandang's erudite mastery of ancient classic texts, the practical knowledge and strategies required of the eldest

---

389 In the explication by Kim Ho of *Yuhandang ŏnhaengnok* (幽閒堂言行錄) in the possession of Seoul National University, it is described as a 'novel-style ethics book', and in Yang Sŭngmin's explication in *Yuhandang Sa-ssi ŏnhaengnok*, it is described as 'a kind of female (life) ethics book'.

390 The existence of the text in literary Sinitic was first reported in a previous study by Yi Chiyŏng. Yi Chiyŏng, "*Yuhandang Sa-ssi ŏnhaengnok* ŭl t'onghae pon Chosŏn sidae yŏsŏng chisŏng ŭi ŭisik kwa chihyang" (Consciousness and orientation of female intellectuality in the Chosŏn dynasty through *Yuhandang Sa-ssi ŏnhaengnok*), *Han'guk kojŏn yŏsŏng munhak yŏn'gu* 28, Han'guk Kojŏn Yŏsŏng Munhakhoe, 2014, 75.

391 Sŏ Kyŏnghŭi, "Kyuhun sosŏl ŭi sŏngnip paegyŏng kwa t'ŭksŏng e kwanhan yŏn'gu" (A study on the background and characteristics of the establishment of didactic novels for women [*kyuhun sosŏl*]), *Onji nonch'ong*, 47, 2016, p. 71. "These works can be categorized as 'didactic novels for women' (*kyuhun sosŏl* 閨訓小說), which are completely materialized by setting up fictional characters and situations to illustrate the content or practice of virtues that have traditionally been emphasized for women. They can be defined as works of art."

daughter-in-law of the family, and the moral norms required of a woman in the Chosŏn dynasty are all presented in a complex way.

In addition to this, the possibility of the work belonging to the novel genre can also be considered. There are numerous books cited in Yuhandang's words, among which are many Chinese 'novels of the bizarre' such as *Yiyuan* (異苑), *Shiyi ji* (拾遺記), and *Soushen ji* (搜神記). This suggests that *Record of the Words and Deeds of Yuhandang Sa-ssi* is itself not far from the novel genre. In addition, there is a similarity to the novel *Record of Lady Sa's Journey South* (*Sa-ssi namjŏng ki* 謝氏南征記), which was widely read during the Chosŏn dynasty. *Record of Lady Sa's Journey South* is also set in Ming dynasty China, and the male protagonist Yu Yŏnsu (C. Liu Yanshou 劉延壽) is a descendant of Liu Ji (Liu Bowen). And Yu Yŏnsu's aunt, who helps the main character, marries Honglüshaoqing Tu Kang (C. Du Qiang 杜强) and is called 'Lady Tu' (Tu puin). Sa Chŏngok (C. Xie Zhenyu 謝貞玉), the main character of *Record of Lady Sa's Journey South* has many similarities in appearance with Yuhandang and is also "embodied as an ideal moral subject who realizes the moral principles she internalizes."[392]

---

392 Ryu Chŏn'gyŏng, "*Sa ssi namjŏngki* rŭl t'onghae pon sosŏlsa ŭi chŏnbyŏn ŭi han kungmyŏn—Sa ssi hyŏngsang ŭi hyŏngsŏng paegyŏng kwa ŭimi" (A phase in the history of the novel as seen through *Sa-ssi namjŏnggi* [Lady Sa's journey south]—the background and meaning of the form of *Sa-ssi namjŏnggi* [Lady Sa's journey south]), *Kungmunhak yŏn'gu* 31,

Record of the Words and Deeds of Yuhandang Sa-ssi is a literary work worthy of attention, but research on it is still scarce. In the future, it is necessary to study in depth the differences between the various versions and the genre characteristics of the work.

Kungmun Hakhoe, 2015, p. 26.

References

Kim Tonguk (Kim Dongwook). "*Yuhandang Sa-ssi ŏnhaengnok* yŏn'gu" (A study on *Yuhandang Sa-ssi ŏnhaengnok* [*Record of the words and deeds of Yuhandang Sa-ssi*]). *Chindan hakpo* 134, Chindan Hakhoe, 2020, pp. 309–329.

Ryu Chŏn'gyŏng (Ryu Junkyung). "*Sa ssi namjŏng ki* rŭl t'onghae pon sosŏlsa ŭi chŏnbyŏn ŭi han kungmyŏn—Sa ssi hyŏngsang ŭi hyŏngsŏng paegyŏng kwa ŭimi" (A phase in the history of the novel as seen through *Sa-ssi namjŏnggi* [Lady Sa's journey south]—the background and meaning of the form of *Sa-ssi namjŏnggi* [Lady Sa's journey south]), *Kungmunhak yŏn'gu* 31, Kungmun Hakhoe, 2015, pp. 7–38.

Sŏ Kyŏnghŭi (Seo Kyunghee). "Kyuhun sosŏl ŭi sŏngnip paegyŏng kwa t'ŭksŏng e kwanhan yŏn'gu" (A study on the background and characteristics of the establishment of didactic novels for women [*kyuhun sosŏl*]). *Onji nonch'ong* 47, Onji Hakhoe, 2016, pp. 69–101.

Yi Chiyŏng (Yi Jiyoung). "*Yuhandang Sa-ssi ŏnhaengnok* ŭl t'onghae pon Chosŏn sidae yŏsŏng chisŏng ŭi ŭisik kwa chihyang" (Consciousness and orientation of female intellectuality in the Chosŏn dynasty as seen in Yuhandang *Sa-ssi ŏnhaengnok* [*Record of the words and deeds of Yuhandang Sa-ssi*]). *Han'guk kojŏn yŏsŏng munhak yŏn'gu* 28, Han'guk Kojŏn Yŏsŏng Munhakhoe, 2014, pp. 63–93.

Index

A

B

C

D

E

F

G

H

I

J

L

M

N

O

P

Q

R

S

T

V

W

X

Y

Z

About the translator

Michael C. E. Finch is a professor in the Korean Language Education Major, College of Humanities and International Studies, Keimyung University. He is the author of *Min Yŏng-hwan: A Political Biography* and the translator of *Min Yŏnghwan: The Selected Writings of a Late Chosŏn Diplomat*. He is currently working on a translation of *Swaemirok* (Record of a refugee) by O Hŭimun (1539–1613).

About the editor

Lee Jonghan is a professor in the Department of Chinese and Chinese Studies, College of Humanities and International Studies, Keimyung University and Director of Dongsan Library. He is interested in the study of Chinese prose, including the works of Han Yu, as well as the translation of Chinese classics. His publications include *The Prose Works of Hanyu: A Korean Translation with Annotations* (5 volumes, selected as an outstanding publication by the Korean Academy of Sciences in 2013).

About Keimyung University Dongsan Library

Keimyung University Dongsan Library has over 78,000 old books, including 22 types and 96 volumes of state-designated treasures such as *Yongbi ŏch'ŏn ka* (Songs of flying dragons) and 8 types and 18 volumes of tangible cultural heritage of Daegu such as *Taegu ŭpchi* (Daegu county gazetteer). As one of Korea's representative institutions housing an extensive collection of old books, Dongsan Library contributes to the systematic management of Korea's traditional cultural heritage and the promotion of Korean studies research by holding exhibitions as well as publishing catalogs, annotated texts and translations.